Praise for *Spirituality in Counseling and Psychotherapy: An Integrative Approach That Empowers Clients*

"In this book, there are many useful ideas for therapists to reflect upon in incorporating client-defined spiritual beliefs and practices into the therapeutic process. Dr. Johnson illustrates through many brief case examples, how exploring a client's spiritual journey can enhance the counseling experience. The message developed in this book is that it is never the place of therapists to impose their spiritual agenda, but to always work as collaborative partners with clients to discover how they can empower themselves by identifying and defining their spiritual path. The author shows how client self-defined spiritual practices can support life-affirming choices and activities, which promote healing and change."

Gerald Corey, EdD, ABPP
Professor Emeritus of Human Services and Counseling
California State University, Fullerton

"Unless clients bring up the topic of their spiritual beliefs spontaneously, most therapists won't go there and many become uncomfortable and change the subject when clients do. In doing so, therapists ignore the most important aspect of many clients' lives and a source of great comfort and potential healing. Drawing from a wide range of spiritual and psychotherapeutic traditions and integrating them through the concept of True Self, Rick Johnson emboldens us to help clients explore and strengthen their relationship to their True Selves and, thereby, to their sense of interconnectedness, wonder, purpose, inner leadership, and wisdom. The book is well written, scholarly yet personal, and comprehensive. I recommend it strongly."

Richard C. Schwartz, PhD
Developer of the Internal Family Systems Model of Psychotherapy

SPIRITUALITY IN COUNSELING AND PSYCHOTHERAPY

SPIRITUALITY IN COUNSELING AND PSYCHOTHERAPY

AN INTEGRATIVE APPROACH THAT EMPOWERS CLIENTS

RICK JOHNSON

WILEY

Published by John Wiley & Sons, Inc., Hoboken, New Jersey

Published simultaneously in Canada

For general information about our other products and services, please contact our Customer Care Department within the United States at (800) 762-2974, outside the United States at (317) 572-3993 or fax (317) 572-4002.

Wiley publishes in a variety of print and electronic formats and by print-on-demand. Some material included with standard print versions of this book may not be included in e-books or in print-on-demand. If this book refers to media such as a CD or DVD that is not included in the version you purchased, you may download this material at http://booksupport.wiley.com. For more information about Wiley products, visit www.wiley.com.

Library of Congress Cataloging-in-Publication Data:

Johnson, Rick, 1964 July 21–
    Spirituality in counseling and psychotherapy : an integrative approach that empowers clients / Rick Johnson.
        pages cm
    Includes bibliographical references and index.
    ISBN 978-1-118-14521-0 (pbk.)
    ISBN 978-1-118-26374-7 (ebk.)
    ISBN 978-1-118-23910-0 (ebk.)
    ISBN 978-1-118-22576-9 (ebk.)
    1. Psychotherapy—Religious aspects. 2. Spirituality. I. Title.
    RC489.S676J64 2013

    616.89'14–dc23

                                                                                2012041400

Printed in the United States of America

10 9 8 7 6 5 4 3 2 1

For Joellyn, Madelyn, and Mia.
For those who endeavor to embrace what is meaningful and life-affirming,
and to help others do so in their own unique ways.

CONTENTS

Preface   *xiii*
Acknowledgments   *xxi*
About the Author   *xxiii*

1 ◆ Spiritual Competencies and Premises   *1*
    Central Premises   *5*
    Spirituality and Religion   *20*

2 ◆ Client-Defined Spirituality   *23*
    Remembering   *28*
    External Presence and Inner Knowing   *29*
    Transcendent and Ordinary Experiences   *31*
    Present Moment Awareness   *32*
    Interconnectedness   *33*
    Love and Fear   *35*
    Free Will   *36*
    Creativity and Artistic Expression   *38*
    Nature and Natural Beauty   *39*
    Openheartedness   *40*
    Personal Relationship   *41*
    Thematic Integration   *42*

3 ◆ Integrating Spirituality With Psychological Theories   *45*
    Freud   *45*
    Jung   *46*
    Object Relations and Attachment Theories   *48*
    Interpersonal Theory: Horney   *51*
    Humanism: Rogers   *52*
    Control-Mastery Theory: Weiss   *54*
    Internal Family Systems Theory: Schwartz   *57*
    Dialectical Behavior Therapy: Linehan   *59*
    Transpersonal and Integral Theories   *60*
    Life Span Development Theories   *62*
    Thematic Integration   *65*

4 ◆ Getting Lost: Psychological and Spiritual Perspectives   *69*
    Why Clients Get Lost   *71*
    A Spiritual Perspective   *87*

5 ◆ Spiritual Health and Abundance: Practical Steps   *101*
    Being Open to Client-Defined Spirituality   *101*
    Utilizing Spirituality for Resourcing   *109*
    Inviting Spirituality to Inform Personal Integrity   *111*
    Evaluating Life Structures   *113*
    Remembering and Committing to Spiritual Practice   *123*

6 ◆ Integrating the Shadow   *125*
    The Shadow   *126*
    How Shadows Form   *129*
    When Clients Marry Their Shadow   *134*
    Integration   *141*

7 ◆ Self and No-Self   *149*
    No-Self   *150*
    An Integration of Self and No-Self   *157*
    Helping Clients Reclaim Their Real Self   *160*

8 ◆ How Spiritually Oriented Therapy Helps *169*
      A Collaborative Team *172*
      Self-Awareness *174*
      Insight *179*
      Reexperiencing Relational Dynamics *181*
      New Relationship With the Real Self *184*
      Embracing Inner Health *187*
      Embracing Relationship Health *189*
      Utilizing Spiritually Oriented Therapy *190*
      Final Thoughts *193*

9 ◆ Spiritual-Differentiation *195*
      The Identity and Differentiation Process *196*
      Characteristics of Well-Differentiated Individuals *201*
      Increasing Differentiation *213*
      Increasing Therapist Spiritual-Differentiation *217*

      References *223*
      Author Index *245*
      Subject Index *249*

PREFACE

For as long as I can remember, I have been drawn to philosophical ideas of existence. I have had a sense that there is more to life than day-to-day tasks, or even longer-term goals. I have often been acutely aware of a sense of existential anxiety and a yearning for deeper meaning. My searching, as it does for many people, led me to focus on learning about and experiencing various forms of spirituality, which often brought comfort as well as more questions. As a therapist, for the past 25 years I have learned about and integrated many theoretical approaches and models. As a professor, I have specialized in teaching therapy theories and techniques. Over time, my interest in spiritual ideas and practices, therapeutic models, and psychotherapeutic change have increasingly blended together.

I have had many experiences with clients, in particular, that have inspired the ideas in this book. One that stands out is my work with Maria, a 32-year-old Mexican American client who entered therapy due to involvement from state child protective services. Her caseworker was threatening to remove her children if Maria allowed her boyfriend to return to live with her. Maria had already been in state-mandated therapy several times with different therapists, with little observable change. She dutifully described a family history with parental alcoholism and neglect as well as her relationships with angry and sometimes abusive men. For several months, she came to therapy and talked primarily about her interactions with her caseworker as well as the behavioral changes she planned to make so that her children wouldn't be placed into foster care. Despite my efforts to empower her, and although she seemed to enjoy talking with me, the therapy had the feeling of being a task she needed to complete. She implemented few of her proposed plans.

That all changed when we started to discuss the "warm/light feeling" in her chest and heart, which she "had never told anyone about." Maria said that when she was a child she would notice the warm/light feeling, but for much of her adult life, she had forgotten about it. When I eagerly listened and invited her to mindfully notice the warm/light feeling, she described a sense of calm that would come over her. Throughout our work together we discussed how she could intentionally access the warm/light feeling and utilize it for her benefit. She remarked that for all the times she had been instructed by well-meaning social service providers about what she needed to do to improve her life and her kids' lives, it felt out of her grasp. But now that she was connecting with the warm/light feeling in her chest, *she seemed to know what was best for her* and was increasingly able to put her clarity about what was life-affirming into action. Maria revealed that she thought that the warm/light feeling was "love sent by God." I didn't care what Maria called the warm/light; I was simply thrilled and amazed by the transformation that I was witnessing and pleased to have a co-therapist, that is, her personally defined, life-affirming spiritual practice.

Maria was an inspiration to me and, along with other similar clinical experiences, deeply affected my thinking about the role of spirituality in psychotherapeutic process. I began to become convinced that therapeutic change could be greatly enhanced and supported by the inclusion of client-defined spiritual views and practices. It also became clear to me that most therapists are not well trained in how to do so. Although this has been changing over the past few years, quite a few therapists and clinical educators with whom I have spoken have been vocally skeptical and even critical about integrating spirituality into therapy, often because of fundamental beliefs in Western psychology as well as their own emotional reactivity toward religion/spirituality based on their personal life experiences.

Due to my experiences with clients like Maria, as well as with clinical graduate students and my own personal spiritual experiences and journey, I wrote my first book, *Reclaiming Your Real Self: A Psychological and Spiritual Integration* (Johnson, 2009), which focused on how individuals could access a life-affirming and personally defined spiritual energy to increase their intuitive wisdom and take greater ownership for their lives. That book evolved into this one, by shifting the focus to how therapists can ethically and competently address and utilize spirituality with their clients.

Target Audience and Book Organization

The target audience for this book is therapists who are looking for a practical integration of psychology and spirituality that builds upon existing psychological theories. Therapists from a variety of theoretical orientations can benefit from the proposed model that integrates a thematic and inclusive view of spirituality, as well as suggests how therapists can decrease their emotional reactivity to client-defined spirituality, thus enabling spirituality to be a great source of support to the therapeutic change process. The book is organized to lead toward this practical integration, with clinical examples embedded in most chapters.

The book begins with a discussion of foundational premises and competencies for therapists when they work with spirituality, including viewing spiritually oriented therapy as a form of multicultural therapy. In Chapter 1, I also propose common reasons why therapists may struggle with spirituality in the psychotherapeutic process, as well as introduce an integrative model that focuses on client-defined spiritual views and practices. The chapter concludes with a discussion of similarities and differences between religion and spirituality.

The focus in Chapter 2 is on the various ways that clients may speak about spirituality. Much of what is reported is based on informal, qualitative research that I conducted, as well as citations from other sources. Although spirituality is uniquely defined and experienced, common themes emerge, including a sense of already possessing spiritual knowledge, experiencing spirituality both internally and externally, transcendent and ordinary experiences, present moment awareness, interconnectedness, love versus fear, potentialities, creativity and artistic expression, nature and natural beauty, openheartedness, and personal relationships. These themes provide a broad and inclusive foundation for therapists to listen for and understand how their clients may define, access, and experience spirituality.

In Chapter 3, I discuss select psychological theories, which focus on the idea that the personality has various conceptual structures, including a central, organizing essence of self, the Real Self. The goal of the chapter is to provide therapists with a psychologically based foundation through which to conceptually integrate client-defined notions of spirituality. I propose that the Real Self contains not only psychological wisdom but also spiritual potential. Theories that are highlighted include Freudian, Jungian, object relations/attachment, interpersonal, humanistic, control-mastery, internal family systems, dialectical behavior therapy, transpersonal/integral, and lifespan development.

In Chapter 4, I provide an integrative perspective on reasons why clients disconnect from their Real Self and therefore lose touch with their most significant source of knowledge and actualizing potential. Common causes of losing touch with the Real Self include traumatic experiences in childhood, learned compensatory patterns, and the frenetic nature of modern Western life. When clients are disconnected from their Real Self, they are not only psychologically lost but also spiritually lost. When they forget to embrace the wisdom, guidance, and life-affirming energy of the Real Self, they get caught up in minutia in their lives and lose perspective on their values and priorities. Clients end up losing touch with their personal integrity and personal barometer of health. The consequences of getting lost spiritually include: reactivity versus spiritual stillness, thinking versus experiencing, losing balance, incongruence, fighting against versus embracing a natural flow, fear versus love, scarcity versus abundance, losing perspective on suffering, sleepwalking, existential vacuum and meaninglessness, unbalanced responsibility, and alienation.

There are many ways that spirituality can inform and support clinical progress. In Chapter 5, I discuss how therapists can assist clients in utilizing a life-affirming spiritual practice to increase their coping and develop personal integrity as a guide in defining and achieving health and growth. When clients make decisions based upon their personal integrity, their choices reflect their core values and make their lives more meaningful and congruent. There are five key steps involved in the process of helping clients use their spirituality in therapy. They are:

1. Being open to client-defined spirituality.
2. Utilizing spirituality for resourcing.
3. Inviting spirituality to inform clients' personal integrity.
4. Evaluating life structures.
5. Remembering and committing to spiritual practice.

Regular spiritual practice can support positive growth by cultivating clients' personal integrity, which can become a moral barometer and guiding voice. Unfortunately, a moral code can also become restrictive and legalistic, leading to a variety of psychological and spiritual problems, including disconnection from the Real Self. Some clients' needs and conscious self-understandings might then become unacceptable, thus fostering the development of a *shadow* part of the personality. By remaining unaware of shadow parts, clients can reduce anxiety in the short term, but do so at great peril in the longer term. They are likely to act out their shadow needs in ways that contradict their personal integrity. A sustainable life vision must include a realistic and holistic understanding of the personality. Therapists need to assist clients to be aware of and integrate their shadow. When acknowledged and assimilated, the shadow can become a great source of creativity and balance. In Chapter 6, I discuss how and why restrictive moral visions develop as well as the theoretical and clinical significance of integrating the shadow.

A philosophical and practical integration of psychological and spiritual views of the self is discussed in Chapter 7. Faith traditions, especially Eastern ones, tend to emphasize ideas of selflessness, while psychology tends to help clients define and build a stronger sense of self. The practical application is that therapists can help clients maintain healthy psychological boundaries while embracing notions of interconnectedness and selflessness.

In Chapter 8, I provide a summative discussion of how therapists can practice spiritually oriented therapy, which assists clients to function more effectively in their lives and reclaim their connection with their Real Self. The approach integrates various psychological models with spiritual themes and incorporates research highlighting the factors that account for psychotherapeutic change.

The final chapter provides an in-depth discussion of differentiation, with particular emphasis on the therapist. More than any other psychological concept, differentiation of self captures the elements and characteristics associated with healthy psychological functioning that occurs when individuals embrace their Real Self, including: healthy interpersonal boundaries, low levels of emotional reactivity, balanced ownership of responsibility, balance of thoughts and emotions, inner-generated convictions, ability to self-soothe, direct communication, adult-to-adult relationships with parents, personal authority, and personal integrity. These characteristics provide markers and goals of psychological health that therapists can use with their clients and themselves. The chapter concludes with a focus on how therapists can increase their own levels of differentiation, especially their spiritual-differentiation, which is essential to providing competent and ethical spiritually informed therapy.

ACKNOWLEDGMENTS

This book could not have been written if not for the many clients who have had the courage to share with me what touches their hearts and provides them with a sense of meaning, wisdom, and peace. I am grateful and honored to be part of my clients' journeys of discovery and growth. Their courage and impulses for health are the essence of this book.

I am also grateful to my wife and daughters, extended family, and friends for their support and encouragement. Thanks to Rachel Livsey and Robin Bagai, PsyD, for their editorial guidance. I am particularly thankful for the graduate students at Portland State University, with their deeply personal sense that spirituality is vitally important to their own and their clients' health and growth, for being increasingly insistent about learning how to effectively and ethically practice spiritually oriented therapy. Lastly, I am appreciative of the reviewers who read and critiqued drafts of the manuscript: Cara Carlson, PhD, University of St. Thomas/St. Catherine University; Robin Trippany, EdD, Walden University; and Naomi Chedd, licensed mental health counselor and educational consultant, Brookline, MA; their feedback was essential to the development of the focus and organization of the book.

ABOUT THE AUTHOR

Patrick "Rick" Johnson, PhD, is the chair of the counselor education department at Portland State University (PSU). Previously, Dr. Johnson was an assistant/associate professor at Montana State University. He received his PhD in counseling psychology from New Mexico State University. His scholarly agenda has focused on the effects of various family experiences on psychological and relational development in adolescence and adulthood as well as spiritually oriented therapy. His research has led to numerous journal publications and professional presentations. His first book is entitled *Reclaiming Your Real Self: A Psychological and Spiritual Integration* (2009). In addition to his work at PSU, Dr. Johnson maintains an active private practice, focusing on individual adult psychotherapy and couple therapy as well as clinical supervision and consultation. His theoretical orientation is an integration of relational psychodynamic, family systems, humanistic/existential, and various contemporary, experiential models. Areas of clinical expertise include relational issues, marriage/divorce, childhood trauma, addiction issues, parental alcoholism, depression, anxiety, and spirituality. He is a licensed psychologist in Oregon and a clinical member of the American Association for Marriage and Family Therapy.

CHAPTER 1

SPIRITUAL COMPETENCIES
AND PREMISES

Kristi, a mental health therapist in private practice, had just listened to a phone message from a potential client. (The term *therapist* will be used throughout the book to refer to various mental health clinicians, including psychologists, social workers, marriage and family therapists, and professional counselors.) On the voice mail, the client reported that she had the names of three therapists, and she was looking for the best fit. The client indicated that she wanted a therapist who could work with her nagging feelings of depression as well as her relationship issues. She described herself as "very spiritual" and needed her therapist to be a "good match" with her spiritual beliefs and practices. The client wanted to speak with Kristi, to ask questions about Kristi's theoretical orientation as well as her spiritual beliefs in order to determine if they could work well together.

Although eager to build her practice and interested in talking with the client, Kristi experienced some apprehension about how to respond to the client's desire to learn about *her* spiritual beliefs. Similar to many therapists, Kristi's professional training had provided little guidance about how to respond to such requests, other than to not engage in excessive, personal self-disclosure. For the most part, she was diligent about keeping her personal values separate from her professional practice. In this case, she didn't want to come across to the client as rigid, distant, and unapproachable. Yet, discussing her personal beliefs with the client felt invasive and complicated.

Kristi wasn't entirely sure she knew what her own spiritual beliefs were. So, how could she discuss them in a therapeutic manner with the client? She had been raised in a family that did not attend church. She saw religion and spirituality as foreign to her, preferring to live her life based on rationality rather than faith. In addition, it seemed that the client wanted to integrate spirituality into the therapy process; Kristi had very little idea about how to do that, or even what the client meant by spirituality. She had received no training on how psychological theories and techniques could interface with religion and spirituality. Specifically, she wondered if her psychodynamically oriented approach was compatible with the client's self-defined spirituality. Maybe the client needed a referral to a pastoral counselor instead of a therapist? The more she thought about it, the more unsettled she felt.

Carlos, a therapist working at a community mental health agency, had been seeing a 40-year-old client in weekly, outpatient therapy for five sessions. The therapy was focused on addressing generalized anxiety and panic attacks. Carlos had introduced various cognitive-behavioral techniques, including mindful breathing and thought stopping and thought replacement, which seemed to be helping reduce the client's anxiety. In the sixth session, the client articulated that she "is a strong Christian" and attends church services several times a week. The client asked Carlos if he felt comfortable with her talking about the Bible and her "personal relationship with Jesus." She indicated that she wanted to make sure that the therapy supported "God's plans" for her.

Carlos was hit instantly by a wave of emotions, most notably anxiety and irritation. Carlos suddenly felt less comfortable with and trusting of his client. Part of him wanted to challenge the client's beliefs while another part felt exhausted and unable to address her questions. The client's words had obviously activated strong reactions in Carlos, including memories of his childhood.

Carlos was raised in a Christian family, which at times he experienced as oppressive and judgmental. His parents often used very similar words to the ones his client was now using. In young adulthood, he had a series of painful encounters with his parents whereby he vehemently disagreed with aspects of their beliefs and practices, which culminated in a several-year period of cutoff from his parents and extended family. He has since reinitiated limited contact with his family, and is raising his own kids without organized religion. Based on his strong emotional reactions, Carlos wondered if he could work effectively with the client; he considered referring her to another therapist.

Jana, a student in a clinical graduate degree program, was about to work with her first client at her practicum site. She had completed courses in theories and techniques, assessment, diagnosis and treatment planning, ethics, and basic counseling skills, and was excited to put her newly forming skills into action. She was anxious, however, about the interface between her personal beliefs about health and healing and traditional talk therapy.

Over the past few years she had been engaged in a variety of personal growth activities, including mindfulness practices, body-oriented therapy, yoga, and Buddhist meditation retreats. She had been in a great deal of talk therapy in the past, but nothing helped as much as the experiential approaches that she now utilized. She believed strongly that traditional therapy models were too restrictive and wouldn't produce the lasting change that "spiritually oriented" techniques would. She felt that it was her responsibility to provide the best care for her clients, which included an infusion of spiritual practices and beliefs, although she was conflicted about this because of clinical concerns and ethical cautions raised by her professors. The concerns and cautions focused on the need to not impose her beliefs and practices on her clients. She wondered if she could be true to her beliefs and still be accepted into the traditional therapy community. Specifically, how could she integrate the therapy approaches she had been learning in graduate school with her spiritual beliefs?

These are just three of the many possible examples of the interface between therapy and religion/spirituality. Scenarios like these tend to generate a variety of reactions and questions for therapists, such as:

- What is spirituality, and how is it similar to and different from religion?
- Do clients have a right to know about therapists' spiritual and religious beliefs when choosing a practitioner, much like asking about their theoretical orientation or cultural background?
- Is it even appropriate to address spiritual and religious issues in therapy?
- If yes, how does this happen without imposing the therapists' beliefs and values onto the client?
- What should therapists do if they have strong beliefs about spirituality and religion, especially if they differ to a large degree from their clients' beliefs?
- How do therapists deal with clients who espouse spiritual and religious beliefs and practices that the therapist views as unhealthy?
- What should therapists do if they are unclear about their own spiritual and religious beliefs?
- How should therapists manage their emotional reactivity to spiritual and religious issues that are based on their own upbringing and life events?
- How can spiritual and religious beliefs and practices be integrated with traditional therapy approaches?
- Are there models in the therapy field that provide a framework for addressing and integrating spiritual and religious issues?
- How could addressing spiritual and religious issues in therapy be useful to the therapeutic change process?

To address questions such as these, the following are central premises of the approach described in this book.

Central Premises

Premise 1: Spiritual, religious, and philosophical reflections, beliefs, and practices are foundational to the human experience and, therefore, are an essential aspect to consider in effective therapy.

Premise 2: Spiritually and religiously informed therapy is a form of multicultural therapy.

Premise 3: Many therapists struggle with addressing spiritual and religious issues in therapy based on foundational theoretical paradigms in the mental health field.

Premise 4: The therapist's own level of *spiritual-differentiation* most often predicts his/her effectiveness with addressing spiritual and religious issues in therapy.

Premise 5: Utilizing a model that integrates psychological theories with a broad-based, thematic, and inclusive view of spirituality increases therapists' competency in assessing and addressing spiritual and religious issues with clients from a variety of faiths and spiritual and philosophical positions.

Premise 6: The concept of the *Real Self* provides a conceptual link between psychological theories and client-defined, spiritual, and religious beliefs and practices.

Premise 7: Utilizing a client-defined sense of spirituality and religion in therapy can be a significant avenue for connecting with clients and a great asset and ally in the therapeutic change process.

Each of these premises is now discussed in greater detail.

Premise 1: Spiritual, Religious, and Philosophical Reflections and Practices Are Foundational

Research has consistently shown that a high percentage of Americans believe in God, pray, are church members, and attend religious services (Harris Interactive, 2009; Kosmin & Keyser, 2009). Many other people engage in a variety of ways of understanding and practicing spirituality outside of organized religion. Ninety-three percent of Americans consider themselves to be religious and/or spiritual (Gallup, 2007), with nearly 75% describing spirituality and/or religion as integral to their worldview, sense of self, and part of their daily lives (Hagedorn & Gutierrez, 2009). Virtually everyone has some philosophical beliefs about existence and meaning, which have significant implications for how they live life. People that define themselves as atheists or agnostics also have some philosophical notions about their lives.

Increasingly clients are seeking spiritual answers in therapy and view spiritual development as essential for dealing with concerns in their lives (Morrison, Clutter, Pritchett, & Demmitt, 2009; Sperry, 2003). A vast amount of research has shown that spirituality is positively related to health and inversely related to physical and mental disorders (Miller & Thoresen, 2003). Therefore, it behooves therapists to understand and address clients' spiritual beliefs and philosophical notions as well as the practical implications of these beliefs and reflections, especially as they relate to clients' thought processes and behavioral choices.

In response to client needs and research data, professional organizations and accreditation bodies (e.g., American Psychological Association, American Counseling Association, Council for Accreditation of Counseling & Related Educational Programs, National Association of Social Workers, Council on Social Work Education, American Association for Marriage and Family Therapy, Commission on Accreditation for Marriage and Family Therapy Education) have increasingly recognized spiritual and religious issues as foundational to the human experience, and as an important client variable to be assessed in therapy. Along with other cultural variables, having the clinical skills to address spiritual and religious issues is now viewed as an expectation for effective therapy and graduate-level clinical training. Specific competencies for addressing spiritual and religious issues in counseling have been created by the Association for Spiritual, Ethical, and Religious Values in Counseling (ASERVIC) and have been adopted by the American Counseling Association.

ASERVIC (2009) lists 14 competencies across six categories for addressing spiritual and religious issues in counseling. The six categories are: (1) culture and worldview, (2) counselor self-awareness, (3) human and spiritual development, (4) communication, (5) assessment, and (6) diagnosis and treatment. Although the language of the competencies is focused on professional counselors, the message is aimed at all clinical mental health professionals. The complete ASERVIC standards can be accessed at www.aservic.org, and require that therapists are able to:

- Recognize the centrality of spirituality and religion in many clients' lives as well as have an understanding of various spiritual systems, major world religions, agnosticism, and atheism.
- Have a high level of self-awareness of their own spiritual attitudes, beliefs, and values and how their attitudes, beliefs, and values may impact the therapeutic process.
- Apply theoretical models of spiritual and religious development.
- Identify spiritual and religious themes and communicate with clients about spiritual and religious issues with acceptance and in ways that match clients' worldviews.
- Consider spiritual and religious issues when conducting client assessments.
- Consider and utilize clients' spiritual and religious views when diagnosing and treating clients' issues in ways that match clients' preferences.

The development and adoption of the ASERVIC competencies point to the foundational importance of spiritual and religious issues in the lives of many individuals and the associated need for therapists to have the skills to address these issues. Unfortunately, many therapists feel unprepared to integrate these issues into the therapeutic process. In one survey, 73% of therapists reported that spiritual issues are important to address but did not believe that they possess the necessary competency to do so (Hickson, Housley, & Wages, 2011). Furthermore, although graduate faculty indicate that integration of spiritual and religious issues are important, many educators do not feel prepared to teach these topics to students (Kelly, 1995; Robertson, 2010; Young, Cashwell, Wiggins-Frame, & Belaire, 2002). Not adequately addressing spiritual and religious issues in therapy misses a central aspect of client functioning and fails to utilize a primary resource in clients' lives (Robertson, 2010; Robertson, Smith, Ray, & Jones, 2009).

Premise 2: Spiritually Informed Therapy Is a Form of Multicultural Therapy

A multicultural perspective reminds therapists to conceptualize client worldviews as containing a variety of factors that combine to create a lens through which they define and experience themselves and the world. Cultural factors may include ethnicity, race, age, sex, gender identity and expression, sexual orientation, disabling conditions, spirituality and religion, political ideology, immigration status, and socioeconomic status, to name a few. Both clients and therapists bring their cultural lens to the therapy room. To raise awareness of the impact of culture for both therapists and clients, a commonly accepted process in multicultural therapy includes three general steps (e.g., Vacc, DeVaney, & Wittmer, 1995). Therapists should:

1. Be open to learning about and knowing themselves culturally.
2. Be open to learning about and knowing their clients culturally.
3. Be open to discussing the interface between their own and their clients' cultural worldviews.

Although most therapists have embraced these steps as a minimum expectation for multicultural competency, many struggle with the execution of this process related to spirituality and religion, despite the generally accepted view that spirituality and religion are intertwined and interrelated with culture (Fukuyama, Siahpoush, & Sevig, 2005). For example, most therapists do not have difficulty addressing racial or sexual orientation differences between themselves and clients, but spiritual and religious issues seem to be a different story. This struggle is partly due to the personal and private nature of spiritual and religious values and experiences. In addition, spiritual and religious beliefs are often in flux and in process, which tend to make quick, sound-bite responses much more difficult for therapists.

Some therapists do not have a clear idea of their spiritual and religious beliefs, while others have very strong convictions. Either way, it can be quite intellectually and emotionally complicated to understand and then articulate one's beliefs to others, especially clients, who may be engaged in their own spiritual identity process and journey.

Although challenging for many therapists, it is increasingly likely that clients will ask therapists about spiritual and religious beliefs, just as they might ask about a therapist's theoretical orientation or other cultural variables. There is an increased expectation from clients that therapists will understand spiritual concerns and utilize holistic interventions (La Torre, 2002; Sperry, 2003).

One source of this increased expectation is the consumer/survivor movement within the mental health field, which attempts to improve mental health services, increase accessibility of services, and encourage educated and informed choices for consumers as well as transparency and collaboration from providers. From this perspective, consumers should be well informed about the services they are purchasing. If spiritual and religious issues are important to them, clients should inquire about how potential therapists would address these issues in therapy, similar to asking a therapist about his/her theoretical orientation and, for example, experience with and beliefs about gay and lesbian issues, or any other cultural variable.

Thus, therapists need to understand their own spiritual and religious beliefs, be interested in learning about their clients' spiritual and religious worldviews, and be able to respond to client inquiries about the interface of spiritual and religious issues and the therapy they provide. In general, therapists need to have the skills to individualize treatment to match their clients' needs and preferences (Norcross & Wampold, 2011a; Swift, Callahan, & Vollmer, 2011). In particular, research suggests that for clients who specifically request that religious and spiritual issues be addressed in therapy, the match between the client's beliefs and the therapist's ability to accommodate treatment to address these issues significantly affects psychological and spiritual outcomes in therapy (Smith, Bartz, & Richards, 2007; Worthington, Hook, Davis, & McDaniel, 2011). Even when clients do not specifically request that therapy have a spiritual and religious focus, clients seem to benefit from treatment that incorporates their spiritual and religious framework (Norcross, 2002; Pargament & Saunders, 2007; Worthington & Atten, 2009).

Premise 3: Therapists Often Struggle With Spiritual and Religious Issues in Therapy

Kristi, Carlos, and Jana, the therapists in the scenarios at the start of this chapter, are not alone with their difficulties in addressing spiritual and religious issues in therapy. Along with the aforementioned challenges of executing a multicultural process with regard to spiritual and religious issues due to the private, personal, and ongoing nature of one's spiritual identity development process, there has been a deep-seated tension between the practice of therapy and spirituality and religion that has been a foundational aspect of modern psychology and clinical training, largely due to three pervasive perspectives. The first is Freud's views on religion as well as his ideas about the therapist's role in the psychotherapeutic change process.

Freud

Although most practicing therapists do not adhere to a classical psychoanalytic perspective, almost all have been heavily influenced by psychoanalytic ideas related to maintaining the analytic framework. This includes the creation and maintenance of a holding environment for clients with firm boundaries between therapists and clients, consistent meeting times, and very little therapist self-disclosure, primarily as a way to facilitate client transference and projection processes. A key aspect of the change process occurs when clients reexperience past relational dynamics with the therapist. From this perspective, therapist self-disclosure can interfere with these dynamics, and is often seen as gratifying the therapist's needs at the expense of the therapeutic process.

The admonitions regarding therapist self-disclosure, in particular, can make addressing spiritual and religious issues in therapy quite challenging. Spiritual and religious issues are often very personal, for both clients and therapists. While most therapists feel comfortable discussing their theoretical orientations with clients, the personal nature of spiritual and religious issues leaves many therapists feeling unsure of the appropriate boundaries. They tend to either refuse to discuss the topic with clients or end up feeling as if they revealed too much.

Although therapeutic boundaries and a healthy holding environment are often crucial for therapeutic success, for some clients the ability to have discussions with their therapists regarding spiritual and religious ideas promotes the therapeutic alliance and contributes to the development of a holding environment. Many therapists need guidance on how to navigate therapeutic boundaries when clients are revealing their spiritual and religious beliefs and experiences and are asking therapists to reveal their own.

Another influential belief that Freud espoused was that religion served the neurotic purpose of gratifying an individual's infantile needs to be cared for by an omnipotent father figure. Once individuals emotionally and psychologically matured, it was argued, they would no longer need such childish security blankets. Freud also saw religion as providing overly simplistic explanations and prescriptions for the ills of people and society. He argued that therapy, in his case psychoanalysis, should remain morally neutral, focusing on the facilitation of deep psychological self-awareness as the key to softening neurotic suffering. The best humans can hope for is a reduction in the intensity of neuroses through increased awareness and understanding of internal dynamics, leading to a transformation of "neurotic misery into common unhappiness" (Breuer & Freud, 1895/1962, p. 304). Thus, we can live an informed and rational life, more aware of our patterned tendencies and without the false hopes of religious salvation.

Within this Freudian framework, there is virtually nothing said about joy, growth, abundance, or any understanding of positive health. As noted in Rubin (2003), *The Standard Edition of the Complete Psychological Works of Sigmund Freud* "contains over four hundred entries for neurosis and pathology and not one for health" (p. 395). Although I wouldn't argue with Freud's point that suffering is an inevitable aspect of living, I do believe that humans are capable of far more than living an informed and rational life and that spirituality, rather than simply creating false and childish hopes, can assist many people in experiencing deeper meaning and holistic health in their lives. Therapists can utilize the integrated model presented in this book to understand how a client-defined sense of spirituality can be a vital aspect of the therapeutic process.

Scientific Rationalism

Related to the Freudian view is modernist thinking, predominately expressed by scientific rationalism. From this view, religion is seen as an attempt to explain the unknown. God simply fills the gap until more reasonable explanations can be found. The core of this belief system is that science, and specifically the scientific method, will eventually find the answers to all of life's mysteries, thereby rendering religion as archaic and unnecessary. Underlying this view is the idea that empirical knowing and intellectual thought are superior to affective and intuitive knowing. The bottom line is that, similar to Freud's view, rational people should let go of whatever can't be proven through the scientific method. This paradigm espouses an acceptance of and absolute faith in science and a dismissive and pathologizing view of spiritual and religious faith.

In addition to Freud, an example of this pathologizing view comes from Albert Ellis (1980), founder of rational-emotive behavior therapy, who indicated, "Religiosity is in many respects equivalent to irrational thinking and emotional disturbance" (p. 637). He contended that atheism is the only reasonable and rational choice for those interested in optimal human functioning.

Scientific rationalism continues to offer a great deal to the world, with few arguing that scientific, medical, and technological advances don't carry with them enormous potential for improving the quality of life. The problem is that excessive rationalism, or the belief that reason is superior to all other forms of knowing, is quite limiting and can be experienced as condescending by faith-oriented clients, especially clients who embrace fundamentalist views. Clients who have experienced profound spiritual experiences, for example, often feel misunderstood, minimized, and judged by therapists. Again, the model presented in this book can assist therapists to respectfully utilize a client-defined sense of spirituality as an aspect of the therapeutic process.

Value-Free Therapy
A third voice in the field that has contributed to therapists having difficulty with addressing spiritual and religious issues in therapy

is the belief that therapy should be value-free. This view, which is perhaps most strongly represented by humanistic thought, is that all individuals are completely unique. Consequently, it is disrespectful and unhelpful for therapists to impose their own values or belief-systems onto clients. Individuals are capable of choosing their own beliefs and of finding their own way in the world. Attempts to integrate religion or spirituality into the therapy process are viewed with skepticism, particularly of the therapist's motives. The very personal nature of spiritual and religious beliefs and practices makes the process even more complicated for therapists and clients.

This view about managing one's own personal values is warranted and carries an important caution. As a general rule, therapists should be careful not to impose their values or beliefs onto clients. Therapists have a sacred responsibility to manage their power appropriately, especially when working with clients in pain or crisis who are eager to relieve their suffering and may be vulnerable to blindly adopting the values of others. In the broadest sense, extreme religious views and fanaticism have certainly caused great destruction and suffering in the world. When a person or group of individuals thinks that they have *the answer* and the right way to live life, there is great potential for intolerance and oppression. However, to throw the baby out with the bath water, while possibly the safest route, also seems extreme.

Furthermore, to assume that therapy can be value-free is simply erroneous. Every therapy theory and approach is value-laden, even humanism, which values not imposing values! Therapists need to recognize the values and beliefs about health and pathology that are embedded in their personal worldviews and their theoretical approaches to helping. Part of effective therapy is a dynamic process of developing shared and hopefully more functional realities with clients. As with any topic, a discussion of spirituality and religion needs to be handled with respect for different worldviews, including cultural beliefs and unique phenomenological perspectives.

Premise 4: Spiritual-Differentiation Predicts Effectiveness With Spiritual and Religious Issues

Along with these foundational sources of difficulty, I have found that it is the therapists' own level of differentiation that is most predictive of their ability to address spiritual and religious issues as they emerge in therapy. *Differentiation of self* refers to an individual's ability to function in an autonomous and self-directed manner while staying in contact with significant others (Bowen, 1978; Kerr & Bowen, 1988). Differentiated individuals are able to separate themselves from unresolved emotional attachments in their families without emotionally cutting off from significant relationships. Undifferentiated individuals, on the other hand, tend to remain fused in relationships with parents and significant others and/or emotionally cut off from these relationships (Kerr & Bowen, 1988; Skowron, Holmes, & Sabatelli, 2003; Titelman, 1998a). Thus, fused relationships are characterized by enmeshment and emotional reactivity whereas emotional cutoffs are characterized by reactive disengagement (Johnson & Waldo, 1998).

A central barometer of differentiation is an individual's level of emotional reactivity, often seen in the ability to separate thoughts and feelings (Bowen, 1976, 1978; Johnson & Buboltz, 2000; Skowron & Dendy, 2004; Titelman, 1998b). Differentiated individuals are not overwhelmed by emotionality at the expense of their intellect whereas undifferentiated individuals tend to be ruled by their emotions. Differentiated individuals are "inner-directed" and readily take an "I position" rather than act reactively in response to external events and others' emotionality (Johnson, Buboltz, & Seemann, 2003; Kerr & Bowen, 1988). The key components of differentiation, then, include an individual's level of fusion versus emotional cutoff, and *I position* versus emotional reactivity (Skowron & Friedlander, 1998).

The ability to differentiate is largely determined by how an individual's nuclear family manages anxiety related to balancing the issues of separateness and togetherness. Projection of anxiety onto children typically produces lower levels of differentiation (Bowen, 1978). When individuals are overwhelmed by emotionality and anxiety in their family, they are likely to remain fused or emotionally cut off.

Assessing the various dimensions of differentiation not only provides markers of psychological health and dysfunction for clients, but also for therapists. High levels of differentiation allow therapists to be near others' anxiety without owning it or becoming emotionally reactive (Chen & Rybak, 2004). This is vital when addressing spiritual and religious issues, which tend to have great potential for reactivity. Emotional reactivity by therapists makes the three steps of multicultural process very challenging.

Spiritual-differentiation, in particular, refers to one's level of resolution and ownership versus reactivity in regard to spiritual and religious issues. Everyone, including therapists, has had some experiences with religion and spirituality, which influence the development of beliefs, values, and practices. When past experiences with religion and spirituality are intrusive, the process of developing and choosing one's own beliefs and practices, without blindly adopting and/or reacting against those experiences, can be quite challenging (Johnson, Buboltz, et al., 2003). For therapists, like Carlos in the vignette, who have experienced *spiritual-violence*, also referred to as "religious wounding" (Fukuyama et al., 2005), which is judgment, abuse, oppression, and/or restriction of a person's authentic self in the context of religion or spirituality, it can be very difficult to work with spiritually and religiously oriented clients due to the therapist's own sensitivities and associated reactivity. Due to the importance of spiritual-differentiation for therapist competency, the last chapter of the book will be devoted to this topic.

Premise 5: An Integrated Model Increases Competency

Many therapists are simply lacking a model for how to conceptualize and address spiritual and religious issues in therapy, largely due to the foundational tensions within the therapy field. Despite these impediments, there are several theorists who have attempted to bridge the gap between psychology and spirituality. Of great importance is the work of Carl Jung. Jung broke radically from Freudian thought by focusing on what could be termed *psychoanalytic mysticism*. He believed that religion held more healing and redemptive power than did psychological analysis alone. He argued that each person has potential access to a deep pool of collective knowledge (i.e., the collective unconscious) and that the kernels of knowing exist inside everyone, in the form of archetypes. He proposed the idea of the Self as an archetype that represents human striving for unity. The Self strives for wholeness, especially through the avenues associated with religion and spirituality, and is described as "the only accessible source of religious experience" (Jung, 1957, p. 101).

More recently, the integration of psychology and spirituality has been given fresh energy, as the definition of spirituality has been broadened and clarified as potentially distinct from organized religion. This broadening has engendered a more inclusive view of spirituality that is sparking interest in many who have felt unrepresented by and reactive to organized religion. Movements in the field of psychology, such as dialectical behavior therapy (e.g., Linehan, 1993a, 1993b), acceptance and commitment therapy (e.g., Hayes, Follette, & Linehan, 2004; Hayes & Smith, 2005; Hayes, Strosahl, & Wilson, 1999), transpersonal and integral psychology (e.g., Boorstein, 1996; Cortright, 1997; Forman, 2010; Vaughan, 2000; Walsh, 1999; Wilber, 1996, 2000, 2006), body-oriented therapies (e.g., Eisman, 2001; Kurtz, 1987, 1990; Ogden, 1997; Roy, 2003), mind-body medicine (e.g., Benson & Proctor, 2010; Proctor & Benson, 2011), and Buddhist psychology (e.g., Brach, 2003; Epstein, 2007; Germer, Siegel, & Fulton, 2005; Magid, 2002; Prendergast, Fenner, & Krystal, 2003; Safran, 2003; Welwood, 2000) are connecting with people who are interested in learning about various forms of holistic, reflective practice.

A primary goal of this book is to provide readers with a model that integrates traditional and contemporary psychological theories with a broad-based, thematic, and inclusive view of spirituality. Using a model that integrates various psychological theories provides therapists from different theoretical orientations with increased competency in assessing and addressing spiritual and religious issues with clients from a variety of faiths and spiritual and philosophical positions, especially when such competency is combined with a high level of spiritual-differentiation.

Premise 6: The Real Self *Provides a Link Between Psychological Theories and Spirituality*

A number of theories from different schools of psychological thought converge around the idea that there is a core self, a higher self. There are different names for it (e.g., inner knowing, Self, ego, wise mind, natural self, authentic self, core self), but the idea seems to be the same. That is, there is a part of everyone that exists at the center of one's being, which holds great potential for growth, health, and creativity and possesses knowledge about what is life-affirming and life-enhancing. Borrowing from Karen Horney, a post-Freudian analyst, I call this the *Real Self.* The Real Self has access to the collective knowledge described by Jung and is each person's guide to healing, growth, abundance, and the potential for transcendence. Horney (1950) defines the Real Self "as that central inner force, common to all human beings and yet unique in each, which is the deep source of growth" (p. 17).

Throughout this book, I propose that the Real Self provides a conceptual and practical link between psychological ways of understanding health and healing and a broad-based, thematic, and inclusive view of spirituality. Being out of touch with the Real Self has both psychological and spiritual consequences, which lead to the majority of difficulties that motivate clients to seek mental health treatment. Assisting clients with embracing their Real Self enables them to regain the most significant source of guiding wisdom in their lives.

Premise 7: Client-Defined Spirituality Is an Asset in Therapy

Understanding client-defined spiritual or religious beliefs and practices can be a significant avenue for connecting with clients and very useful for therapeutic change. When therapists are open to learning about their clients' philosophical, spiritual, and religious views, they will come to understand their clients on a deeply personal level. For clients who have a preference for discussing these issues, matching clients' preferences significantly improves therapy outcomes (Smith et al., 2007; Swift et al., 2011; Worthington et al., 2011).

Even for clients who do not specifically request that spiritual or religious issues be addressed in therapy, a broad-based and inclusive view of spirituality can inform and support therapeutic change. The therapist's task is to listen for how clients talk about existential issues of meaning, values, mortality, and sense of self in the world. Philosophical notions of existence will often reflect spiritual beliefs and practices, broadly defined. The goal is to be open to how clients define, experience, and access whatever helps them stay connected to their core values and the inner wisdom of their Real Self. Some clients will experience and access spirituality through traditional methods such as prayer and meditation, while others may connect to personal clarity through a variety of nontraditional ways. It shouldn't matter to therapists *how* their clients connect with spirituality. What matters most is whether the spiritual practices are life-affirming and support personal integrity.

Personal integrity provides an inner compass, based on core values. I often ask clients to consider how their lives and choices would be if they were based on the wisdom of their Real Self. When choices are made from the centered wisdom of the Real Self, clients lead a *value-driven life.* They tend to make choices that are congruent with their core values. Helping clients define, experience, and access their own life-affirming spiritual beliefs and practices (even if they don't refer to them as "spiritual") supports them in leading a discerning and intentional life and is a tremendous ally in the therapy process.

Spirituality and Religion

There is no clear consensus on what is meant by the terms *religion* and *spirituality,* although there seem to be some common themes associated with the two concepts. For example, Hodges (2002, p. 112) provided the following list of similarities between religion and spirituality; both provide:

- Meaning in life
- Intrinsic values as the basis for one's behavior
- Transcendence
- A relationship with a Higher Power
- A belief in a creative and universal force
- A shift of "locus of centricity to humanicentricity, of egocentricity to cosmicentricity"
- Inclusion within a larger collective
- Guidance through a divine plan
- An experience, a sense of awe and wonder when contemplating the universe
- Shared values and support within a community

Others have articulated the differences between religion and spirituality. According to Hill et al. (2000), religion can be understood as adherence to a belief system and practices associated with a tradition in which there is agreement about what is believed and practiced while spirituality can be understood as a general feeling of closeness and connection to the sacred. The sacred can be a divine being or object, or a sense of ultimate reality or truth. Similarly, Koenig (2008) defines spirituality as a personal desire for connection with the Sacred, transcendent, or ultimate truth/reality, while religion:

◆ Is a system of beliefs and practices of those within a community with rituals designed to acknowledge, worship, communicate with, and come closer to the Sacred, Divine, or ultimate Truth or Reality.

◆ Usually has a set of scriptures or teachings that describe the meaning and purpose of the world, the individual's place in it, the responsibilities of individuals to one another, and the life after death.

◆ Usually has a moral code of conduct that is agreed upon by members of the community, who attempt to adhere to that code.

Many individuals experience spirituality through religion, while many others do not equate their spiritual beliefs and practices with religion (Worthington et al., 2011). Spirituality can be viewed as the umbrella concept, with religion being one of many avenues for connecting with the sacred and divine. Kelly (1995) described religion as "creedal, institutional, and ritual expressions of spirituality associated with world religions and denominations" (p. 5). As cited in Gold (2010), spirituality is "broad enough to accommodate the uniqueness of all individuals . . . and indeed the whole of humanity irrespective of beliefs, values, or religious orientation" (Hollins, 2005, p. 22).

For the remainder of the book, I will exclusively use the term spirituality as an overarching concept that refers to religion as well as broader spiritual and philosophical beliefs and practices. Borrowing from Hodges (2002), I conceptualize spirituality as any beliefs and practices that foster meaning, intrinsic value, and integrity as a basis for one's behavior, and a life-affirming conception of and connection with something larger than oneself. In short, spirituality helps individuals move from a narrow, egocentric position to a sense of connection with a greater whole and a divine force or purpose. This broad definition allows for an inclusive and client-defined view of spirituality. The focus for therapists is on being open to the unique ways that clients define, experience, and access life-affirming spiritual beliefs and practices.

In the next chapter, I provide a discussion of the many ways that clients may define, experience, and access spirituality. Having an understanding of how clients may speak about spirituality provides therapists with an avenue to nonjudgmentally invite a collaborative exploration of the role of spirituality in their clients' lives.

CHAPTER 2

CLIENT-DEFINED SPIRITUALITY

Dan was a 48-year-old client who entered therapy primarily due to alcohol addiction issues, feelings of inadequacy, and relationship conflict with his wife. He had been sober for about two months after completing a 30-day residential treatment program. Although he was feeling some increased self-esteem as he progressed in his recovery process, he indicated that most days he felt quite "overwhelmed and disoriented." He had "always coped" through the use of alcohol and by avoiding relational intimacy. His wife had been overtly critical of him for several years. She was frustrated and lonely due to his "withholding of affection" as well as the many broken promises and lies related to his drinking. Dan carried a great deal of guilt and regret about his drinking and deceptive behaviors, especially in relation to his wife and teenage children, which contributed to his feelings of being relationally incompetent. On many occasions, Dan reported that he didn't know how to live life sober. He felt most comfortable when he was at AA meetings, although he was somewhat confused and conflicted about the focus on embracing a higher power.

Dan was raised in a moderately religious, nondenominational Christian family that attended church regularly. He reported some experiences of judgment in the context of religion, and he didn't feel a connection to the Christian faith. For most of his adult life he distanced himself from organized religion, although this carried some guilt for him as well. When individuals at AA meetings spoke about their connection to spirituality, he experienced a range of emotions. He was simultaneously confused about what they meant (his understanding of spirituality had been exclusively associated with organized religion), scared that he might be "preached at," and deeply intrigued by the possibilities. Something about the way that spirituality was discussed by his sponsor, in particular, interested and captivated him.

When I showed sincere and nonjudgmental interest in him and his reflections on spirituality, he increasingly shared about his childhood experiences with religion and his unfolding sense that there "may be something to this spirituality thing." In one session, our dialogue occurred as follows:

Dan: I think I am getting glimpses of what Dave (his AA sponsor) is talking about.

Rick: Glimpses of what? Tell me more.

Dan: I don't know. He's always talking about being open to God, or a higher power. But it's different than my usual idea of God. He talks about opening your heart in the moment. He says that he has found more peace when he connects to something bigger than himself. Dave's kinda Buddhist, I think. I know he meditates, but he talks about God. Over the last few days I have been noticing my heart more. I have been having these feelings of peace. It's weird, (pause) but good.

Rick: You and I have been talking about opening yourself up and taking risks in relationships, with your wife and kids, and about your childhood. This sounds like another level. Say more.

Dan: Yep. It feels like that, but different. I'm not sure. It just feels like there may be something else. I'm not ready to call it God.

Rick: It sounds like it matters what you call it?

Dan: I don't know. It's weird. It's like when I'm open to a higher power, I notice something in my heart, like Dave talks about.

Rick: What happens when you feel it in your heart?

Dan: I feel calmer, (pause) and better, like it's going to be okay, that I'm not such a bad guy.

Rick: Wow! This is really exciting. Tell me more. When are you having these feelings?

Dan: Mostly when I go for walks in the morning. I try to just focus on the beauty around me and focus on my breathing. Sometimes I worry a lot, but sometimes I can relax and just walk and breathe.

Rick: What do you think is happening in those moments?

Dan: I don't know. I think it's like a higher power or something. I guess it's spiritual. It doesn't make a lot of sense to me, but it's cool. It's helpful.

Dan and I continued in our discussion by further exploring these spiritual experiences, including how he could intentionally access this form of spirituality as well as what these experiences may mean for his life. With my and his sponsor's encouragement, he learned to utilize these spiritual experiences as an effective coping strategy and a grounding force in his life. His morning walks, in particular, became a vital resource for his recovery as well as a source of wisdom and self-esteem. Dan found that the peace he experienced when he "got in touch with a higher power" on his walks was antithetical to being self-critical. His ability to maintain his sobriety, challenge negative self-talk, and take relational risks with his wife and children were greatly enhanced by the inclusion of spirituality in his life. Over time, his personally defined spiritual practice became a foundational part of his holistic health and growth.

For therapists to competently address spiritual issues, it helps to have a familiarity with the various ways that clients will talk about spirituality. Therapists can listen for clients' oftentimes unique ways of making sense of the world and their place in it. When therapists attune to their clients' personal ideas of spirituality, therapy outcomes tend to improve (Robertson, 2010; Robertson et al., 2009; Worthington et al., 2011).

Partly due to my personal interest and partly as a way to increase my competency with addressing spiritual issues in therapy, several years ago I conducted informal, qualitative research on how people experience spirituality, by asking almost 100 people (clients, students, workshop attendees, friends, colleagues, and so forth) three questions:

1. What is your personal definition of spirituality?
2. How have you experienced spirituality in your life?
3. How do you access or practice your spirituality?

What I found is that spirituality is uniquely defined and experienced, yet common themes emerge. These themes provide a foundation for therapists to conceptualize and address the very personal topic of spirituality in broad and inclusive ways.

People of faith often answer questions about their spirituality with certainty and with language that is true to their faith structures. Many people believe that their way of knowing spirituality is the only *right* way. For some, spirituality is based on a relationship with an active, personal, and intentional force or entity that is external to them (i.e., usually "God"). For others, the experience of spirituality is internal. Other people experience an external sense of spirituality that is not intentional and personal (e.g., nature, the cosmos). Still others view spirituality as synonymous with religion and religious doctrine, while many others separate spirituality from organized religion.

Along with a multitude of ways of conceptualizing spirituality, individuals use various words to express personal and paradigm-based definitions of spirituality. Although far from an exhaustive list, some of the names for or ways of understanding spirituality that many use include: God (as defined by different religious faiths),

Higher Power, Holy Spirit, Great Spirit, Soul, Essence, Higher Self, Source, Transcendence, Divine, Universal Love, Joy, Purity, Oneness, Interconnectedness, Interbeing, Energy-Between-Things, Light, Clarity, Divine Potentials, Flow, Nature and Natural Beauty, Creative and Artistic Expression, Vision, Guiding Force, Universal/ Life Force, Life Energy, Sacree, Creator/Creatress, Unity Consciousness, Sacred Mother/Feminine, and Sacred Father.

Others describe physical sensations and sensory perceptions they associate with spirituality. Just a few of the many sensations I have heard described include:

- Feeling like a comforting presence is near or enveloping them
- Sensations of being held or comforted
- A deep knowing in their chest or stomach
- A knowing that they are not alone
- Feeling like they are deeply cared for by a larger force
- "Tingly" and warm feelings on their body or skin
- A warm light or sensations entering their body, head, eyes, or heart
- Spontaneous relief from emotional or physical suffering
- Feelings of peace and clarity
- Experiencing coincidences and connections
- "Hearing" or feeling intuitive wisdom and direction
- A sense of being part of something larger than themselves
- Feelings of being interconnected with all things
- "Seeing" or sensing energy fields
- Moments of clarity and perspective on time and space
- "Seeing" or feeling glimpses of truth in the world or in one's sense of being

It is easy to offend or alienate people (and clients) when talking about spirituality. If the *wrong* words are used, individuals often turn away from the message; they believe the words don't represent their relationship with or understanding of spirituality. Simply put, spirituality is often a very personal issue, for clients and therapists.

In this book, therapists are encouraged to work within their clients' personal definitions and views of spirituality. Based on my intention to discuss an accessible and inclusive view of spirituality, the remainder of this chapter will focus on integrative themes that cut across the many ways of knowing and relating to spirituality, which can assist therapists by providing a framework for understanding their clients' as well as their own spiritual beliefs and experiences. Faiver, Ingersoll, O'Brien, and McNally (2001) highlighted the usefulness of spiritual, "trans-cultural themes" that are "universal to human existence" (p. 18). The spiritual themes they proposed are: hope, virtue, sacred ground, polarities, facing oneself, compassion, love, meaning, and transcendence. The themes I chose to highlight emerged largely from the interviews I conducted, where I asked about the many ways that people define, experience, and access spirituality in their lives, but also from various sources across faith traditions. Because I am most familiar with Christian and Buddhist perspectives, examples and supporting citations will mostly be from these two perspectives.

I will not attempt to summarize the many different faith traditions, to provide an in-depth comparison of different faiths, or to provide a comprehensive discussion of any particular perspective on spirituality. Rather, the purpose of the chapter is to discuss key themes that are relevant across faith traditions and are useful for integrating with psychological approaches to growth and healing. As Wayne Teasdale (1999) writes in his book *The Mystic Heart*, when spiritual traditions meet, "interspirituality" occurs and greater truths can be realized.

Remembering

The first theme I want to discuss is the heartfelt sense many people have that they already possess spiritual knowledge. When people experience spiritual insights, they often describe the feeling as being confirmatory, as though they are remembering something rather than learning it for the first time. Many describe it as a feeling of "already knowing," or at least having glimpses of knowing. For most, this feeling of knowing is hard to put into words. It occurs on an intuitive level and can emerge through many different avenues, such as looking deeply at a sunset or a piece of art, listening deeply to the sounds of a stream rippling over rocks, and opening one's heart during prayer and spiritual reflection. The remembering inevitably brings perspective and clarity to their life as well as feelings of certitude, calmness, joy, and solidity.

It is important for therapists to embrace the idea that clients already possess, and have access to, a certain amount of spiritual wisdom. If spirituality is, at least partially, something that is remembered by clients, then therapists don't need to teach about spirituality, and thus they avoid the ethical and clinical problems associated with imposing their beliefs onto clients. Clients' inner wisdom should be viewed as an ally and a resource. From this perspective, a central focus of therapy is on facilitating connection to clients' inner knowing and intuitive clarity.

External Presence and Inner Knowing

A sense of remembering and knowing spiritual wisdom seems to come from both internal and external sources and is described by people of many faiths. One way to understand external spiritual presence is reflected in ideas of God that cut across many faith structures. Many people describe the feeling that God (personally defined) has always been available to them, even when they have chosen to not access him or have had only a faint sense of his presence. (Many, but not all, individuals refer to God in the masculine.) It's a feeling or sense that God is waiting to be invited into their lives. This experience is exemplified by comments a client made to me: "Even when I turned my back on God, I knew he was there waiting for me. I always felt his presence, even though I wasn't ready to accept him into my life."

Along with prayer and reflective practice, external presence is often known and experienced through both transcendent and ordinary experiences, including relationships with others, beholding nature and natural beauty, and creative and artistic expression, themes which will be expanded upon later in the chapter. Thus, an aspect of spirituality that is commonly discussed by people is a feeling of remembering what they already know and remembering to connect with an external presence that is available, most often cited by people as God.

Inner spiritual knowing is also described by those from many different faiths. From a Christian perspective, connecting to inner knowing is often equated with connecting with the Holy Spirit within us. "We know that we live in him and he in us, because he has given us of his Spirit" (*New International Version Bible*, 1984, I John 4:13). The Holy Spirit is understood generally as the energy sent by God. David Steindl-Rast (1995) defined the *Holy Spirit* as the breath of divine life and argues that, "From the biblical perspective, there has never been a human being that is not alive with God's own life breath" (p. xiv).

Buddhists provide other ways of understanding this sense of inner knowing, including reincarnation and the belief that all people possess *Buddha nature*. Buddha nature is the seed of enlightenment and spiritual knowledge that exists in every person. Buddha nature represents the inner potential to become fully awake.

In his immensely powerful and inclusive book *Living Buddha, Living Christ*, Thich Nhat Hanh (1995), a prominent Vietnamese Buddhist monk and teacher, provided a beautiful integration of not only Buddhism and Christianity, but also the concepts of Buddha nature and the Holy Spirit. He proposed that when individuals live life being aware of and awake in the present moment, they activate their inner potential and connect with the Holy Spirit. Thereby, they invite the Holy Spirit into their hearts and lives. From both Christian and Buddhist perspectives, then, all people possess the potential for knowing deep truths, with every moment offering opportunities to be awake to spirituality within and around them.

Transcendent and Ordinary Experiences

While sitting atop a mountain or hilltop with a view of the surrounding environment, it is easy for many people to embrace the majesty and profound beauty of the world. During periods of intense prayer and spiritual practice, people can experience intense bodily and emotional sensations. Peak experiences such as these tend to interrupt the perceptions of everyday experience of life and provide individuals with glimpses of a transcendent perspective. During moments of transcendence, some people report having visions of being part of an intricate interconnected web of life, being connected to God or spiritual energy, having glimpses into the nature of reality, or reevaluating their core values and priorities, to name a few reactions. Yalom (2009) refers to these "awakening experiences" as "existential shock therapy" (p. 31). The point is that entering into peak or transcendent experiences allows many individuals to have insights and perspectives that they don't normally have in day-to-day living, which can be quite useful to the therapeutic process. Peak experiences tend to increase clients' openness to reflections on themselves and their lives.

In addition to transcendent experiences, many people report having spiritual experiences throughout their everyday lives. Whether looking at a tree while walking during a lunch hour, compassionately seeing the beauty and suffering in another person's face, or simply washing the dishes after dinner, each moment contains possibilities to see deeply into the nature of life. This idea is captured in a famous Buddhist saying: "Before enlightenment the Monk chops wood and carries water. After enlightenment the Monk chops wood and carries water." After enlightenment, the Monk does the same chores; however, the Monk's experience of his chores is different. He is more awake to the present moment and to the experience of the chore. Each moment contains all of life.

In his book *Ordinary Mind*, Barry Magid (2002) describes the ideas of transcendent and everyday spiritual practices as "top down" and "bottom up." Top down spiritual practice is intended to induce a peak experience, usually through focused concentration that eventually brings flashes of insight and understanding. Bottom up practice, on the other hand, supports spiritual growth by being in the moment and becoming attuned to emotional and physical sensations that naturally occur as an aspect of being.

An important theme, therefore, is that spirituality can be accessed through ordinary as well as exceptional experiences. As therapists, it is important to be able to listen for and explore spiritual experiences as clients describe them in everyday and transcendent forms.

Present Moment Awareness

Many people report that spirituality is most accessible to them when they are awake in the present moment. Although this theme is most associated with Buddhism and other Eastern traditions, the idea cuts across faiths. For example, many people describe the intensity of their prayer sessions being increased when they are fully present with the experience in the moment. Buddhism teaches that any moment can be a spiritual moment, when experienced with conscious presence.

As therapists we often see our clients (and ourselves) not embracing present moment awareness. Many people spend the majority of their conscious awareness focused on experiences that have already occurred or on those they are anticipating. So much suffering is caused by the continual addiction to thinking about how life *should have been* or how it *needs to be*. "If only this hadn't happened, then I could be happy. If only this would change, then I could be happy. If only I had this relationship, then I could be happy." This isn't to say that life isn't hard. However, most of the time clients create more misery by making happiness contingent upon certain conditions being met, which may be largely out of their control. And when the conditions they deemed necessary for their happiness are met, they painfully realize that the conditions are transitory. They cannot hold on to and possess the conditions. So, they feel pain and then rush to find new conditions they hope will create and support their happiness. This is a very unwise and painful cycle.

When not focusing on the past or future, many people are simply not awake. They are mindlessly following ritual and routine, not aware of what is occurring within them, and not intentionally engaged in their lives. They often suffer from chronic feelings of boredom and alienation.

Years of attempting to live an aware and intentional life have only strengthened my belief in the power of present moment awareness. The present moment is where life is always lived. Even when reminiscing about the past or planning for the future, there can be an awareness of present experience. The present moment is where the breath is in one's consciousness, where the mind can calm down, and where there is an awareness of one's heart.

Interconnectedness

Several years ago, I attended a talk by Mark Epstein, a psychiatrist who focuses on integrating psychoanalysis and Buddhism. After his talk and as he was leaving to read from his new book at a local bookstore, I asked him the same question I have asked many other people, "What is your definition of spirituality?" He said,

"Spirituality is anything that helps us realize we are not separate selves, anything that allows us to see we are interconnected with everything else." Dr. Epstein's answer to my question mirrored what I have heard from many people, especially those who practice Eastern traditions: that interconnectedness is an aspect of their spiritual wisdom.

From Taoist and Buddhist perspectives, spirituality is primarily experienced through moments of knowing or experiencing oneness. Voices from various fields of study, such as quantum physics, systems science, psychology, communications science, and ecology, are joining and supporting the Eastern philosophical view that all of life is interconnected by dynamic patterns of energy. Thich Nhat Hanh (1995) described this idea as "interbeing—the Buddhist teaching that nothing can be by itself alone, that everything in the cosmos must 'interbe' with everything else" (p. 203). As Joan Halifax (1993) noted, "Buddhist practice and my study of shamanism have helped me see that we are one node in a vast web of life. As such, we are connected to each thing, and all things abide in us" (p. 13).

Although mostly associated with Buddhism and various Eastern faith traditions, oneness can also be understood from a Christian perspective. Christians would likely describe the energy among all things as again being the Holy Spirit. "For the Spirit of the Lord fills the whole universe and holds all things together . . ." (*New American Bible*, 1992, Wisdom 1:7).

For many people, once they begin to grasp the ideas of oneness and interconnectedness, they no longer feel so isolated and alone in the world. They also tend to develop a deeper sense of compassion and responsibility for all beings. They begin to realize that what they do matters and affects everyone and everything else, like energy rippling out and eventually interacting and touching all of life. They feel a sense of harmony in their lives rather than alienation and competition. As Catherine Ingram (2003) says in her book

Passionate Presence, "The deepest contentment comes from recognizing the pervading life force in everything" (p. 188).

Love and Fear

What role, if any, does fear have in healthy living? In short, the answer is that fear should have a very limited role. Fear can be a gift that informs people when something is not right. Humans have a natural, built-in tendency to fear things that can harm them. At its best, fear motivates individuals to act decisively to protect themselves and restore safety by triggering a fight or flight response. In fact, problems can occur when they don't listen to their intuition about fear, when they ignore the signs that something is not right.

Unfortunately, after the danger is gone, fear turns from a gift into an obstacle. Fear overwhelms and paralyzes many people. Think about the vast numbers of clients who enter therapy with anxiety-related symptoms. Fear-based living encourages people to consistently overestimate the dangers in their world, which robs them of spontaneity, joy, and generousness. Thus, although fear can serve the purpose of alerting people to danger, it more often leads to a perception that life is more dangerous than it actually is and fosters limitations in their lives. In other words, fear can inform under limited circumstances, but it should not run one's life.

Although some religions propagate fear as a means to control and direct their followers, many different faiths espouse the idea that spirituality supports a loving energy and presence. In fact, many people report that love is the central aspect of their definition of and experience with spirituality. Marianne Williamson's (1992) book, *A Return to Love: Reflections on A Course in Miracles*, introduced many people to the belief that fear, rather than hate, is the opposite of love. Christians generally believe, "God is love. Whoever lives in love lives in God, and God in him. There is no fear in love. But perfect love drives out fear. . ." (*New International Version Bible*,

1984, I John 4:16). Speaking from a Taoist perspective about the "Way of Love" in her book *The Tao of Inner Peace*, Diane Dreher (1990) writes, "Compassion for ourselves and others breaks down illusions of separation, bringing greater harmony to our world" (p. 201).

The unifying idea is that embracing a loving and compassionate heart allows people to make decisions based on joy and abundance instead of fear and scarcity. Therapists can support clients by helping them to focus on embracing what is life-affirming and nourishing rather than avoiding what scares them.

Free Will

The interplay between free will and determination is one of the most hotly contested and controversial topics in various fields of study, including religion, psychology, physics, and philosophy. Some, including many I interviewed, placed almost limitless faith in each individual's ability to create his or her own reality while others argued that life is largely predetermined. Although varying and competing points of view exist, some convergence of ideas is possible.

First, there seems to be an interaction between free will and a larger purpose or possibilities. Most people, especially those from Western cultures, embrace the idea of free will, focusing their ideas of spirituality on the process of choosing their paths in life and determining their realities. On the other hand, many people experience a guiding force in their lives, alerting and encouraging them to choose life-affirming options. From a Christian perspective, God gave humans free will *and* he has a higher purpose in mind for each person. As discussed in Rick Warren's (2003) book, *The Purpose Driven Life*, each person's mission should be to understand and get in line with God's purpose and plan for him/her.

Although it is nearly impossible to grasp and hold the entire, complete meaning of one's life, when individuals more clearly understand their purpose in the world, they can intentionally direct their energies, prayers, and choices in accordance with this deeper understanding. Generally speaking, when their intentions and behaviors are in line with a spiritually based sense of purpose, their lives are more joyous, meaningful, and successful.

A Zen Buddhism perspective adds to the discussion of this interplay of free will and determination by espousing concepts such as *flow* and *naturalness*. In *Zen Mind, Beginner's Mind*, Shunryu Suzuki (1973) uses the image of a plant growing naturally out of the ground: "The seed has no idea of being some particular plant, but it has its own form and is in perfect harmony with the ground, with its surroundings. As it grows, in the course of time it expresses its nature. . . . That is what we mean by naturalness" (p. 108). From this perspective, there is a natural course of development and growth that flows through life. Difficulties occur when choices are not in accordance with these natural processes and one's true nature.

Another way of thinking about free will and determinism is an image of a tunnel. Most people see their lives and options as very narrow, as if contained within a tunnel. They are largely unaware of the many possibilities swirling just outside their tunnel. Fear-based thinking drives this tunnel vision and defines reality. Conversely, when they embrace love in their lives they become awake to the many possibilities available to them.

Thus, some individuals describe spirituality as seeming to offer an *invitation* to live life in accordance with a deeper purpose and meaning; they still have the freedom to choose whether to accept the invitation. Many Christians talk about this invitation, which is exemplified by the words of Jesus, "Come to me, all you who are weary and burdened, and I will give you rest" (*New International Version Bible*, 1984, Matthew 11:28). Many people talk about the opportunity to accept the invitation and guidance of spirituality, which leads to life-affirming choices and a tendency to experience a flow, congruence, and naturalness in life.

Most therapists tend to emphasize (possibly overemphasize) free will. Along with empowering clients in their attempts to make changes in their lives, it is important that therapists are open to various ideas of determinism. This can take the form of understanding how past events and conditions have influenced and shaped clients' worldviews and behaviors. It may also take the form of a personal relationship with a guiding and intentional force, such as God. It often can be useful to explicitly discuss clients' ideas on free will as well as the events and forces that shape their choices. The central point is to understand how clients address and attempt to resolve the interplay of the two, which can profoundly influence their behaviors and emotional, psychological, and relational health.

Creativity and Artistic Expression

One of the most significant events that impacted my motivation to write about spirituality occurred when I went to a local poetry reading. I have always had an appreciation for the arts and could *see* spiritual energy in various forms of creative expression, including music, dance, and visual arts. However, when I went to this poetry reading I felt as if my heart literally opened up and I experienced clarity about the deep connection between artistic expression and spirituality. As I was driving home from the reading, I had a very strong sensation of warm light pouring into my chest. I pulled the car over and wept, feeling a profound sense of gratitude for life and the presence of spirituality in all things. I also experienced a sense of purpose and clarity related to writing about the link between psychological ideas of health and spirituality. After attending the poetry reading, the outline of my first book poured out of me over the next few days. I couldn't quiet the thoughts and ideas unless I wrote them down. I was totally consumed. I went from having a vague interest in writing a book to having the entire book outlined in just 5 days after the poetry reading.

Creativity and artistic expression were often mentioned by people I interviewed as connected to spirituality. The creative process seems to be touched and guided by energy and vision that are transcendent. It is outside normal everyday perception. And creative arts invite many individuals to experience transcendent glimpses that challenge and expand their ordinary tunnel vision.

Many of my clients are both deeply spiritual and deeply artistic. They embrace many different faiths. Yet, regardless of their specific spiritual and religious beliefs, the common denominator seems to be a connection between spirituality and the creative process. Many of them have read *The Artist's Way*, by Julia Cameron (1992). This wonderful and powerful book provides tools and a structure for harnessing personal, spiritual, and creative potentials. A majority of my clients have some form of regular spiritual and reflective practice in their lives. Creative and artistic expression is often an important part of that practice.

Nature and Natural Beauty

Many individuals report being deeply affected by nature and indicate that participation in the natural world is the primary way they connect with spirituality. In fact, after prayer, engaging with nature was the most common response I received related to how people experience and access spirituality in their lives. Reconnecting with the "Body of the Earth," as Joan Halifax (1993) described in her book, *The Fruitful Darkness*, is a sacred and basic aspect of many people's existence. Unfortunately, modern life often disconnects individuals from nature and, therefore, from their core self. Reconnecting to nature feeds and nourishes one's soul and restores a balanced perspective. For some people, intentionally connecting to geography and nature is a form of pilgrimage, whereby, as Joan Halifax says, "the Earth heals us directly" (p. 51).

Recognizing oneness with nature and the "value of place," as discussed by Rick Bass (1996), creates a convergence of ecology and spirituality. Diane Dreher (1990) indicated, "To study nature is to follow the Tao; to follow the Tao is to know ourselves" (p. 132). When individuals lose touch with nature and natural beauty, they often lose touch with themselves. When intentional engagement with nature is part of a regular spiritual practice, individuals tend to stay connected to the natural rhythms of life and to spiritual energy within and around them.

Openheartedness

Many individuals describe their experience of spirituality as deep, very personal, and heartfelt. Some discuss spirituality in intellectual terms. Most, however, describe an experience that transcends words and rational explanations. Spiritual experience tends to be a matter of the heart. When their hearts are open to the experience, the energy of spirituality tends to change people. It changes their perceptions of themselves, others, and reality. How different reality is when consciousness is based on a loving heart rather than on fear and scarcity. Heartfelt experience seems to lead to a generousness of spirit for many people.

I have heard it said that having children changes you. "Your heart is no longer inside just your body. Part of your heart now resides inside your child." The heart-based love for one's children provides many individuals with opportunities to experience and access a profound sense of connection and spirituality. Although having children certainly provides opportunities to become open-hearted, it is far from the only way to do so. Heartfelt experience is available all the time, in every moment. People often simply forget to notice. They become too busy to be awake to the possibilities. They stay task-focused and closed off from others and their true nature.

As a therapist, I regularly ask clients what happens when they come home after a long day. Does their exhaustion, need to complete tasks, or thoughts about the day interfere with their awareness and ability to be open with their family members or friends? If they are closed off regularly, significant others may pull away from them and stop hoping they might respond with an open heart. Yet, these moments are some of the most available for clients to practice reconnecting with spirituality. If their primary relationships are life-affirming, significant others tend to respond well to openhearted-ness, providing reinforcement for the generousness of spirit.

Personal Relationship

Spirituality is a very personal matter. I have expressed throughout this chapter that there are many ways to define, experience, and access spirituality. As a friend and colleague of mine said when I asked her about her definition of spirituality, "It must be personal for it to be transformative."

The personal nature of one's spiritual beliefs and experiences make it vital that therapists are inviting and accepting of what clients share with them, or they will simply not do so. It also makes it important to not impose beliefs on clients. Spirituality is an area in therapy where teaching clients has some emphasized cautions. Generally speaking, it is best to listen for and work with the words that clients use and to explore and deepen their narratives rather than to teach new ones. An accepting and open approach to the many ways that clients experience spirituality encourages them to discuss their personal views, and increases their consciousness and awareness of spirituality.

Along with the personal nature of spiritual beliefs and practices, spirituality can also be understood as occurring most readily within a personal relationship. In other words, many individuals report having a personal relationship with spirituality, most often described as God. The idea that God meets people where they are, which many Christians believe, is one way of describing this personal relationship.

A personal relationship with spirituality is not exclusive to Christianity. Individuals who regularly engage in various forms of spiritual practice, whether through prayer, mindfulness, connection with nature or the creative arts, or various other means, report having a sense that spirituality is an essential part of their life and routines. Regular practice seems to foster this consciousness and provides a format for the development of a personal relationship with spirituality, which often informs their moral barometer and sense of self. Conversely, when individuals lose touch with this personal relationship, the development of their personal integrity can become inhibited and they can become lost in their lives, an idea that will be expanded upon in a subsequent chapter.

In addition to developing one's own personal relationship with spirituality, many people report that their sense of spirituality is increased when they practice as part of a group, whether that is in a formal religious group or through less formal interpersonal relationships. As would be expected, discussion of spirituality increases awareness and provides support and validation of beliefs and practices.

Relationships, as therapists know, are also a key to personal healing. Most problems that bring individuals into therapy result from disturbances in relationships. Problems oftentimes are rooted in attachment and differentiation issues with parents and family members and are played out in adult relationships. Along with contributing to problems for many people, relationships are also a primary vehicle for healing, with spirituality also emerging in these relational contexts as well. As Charlotte Kasl (2005) says in her book *If the Buddha Got Stuck*, "loving relationships heal trauma."

Thematic Integration

In this chapter, therapists have been encouraged to understand how clients may define and discuss their personal sense of spirituality.

Possible themes include clients *remembering* both inner knowledge and external presence as well as connecting with spirituality through both transcendent and ordinary experiences. Present moment awareness seems to bring many clients the greatest opportunity for embracing spirituality and the accompanying sense of peace and intuitive knowing, regardless of their faith positions. Connecting with spirituality also often brings clarity and perspective about the interconnectedness of life, which tends to increase compassion for others and an awareness of the impact of thoughts and actions on the world.

Many individuals experience spirituality as a loving, compassionate force. Embracing love in their lives, rather than fear, seems to bring joy and abundance rather than reactivity and scarcity. Accepting the *invitation* of spirituality, as many describe it, seems to require an active use of free will and courage to act on convictions and integrity. Spirituality is accessed through various forms of reflective practice, including prayer, meditation, creativity and artistic expression, beholding nature and natural beauty, and openheartedness. Most important, spirituality is personally defined and tends to occur within life-affirming relationships. When clients develop a personal relationship with spirituality, it often becomes a guiding and structuring element in their lives, leading to an increased sense of personal integrity.

In the next chapter, I will discuss various psychological theories, which will provide a foundation for spiritually oriented therapy and point to the idea that there is a wise, core self within all individuals. This core self provides a conceptual and practical link to utilizing client-defined spirituality.

CHAPTER 3

INTEGRATING SPIRITUALITY
WITH PSYCHOLOGICAL
THEORIES

Many therapists report that they lack conceptual and practical skills related to addressing spiritual issues in therapy, including how to integrate spirituality with their theoretical orientations and therapy models (Hickson et al., 2011). In this chapter, some key theories and approaches in the psychotherapy field will be briefly discussed in an attempt to provide a basis through which therapists can incorporate client-defined spirituality. These theories point to the existence of a foundational sense of being within all individuals, the Real Self, which when activated promotes growth, clarity, and meaning and is a conduit to various ways of experiencing and practicing spirituality. The Real Self not only acts as a compassionate and wise guide for clients, but is also an invaluable ally for therapists as they endeavor to assist their clients.

The goal of this chapter is not to provide an exhaustive summary of available counseling theories, nor is it to provide an in-depth discussion of any particular theory. Rather, I hope to provide an introduction to how select theories conceptualize the self as well as self-development, and to set the stage for an integrative view of practicing spiritually oriented therapy.

Freud

Freud (1920/1966, 1949) proposed that the personality consists of three intrapsychic structures: the id, ego, and superego. The id is the primary source of motivation and energy in the personality, the energy being instinctual and expressed mostly through sexual and aggressive drives. The id lives by the pleasure principle and lacks the ability to delay gratification. The ego is the manager of the personality and operates by the reality principle. It manages the archaic and irrational impulses of the id and deals with the demands of the external world, including the superego. The superego represents moral training and develops when the standards of society are internalized. The superego is driven by the perfection principle. The demands of the superego often clash with the id's instinctual needs, which create anxiety. The ego copes with the conflict between the id and superego and the inevitable anxiety that this conflict generates by using of a variety of defense mechanisms, with repression being the most prominent defense in Freud's theory.

Although Freud was largely critical of spirituality, his theory provides a starting point for the idea that the personality is composed of various, and oftentimes competing, parts. His later writings also set the stage for contemporary theories that extended the role of the ego beyond simply mediating between the id and the superego; namely, the ego has its own motivational energy to test reality and provide leadership to the personality.

Jung

Carl Jung (1971, 1981), a contemporary of Freud, proposed ideas that broke from traditional Freudian thought and focused on spirituality and mysticism as transcending forces. Many people consider Jung to be the pioneer of the integration of psychology and spirituality. His work continues to grow in popularity and is currently well represented by James Hollis (1996, 2000, 2005, 2009) and Robert Johnson (1983, 1993; Johnson & Ruhl, 2009), among others. Jung's theory is vast and comprehensive, with several key concepts being important to this book, including his ideas about the structure of the personality and our ability to connect to transcendent experience and knowledge.

For Jung, the ego is the center of consciousness. It is the totality of one's conscious being: memories, thoughts, feelings, and sensory perceptions. Like Freud, he argued that each person has a personal unconscious, which contains experiences that have been repressed from awareness. Unlike Freud, he proposed that each person also has access to a deep pool of knowledge, the *collective* or *transpersonal unconscious.* The collective unconscious contains memory traces from our ancestral past. It is psychic residue of human and animal ancestry that accumulates over many generations and propels psychological and spiritual evolution. The collective unconscious is made up of *archetypes*: symbolic images representing universal thoughts, with corresponding strong emotions. Archetypes are collective motifs or representations that are inherited, "unconscious images of instincts themselves" (Jung, 1981, p. 44). Thus, kernels of knowing exist inside each person in the form of archetypes. The importance of this idea is that everyone has access to knowledge and deep wisdom about themselves and their lives.

Two of Jung's archetypes that are quite useful to this discussion are the *Self* and the *shadow.* The Self is often referred to as the internal wise person, which strives for wholeness, centeredness, and meaning, especially through the avenues associated with spirituality. When connected to the Self, individuals are connected to the wisdom of the collective unconscious and to sustainable meaning in their lives. For most people, the first half of life is devoted to the service of the ego while in the second half, the strivings shift to the realization of the Self. In other words, over time there is increased awareness of the opportunities to live in closer accordance with the "soul's intentions" for life, a process described in James Hollis' (2005) book, *Finding Meaning in the Second Half of Life.* The Self increasingly becomes an intuitive guide as individuals courageously take responsibility for their lives and embrace what is meaningful, a concept that is central throughout this book.

The shadow archetype includes animal instincts that humans inherited through evolution, traits that are often deemed as primitive or uncivilized. The shadow is all that the ego consciously wants *not* to be. It is the unconscious, compensatory side to the ego ideal, that is, what the ego consciously wants to be. Along with repression (i.e., the unconscious exclusion of threatening material from conscious awareness), projection protects the ego from anxiety associated with recognizing the shadow and the potential to act on those needs. Projection involves attributing or seeing qualities in others that are unconsciously denied or disowned, thus keeping individuals safe from recognizing and owning their shadows. For example, if individuals are frightened by anger, it is likely that they have banished (i.e., repressed) their own anger into the shadow of their personality. When they deny their own anger, they will likely be unconsciously drawn to another person who expresses anger more easily than they do, even if it repulses them, which leads them to consciously attempt to eliminate expressions of anger in the other person. In other words, they project their denied anger onto the other person, who acts it out for them even as they try to change that person.

The importance of the shadow and corresponding interpersonal dynamics cannot be overstated, particularly when individuals attempt to embrace psychological and spiritual health, because of the tendency to overvalue the ego ideal (i.e., who they think they *should* be). The more rigidly the ego ideal and shadow are separated, the bigger the shadow becomes, increasing the likelihood that individuals will act out their needs in ways that will be in contradiction to their personal integrity. Chapter Six will be devoted to the importance of assisting clients with integrating their shadow to promote sustainable psychological and spiritual health.

Object Relations and Attachment Theories

Object relations theories consist of a loosely defined cluster of models most represented by the thinking of Melanie Klein

(1975), W. R. D. Fairbairn (1954), Margaret Mahler and associates (Mahler, Pine, & Bergman, 1975), Otto Kernberg (1975, 1976), D. W. Winnicott (1971), James Masterson (1976), Heinz Kohut (1971, 1977), and, more recently, Stephen Mitchell (1988, 2000) and Sheldon Cashdan (1988). Attachment theory is most associated with John Bowlby (1988), Mary Ainsworth (1978), and more recently, Peter Fonagy (2001) and colleagues (Fonagy, Gergely, Jurist, & Target, 2002). Although significant differences in concepts and language exist between object relations and attachment theories, these theories share a focus on the processes through which a sense of self develops within the context of early parent-child interactions.

The core of these relational models is the belief that humans need contact with others and are psychologically formed through their relationships. Humans are pre-wired for connecting with others, mostly for survival reasons. A person's basic sense of self develops in a relational context; individuals learn who they are and what they can expect from others through repeated interactions with significant others, most notably parents. The repeated interactions with parents, caregivers, and others (e.g., siblings) form a kind of foundational *interpersonal* or *relational template,* for a child's emerging sense of self. Relational templates have been given various names, such as self-object templates and internal relational working models.

From this perspective, the process of developing a sense of self occurs through stages or developmental pathways, with the central developmental task being the dialectic between connection and separateness. Specifically, children and caregivers need to form a strong attachment bond, and yet children ultimately need to become separate psychologically. Theoretically, if children can form a strong attachment bond with parents and also feel supported in their attempts at separation and exploring the world, children develop a stable sense of self that allows them to *self-soothe* when not in contact with parents. Children can bring to mind an image of a caring, supportive parent even when they are not in physical contact with their parents. This self-soothing process allows them to develop a stable sense of self and to tolerate the anxiety associated with autonomy. The child's early successes with separation from and connection with parents set a trajectory for healthy development and lead to a variety of self-soothing strategies as the child grows. Strategies for self-soothing may include talking oneself through a stressful event, connecting to a core sense of identity, connecting to feelings of competency or safety, and returning to familiar and grounding activities. The ability to self-soothe in the face of anxiety is a central barometer of health throughout life.

The relational paradigm is particularly useful for therapists as they integrate their clients' spiritual beliefs and practices into the therapeutic process. First, clients' relational templates are often associated with their spiritual templates, that is, their view of themselves and what they expect from the world spiritually. Specifically, clients' ideas of themselves vis-à-vis a higher power or other notions of spirituality often mirror their relationships with significant attachment figures in their lives (Rizzuto, 1979). Their conception of their spiritual position in the world can be thought of as a spiritual, self-in-relation (Hall, Brokaw, Edwards, & Pike, 1998). It can be quite instructive for therapists to inquire about the content of clients' prayer life, for example. The spiritual positions that clients assume in relation to a higher power often reflect their broader interpersonal themes and conflicts. Common themes include trust, power, self-efficacy, forgiveness, and responsibility as well as core feelings of esteem or shame.

A second, and related, highlight of this model is the emphasis on self-soothing, which can be supported through a life-affirming spiritual practice. A personal and client-defined spiritual practice can provide support that is similar to the nurturance of parents being internalized by a child (Rizzuto, 1979). In this case, clients can engage in spiritual activities and/or call upon an internalized loving, supportive image or feeling associated with their spiritual beliefs and practices, which enables them to self-soothe and tackle the inevitable anxiety of living, an idea I refer to as *spiritual resourcing.*

Interpersonal Theory: Horney

Interpersonal theories comprise a number of models that focus on the development of relational strategies, primarily for the management of anxiety. Recent theorists in the area include Michael Kahn (1991), Lorna Benjamin (1996), Donald Kiesler (1996), Myrna Weissman, Gerald Klerman, and associates (Klerman, Weissman, Rounsaville, & Chevron, 1984; Weissman, Markowitz, & Klerman, 2000), Edward Teyber (2000), and Jeremy Safran (Safran & Muran, 2000), while the foundation for the theory was laid primarily by Harry Stack Sullivan (1953, 1954) and Karen Horney (1945, 1950).

Horney provided a model of interpersonal theory that has been termed *psychoanalytic humanism.* She introduced the concept of the Real Self, the part of every person that contains growth potentials. Although similar in some ways to Freud's original view of the ego, Horney's conception of the Real Self has more in common with Jung's Self archetype. The primary motivation of the Real Self is to strive for health, meaning, and life-enhancing experiences.

The Real Self naturally emerges under relatively optimal life circumstances. With favorable parenting and life circumstances (e.g., predictable love, respect, and support) a child develops feelings of belonging and security and the Real Self flourishes. Conversely, when parenting or life is characterized by unfavorable circumstances (e.g., neglect, abuse, traumatic loss, and unsupportive parents) the child experiences *basic anxiety* (generalized feelings of insecurity, discomfort, loneliness, and helplessness) and development becomes based upon the idealized self (very similar to Jung's idea of ego ideal) rather than the Real Self. Put simply, when one's life and upbringing are supportive and without trauma, the natural tendency will be to strive to actualize potentials and flourish in life. The more life is characterized by unfavorable parental and environmental conditions, the more individuals move away from their Real Self and utilize compensatory, interpersonal strategies to cope with life circumstances and the associated basic anxiety.

Compensatory strategies are clearly not as healthy for individuals as behaviors that would be chosen by the Real Self—they are compromises to make the best of a situation. Strategies initially employed by children often become patterned and are used throughout their lives. The more rigidly and persistently strategies are utilized, the more their use can become problematic.

When clients are supported by therapists to connect with their Real Self and associated wisdom, they can attain clarity on not only their lives, but on larger spiritual perspectives. The Real Self is a guide and conduit to spirituality. I conceptualize the Real Self as the Holy Spirit that resides within. It is God's life breath. It is one's Buddha nature, inner essence, and true and natural self. When clients lose touch with their Real Self, they lose touch with the single most important guiding force in their lives, and as a result, they struggle. Assisting clients with embracing their Real Self enables them to access guiding wisdom in their lives. Being out of touch with the Real Self, conversely, has both psychological and spiritual consequences, which will be discussed in detail in the next chapter.

Humanism: Rogers

In stark contrast to the Freudian view that humans are driven primarily by instinctual impulses within the id, that unconscious thoughts and feelings have a dramatic impact on a person's actions, and that the human personality is largely formed during the first 6 years of life, Carl Rogers (1951, 1961, 1980) proposed that humans are innately positive and have free will that can be expressed across the life span. Rogers' approach, termed person-centered therapy, focused on facilitating a person's inner potentials and ownership of options and choices. He believed each person has inner dignity and unique value and possesses the ability to know what is life-affirming and life-enhancing. At their core, individuals have *inner wisdom* and *inner knowing* about what is positive for them in their lives.

Along with other humanistic theorists, Rogers argued that if basic needs are met (e.g., food, shelter, safety, and love), humans have a natural tendency to strive for self-actualization. Self-actualization refers to the process of embracing one's potentials and transcending limitations that are self-imposed or have been internalized. Self-actualization can be expressed and experienced through a variety of creative and unique ways and is individually defined. For some people, self-actualization is experienced through accomplishments or peak experiences, including profound spiritual experiences. For others, it is experienced through everyday activities. The central and defining aspect of actualization experiences is that they contribute to growth and potentials in life-enhancing ways.

Rogers also proposed that humans have a learned sense of self, which is based on the perception of regard by others (i.e., how others, especially parents, evaluate them). Under relatively optimal parenting and life circumstances, individuals will make life-enhancing choices and will devalue experiences that are contrary to the self-actualization process. In other words, if parents and significant others have positive, life-affirming views of children, they will internalize this positive regard and strive to actualize their potentials. Conversely, if parenting and life circumstances are characterized by abuse and life-detracting experiences, individuals internalize those experiences and oftentimes move away from their unique potentials and lose touch with their inner knowing and positive sense of self.

As they become adults, individuals have more and more freedom to make choices in their lives. Sometimes these choices can involve difficult decisions related to listening to their own inner wisdom versus allowing others to dictate to them what they think is good for them. Rogers did not advocate rejecting others' advice per se. He simply believed that if individuals can quiet down and focus their awareness on their own internal wisdom, they will find their own answers and know what is right for them. Unfortunately, many individuals, due to fear of not being loved or accepted by others, stop listening to their innate inner wisdom. This *de-selfing* process is one of the primary ways individuals lose touch with their Real Self and suffer in their lives.

Rogers' immense contributions to the field of psychology focus on his unwavering belief that within all people is an *inner wise person* that can guide and direct them in their lives. His theory punctuates the need for therapists to not impose their beliefs on clients, a caution that is particularly relevant when dealing with spiritual issues. He believed it is disrespectful to assume to know what is best for others, or to tell them what to do with their lives, or how to practice their spirituality. Rather, he urged therapists to turn clients inward to reconnect with their own inner knowing and develop clarity about their needs and choices. Clients are then encouraged to act courageously in accordance with this wisdom, even if it means disappointing others. Generally speaking, it is better for clients to love themselves and take ownership of their decisions than to allow others to define or control them. The key to Rogers' approach is in helping clients grasp the notion that the wisdom and clarity they seek already exists within them, which allows them to experience the exhilaration of their freedom as well as ownership of their personal power.

Control-Mastery Theory: Weiss

Control-mastery theory was originated and developed by Joseph Weiss (1993), with the theory's tenets being researched and tested by Weiss, Harold Sampson, and others (1986) at the San Francisco Psychotherapy Research Group (formerly the Mount Zion Psychotherapy Research

Group). Control-mastery theory is a contemporary, integrative theory that has been termed a cognitive-psychoanalytic theory because it integrates cognitive theory into an extension of Freud's later ideas. The result is a wonderfully rich and useful theory of personality and psychotherapy approach.

Weiss extends Freud's later writings by proposing that the ego is not simply managing anxiety generated through the internal conflict between the selfish demands of the id and moralistic demands of the superego. Weiss argues that the ego has its own energy, which is focused on adapting to the environment, making sense of life events, and maintaining connection with parents. Traumatic and emotionally unsettling experiences, especially those that threaten attachment to parents (e.g., abuse, neglect, and abandonment), create a strong urgency to make sense of these experiences.

Unfortunately, children tend to blame themselves when traumatic events occur, leading to *pathogenic beliefs*. Pathogenic beliefs, acquired as the child infers causality about traumatic experiences, are convictions about how one must behave in order to avoid being retraumatized. Pathogenic beliefs set parameters around what kinds of behaviors are allowable and lead to inflexible behaviors. Pathogenic beliefs and associated inflexible behaviors tend to become overgeneralized to all areas of life, and tend to stick with individuals throughout their lives. These inflexible behaviors also tend to be self-fulfilling. For example, if individuals approach relationships with a rigid style of caretaking or assuming too much responsibility for the lives of others, they tend to attract complementary types (i.e., underfunctioners) and elicit complementary behaviors from others, which then reinforce their pathogenic beliefs and their perceived need for continuing the inflexible behaviors. Thus, they get what they expect and a self-reinforcing cycle ensues.

At the core of control-mastery theory is the belief that individuals have *unconscious plans* to heal past wounds, disconfirm pathogenic beliefs, and increase behavioral flexibility. Individuals attempt to heal and disconfirm pathogenic beliefs by reenacting childhood trauma in current relationships in hopes that better outcomes will result. This tends to emerge in two ways: (1) transference tests and (2) turning passive into active. Transference tests occur when they reenact the same old dynamic and assume the same interpersonal position (e.g., caretaker, responsible one, etc.) as when the pathogenic beliefs first started to form during childhood. Turning passive into active occurs when they re-enact the same old dynamic and adopt the other person's interpersonal position (e.g., Dad's drunken irresponsibility) and find someone who will play their childhood role (e.g., responsible one). Either way, they unconsciously hope the outcome will be different and they will resolve the trauma and disconfirm the pathogenic beliefs.

Thus, control-mastery theory provides a growth-oriented explanation for the repetition compulsion, a term noted by Freud, which is the tendency to repeat relational patterns that were unresolved or troublesome in the past. That is, individuals are not simply repeating what they witnessed or experienced as children; rather, they are drawn to similar relationships again and again in hopes of healing unresolved trauma and disconfirming pathogenic beliefs. Unfortunately, these attempts can be retraumatizing and may end up reinforcing pathogenic beliefs.

In this approach, therapists see their clients as cotherapists and as experts on themselves and what they need. A therapist's job is to help clients become aware of their unresolved traumas and associated pathogenic beliefs, inflexible behaviors, and unconscious plans to heal and grow. Therapists help make unconscious plans conscious, and then support clients as they make cognitive and behavioral changes in accordance with their plans.

This is another theory that supports the notion that each client possesses inner wisdom, spiritual wisdom. The theory highlights that inner health is trying to emerge. Even seemingly ineffective behavior by clients can be conceptualized as the ego's attempts to master conflicts, grow, and transcend. A life-affirming spiritual practice can support this growth-oriented process by providing insights and wisdom as well as spiritual resourcing that aligns with and fosters clients' inner plans.

Internal Family Systems Theory: Schwartz

Internal Family Systems (IFS) is a contemporary theory, which was developed by Richard Schwartz (1995, 2001) as an integration of family systems models, Jungian theory, and various other theorists who propose that our personality is comprised of parts. The resulting integrative theory is an empowering and nonpathologizing view of human functioning and an approach to healing and growth.

Schwartz describes parts within individuals as subpersonalities that interact with each other and the outside world. The parts have healthy preferred roles, which can become extreme and problematic, mostly due to traumatic life experiences. Schwartz divides the personality into four major parts: (1) Self, (2) Managers, (3) Exiles, and (4) Firefighters.

The Self, borrowed from Jung's Self archetype, is the core of the personality. The Self is the part of individuals that seeks meaning and integration. When individuals are emotionally balanced, the Self acts as a wise leader and exhibits characteristics such as calmness, curiosity, compassion, confidence, creativity, connectedness, courage, and clarity. Everyone has a Self. However, extreme behaviors from the other parts can limit the Self from assuming an active and compassionate leadership role within the personality. Sometimes, the other parts have been leading for so long they do not trust that the Self will lead effectively. In situations where people have endured trauma and abuse, they lose touch with their Self and tend to define their personalities as consisting solely of the other parts. In other words, they have very limited ability to connect with or access the full characteristics of the Self.

Managers run the day-to-day aspects of most people's lives. They attempt to keep individuals safe and functional by maintaining control of their world. These are the very responsible parts that remind people to follow the rules, keep their jobs, be on time for appointments, and stay in control in relationships. Managers play roles such as controller, striver, caretaker, pleaser, judge, critic, passive pessimist, and planner. When they are in balance, Managers help individuals function in their lives. When out of balance, they promote fear-based decisions designed to avoid change and eliminate risk. The essence of the fear is that if control is lost, bad things will happen.

Exiles are those parts of the personality that hold painful, raw emotions and experiences. They are the vulnerable parts that have experienced pain and trauma and tend to be isolated from the rest of the internal system. They become extreme when they are not being heard or validated by the other parts, which happens periodically because the other parts avoid the raw and scary emotions contained in the Exiles. Any emotions that are deemed unacceptable can be exiled by the other parts, which is similar to Jung's idea of the shadow archetype. Typical examples are shame, fear, neediness, loneliness, anger, grief, abandonment, and any memories associated with childhood trauma (e.g., verbal, physical, and sexual abuse).

Firefighters are the parts that jump to action whenever an exiled part floods individuals with painful emotions, memories, or sensations that overwhelm the Managers' ability to control the situation. Firefighters act to repress the emerging Exiles and distract them by impulsively seeking stimulation that can override the pain. Examples of firefighting behaviors include addictive behaviors (drugs, alcohol, food, sex, work, shopping, gambling, etc.), rage, violence, self-mutilation, suicidal thoughts and behaviors, and dissociation.

Many people spend the majority of their conscious lives moving between Managers, Exiles, and Firefighters and have lost significant contact with their core Self. Most individuals define who they are almost exclusively from the Manager consciousness. The main goal of IFS is to return the Self to its rightful leadership role of the internal system, which includes supporting the other parts in finding their voice and assuming healthy roles. In other words, all parts need to be heard, but the Self needs to run the show.

The Self clearly has access to not only psychological leadership but also to spiritual wisdom. The calm curiosity of the Self strives for wholeness, integration, and clarity, especially through spiritual pursuits. Thus, the Self provides a natural avenue to integrating client-defined spiritual practice into the therapy.

Dialectical Behavior Therapy: Linehan

Marsha Linehan (1993a, 1993b) originally developed dialectical behavior therapy (DBT) to treat individuals diagnosed with borderline personality disorder. DBT combines traditional cognitive-behavioral techniques with mindfulness to assist clients with increasing their distress tolerance, emotion regulation abilities, and interpersonal effectiveness. Along with treating borderline personality disorder, DBT has been increasingly used by therapists to address many different client issues, including anxiety, mood disorders, impulse-control disorders, addictions, and trauma. DBT skills are being used by therapists across theoretical orientations to support client self-soothing and self-regulation.

The foundational skill in DBT is mindfulness, which can be defined as having three interconnected parts: "(1) *awareness*, (2) *of present experience*, (3) *with acceptance*" (Germer et al., 2005, p. 7). Thus, mindfulness is being awake, present, and nonjudgmental of what *is*. Mindfulness encourages clients to be aware of their thoughts, emotions, and experiences in the present. When they can be accepting of their present experiences, clients tend to have a decrease in negative attributions of their thoughts, emotions, and circumstances and an increase in coping.

Along with having clients practice various mindfulness-based skills, Linehan teaches about various states of consciousness: reasonable mind, emotional mind, and wise mind. Reasonable mind emerges when clients are being logical and rational, which is important to learning skills and dealing successfully with many of the practical issues of living. However, many of life's issues have an emotional component. When emotional mind takes over, individuals are more likely to act impulsively and reactively to life events and circumstances. Wise mind is an integration of emotional mind and reasonable mind, and transcends both. It is a state of mind in which individuals experience themselves as calm and centered; they act in accordance with their inner beliefs, values, and intuition. Wise mind utilizes mindfulness to be aware of emotions and logic, and then makes decisions that lead to feelings of integrity and wholeness.

The connections between DBT and spirituality are obvious. The theory assumes that all individuals have access to wise mind, which is connected to deeper truths about reality and successful living. In addition, all forms of spirituality can be enhanced when clients practice mindfulness and are open to their present experience. The feelings of being calm, centered, and grounded are linked to spiritual insights and experiences for many people across faiths. Many of Linehan's ideas have been adopted by various types of therapy, especially as a form of client resourcing.

Transpersonal and Integral Theories

The field of transpersonal and integral psychology is vast and expansive. Many different theorists and practitioners have made significant contributions (e.g., Boorstein, 1996; Cortright, 1997; Forman, 2010; Vaughan, 2000; Walsh, 1999; Washburn, 2003), with Ken Wilber (1996, 2000, 2006) perhaps being the most well known. The various theories tend to embrace a developmental and holistic perspective that includes personal and transcendent experiences.

Lajoie and Shapiro (1992) define *transpersonal psychology* as being "concerned with the study of humanity's highest potential, and with the recognition, understanding, and realization of unitive, spiritual, and transcendent states of consciousness" (p. 91). Caplan (2009) states, "Transpersonal psychology addresses the full spectrum of human psychospiritual development—from our deepest wounds and needs, to the existential crises of the human being, to the most transcendent capacities of our consciousness" (p. 231).

Various spiritual traditions are incorporated into transpersonal/integral theories, including Hinduism, Yoga, Buddhism, Zen, Taoism, Sufism, Christian mysticism, Shamanism, and Native American beliefs and practices. Common themes that are explored across these theories include spiritual development of the Self, peak and mystical experiences, higher or ultimate potentials, and transcendent states of consciousness. In particular, these approaches clarify differences between the ego and the core Self. Following Jung, the ego is defined as the story of personal identity: It is who individuals usually say that they are, including the totality of their conscious memories. It contains the labels that they tend to use to describe themselves. The ego is fragile and needs regular reminders of its existence. The Self, in contrast, is the transcendent essence at the center of every person that far exceeds ego. In short, the ego is connected to a small mind concerned with individual pursuits and protection while the Self is connected to the big mind of the collective unconscious, and beyond.

Transpersonal and integral psychology, along with DBT and other contemporary psychological approaches (e.g., Brach, 2003; Epstein, 2007; Germer et al., 2005; Hayes & Smith, 2005; Magid, 2002; Prendergast et al., 2003; Safran, 2003; Welwood, 2000), advocate for the use of mindfulness to further psychological and spiritual development. Whether engaging in prayer, meditation, or any activity with transcendent potential, mindfulness provides an opportunity to open oneself to higher states of consciousness and spiritual wisdom.

Life Span Development Theories

A variety of developmental theories have been proposed or adapted to understand the process of spiritual identity formation and attainment, including Allport (1950), Piaget (1965), Erikson (1959, 1968), Marcia (1966, 1980), and Fowler (1981, 1991, 1996). These theories provide views of how an individual's conception of spirituality and a spiritual sense of self develop and lead to various levels of complexity and maturity. Along with the other theories discussed in this chapter, therapists can use developmental models to understand clients' spiritual journey and identity process, especially in the context of their broader cultural lives (Fukuyama et al., 2005; Miller, 2005). The goal for therapists is to meet clients where they are rather than impose an idea of where they should be. Developmental theories are also useful to assess therapists' spiritual identity and how their levels of attainment may influence their ability to competently address spiritual issues with clients. The aforementioned theories will be briefly summarized.

Allport's Religious Sentiment Stage Model

Allport proposed a simple, three-stage model of spiritual identity development: (1) believing what has been taught about faith, (2) doubting what has been taught about faith, and (3) dealing with the ambiguity of what has been taught by fluctuating between faith and doubt (Worthington, 1989). A successful developmental process leads to a mature faith, which is characterized by individuals being (Kelly, 1995; Miller, 2005):

* Well-differentiated: Their views are based on a cognitive, evaluative process that leads to ownership of a faith structure.
* Dynamic: Their faith has shaped their personal and social development in positive ways.

+ Directive: Their actions match their values in caring for others.
+ Comprehensive: Their faith includes an active process of dealing with issues of meaning in life.
+ Integral: Their faith can include scientific information.
+ Heuristic: Their faith can accommodate and integrate new information and experiences.

Piaget's Cognitive-Development Stage Model

Piaget's stages have been applied to spiritual development to highlight how spiritual views can alter based on changes in cognitive abilities. Worthington (1989) summarized the spiritual focus of the stages as:

+ Object permanence: the presence of an unseen God
+ Symbolic representation: symbolizing objects of faith
+ Logical thinking: considering religious questions
+ Formal operational thought: considering complex interactions between faith and various life experiences

Erikson's and Marcia's Psychosocial and Identity Status Models

Within his stages of psychosocial development, Erikson clearly delineated the developmental significance of identity formation, and stressed the importance of an active search for identity during adolescence. As cited in Miller (2005), Kelly (1995) summarized the contribution of Erikson's theory to spiritual development as:

+ Fostering a faith that supports a child's sense of trust and hope, in contrast to religious faith that instills fear.
+ Building up a system (ideology) of values, sometimes manifested in religious tradition, that adolescents may relate to in their expanding search for personal identity.

- Promoting a sense of universalism to undergird the generative care of adulthood.
- Contributing to older adults' formation of a mature sense of the meaningful and integral wholeness of life. (p. 69)

Building upon Erikson's identity versus role diffusion psychosocial stage, Marcia proposed that adolescents and young adults can typically be categorized as being in one of four ego identity statuses: (1) identity achievement, (2) foreclosure, (3) moratorium, and (4) diffusion. Membership in each identity status is determined by the degree of personal exploration and commitment related to ideological and interpersonal issues, including spirituality. Those who attain identity achievement have struggled through their own exploration process before arriving at a place of commitment. Those in foreclosure commit to an identity that is largely based on their parents' beliefs without exploring alternatives of their own. Those in moratorium are actively searching and exploring, but have not come to a place of commitment. Lastly, those in diffusion are neither searching nor are they committed to an identity.

Fowler's Stages-of-Faith Model

Fowler proposed the following six stages of faith development (Miller, 2005):

Stage One—Intuitive-projective (3 to 7 years): focused on imagination, fantasy, and imitation, which are not limited by logic.

Stage Two—Mythical-literal (7 to puberty): focused on the beliefs and symbols of an individual's religious community in a literal way.

Stage Three—Synthetic-conventional (puberty to adulthood): focused on conforming to beliefs and values of an individual's religious community with an emphasis on authority, which unifies values in a sense of identity.

Stage Four—Individuation-reflective (young adulthood): focused on personification of beliefs, symbols, and meanings, which lead to more personal responsibility for an individual's own beliefs.

Stage Five—Conjunctive (mid-life): focused on awareness of paradox, contradiction, and integrating opposites, which lead to more openness to change.

Stage Six—Universalizing: focused on loving others at a universal level that goes beyond an individual's faith, which leads to spiritual awareness in the present moment.

Thematic Integration

Although the various models presented in this chapter are quite different, several themes emerge from these theories. First, there is convergence around the idea that structures exist within the personality, with the core essence of the personality being some form of inner wisdom and intuitive knowing. Whether talking about ego, the Self, wise mind, or the Real Self, a number of these theories propose that on some level all people know what is good for them and what will be affirming in their lives. In this book, I refer to this inner wisdom and core sense of self as the Real Self, the part of every individual that contains the collective knowledge described by Jung and wants to heal from traumatic and unresolved experiences, to grow and actualize potentials, and to provide compassionate leadership in life.

These theories also repeatedly point to the importance of relationships. The basic sense of identity, including spiritual identity, is formed in the context of relationships and culture, especially in one's family. In families, individuals learn about relational themes such as intimacy, conflict, trust, and the dialectic between separateness and relatedness. The types of interactions individuals have throughout childhood and adolescence have a great influence on how they think and feel about themselves and others, how they expect to be treated by others, and the behavioral options and intimate relationships they choose. Their relational templates are also often related to their spiritual templates, and lead to developmental outcomes. Most important, personal, and spiritual relationships provide a primary vehicle for healing, growth, joy, and abundance.

To some extent, these theories focus on the role of anxiety in personality formation and the ability to live a happy and successful life. Anxiety is a natural part of living. A primary source of anxiety comes from actual or perceived threats to significant relationships, first and foremost with parents. A certain amount of anxiety can be beneficial in that it can motivate individuals to tackle difficult tasks and to connect with their strengths, autonomy, and competency. However, too much anxiety can be overwhelming. Thus, everyone needs to find ways to manage anxiety and learn to self-soothe, with the use of interpersonal strategies and spiritual beliefs and practices playing an inevitable and necessary role in this process.

Different theories have various explanations for why individuals seem to repeat painful experiences and dysfunctional relationships over and over. Weiss's theory, in addition to conceptualizing this as a repetition of familiar relational templates, provides a growth-oriented explanation that assumes individuals repeat experiences in an attempt to gain control and mastery over unresolved and traumatic experiences. Once again, the idea is that humans have innate inner wisdom and a hardwired drive to heal and grow.

Jung, Horney, Rogers, Schwartz, Linehan, and the transpersonal and integral theories specifically point to the existence of creative and transcendent energy within everyone. In particular, Jung, Linehan, and the transpersonal and integral theorists emphasize the role of spirituality in health and healing. Building on the foundation of these ideas, a central tenet of this book is that the effectiveness of therapy can be enhanced by an integration of client-defined spiritual practice. When clients' Real Self is aligned with and embraces life-affirming spirituality, a greater capacity to experience guiding and healing energy as well as clarity, creativity, meaning, and sustainable abundance becomes more available to them.

In the next chapter, I will discuss various ways that clients can become lost, psychologically and spiritually. Losing touch with spiritual wisdom and a centered sense of self as guiding and structuring resources are often aspects of why sustained difficulties occur for clients.

CHAPTER 4

GETTING LOST: PSYCHOLOGICAL AND SPIRITUAL PERSPECTIVES

Shawn, a 33-year-old man, entered therapy with depression and a previous diagnosis of post-traumatic stress disorder (PTSD), which was associated with combat duty in the military. Shawn was unemployed and living with his girlfriend and her three young children. They were surviving financially, with much difficulty, through various government support programs. Shawn was receiving group treatment for his PTSD at a local VA hospital, which he reported as helping to reduce his symptoms. He wanted assistance in individual therapy with his chronic "sadness." He experienced the world as an "unwelcoming place." He described his childhood as "troubled," due to having experienced physical abuse at the hands of his unpredictably angry and violent father. Other than knowing that he didn't want to be like his father, he stated that he didn't know who he was. For Shawn, life was dealing with a series of unending crises. He had a strong sense that life could be better, but he "didn't have the map."

Therapy initially focused on a combination of empathic listening and increasing his coping skills. We discussed the idea of "resourcing" as a way to strengthen his coping strategies and as vital to his ability to address his childhood trauma. Our discussions led to a list of activities, which seemed to provide comfort and grounding, with hiking in nature being at the top of his list. He reported that he felt "close to God" and more connected with himself when he was in nature. With encouragement, he talked about his relationship with God and how prayer was increasingly important to him. Over time, his personally defined spiritual practice became an important adjunct to the treatment and an increasingly positive aspect of his life. Slowly, he was able to address his childhood traumas, referring often to a belief and a felt sense that he was becoming "whole."

Alicia, a 42-year-old woman, initially entered therapy at the recommendation of her adult daughter's therapist. Her daughter was dealing with addiction issues and was living in an inpatient facility. In addition to wanting support related to her daughter's substance abuse, Alicia stated that she wanted to deal with her chronic exhaustion, sleep difficulties, and anxiety. Recently, she found herself curled up in a ball on the couch, crying and "paralyzed" by worry and exhaustion.

Alicia was a successful attorney who regularly worked 50 to 60 hours per week. She overfunctioned in most areas of her life and often felt responsible for others, never wanting to let anyone down. When feelings of sadness or anxiety occurred, she would busy herself with her daughter's life, one of her many work projects, or shopping. She was mostly unsatisfied with her marriage but avoided dealing with it. For the past year, her control and avoidance strategies were failing her. Alicia felt as if she didn't know who she was, outside of work and helping others. She felt "so out of balance," with her panic episodes increasing in frequency and intensity. Although it terrified her, she knew that something had to change.

Therapy initially focused on reduction of her anxiety symptoms through the use of mindfulness techniques. Fairly quickly, she was able to substantially reduce her anxiety and moderately improve her sleep. Although her symptoms improved, she continued to feel a chronic sense of lack; something was missing in her life. She then read a book on the basic tenets of Taoism that was recommended by a friend. She resonated with the ideas in the book and began to periodically experience a grounded sense of herself. Therapy continued for almost 2 years, and regularly included her use of mindfulness and her expanding sense of spirituality.

The main commonality between these seemingly disparate cases is the strong sense that each client had: the sense that there is something more to life, and that their attempts to cope were largely missing the mark. Both felt "lost." What were they missing? A key ingredient that was missing at the start of therapy was a connection to their Real Self and the associated spiritual grounding. When clients like Alicia and Shawn are disconnected from their Real Self, they are not only psychologically lost, but also spiritually lost. When lost, clients often forget to trust their inner wisdom or to connect with and be nourished by life-affirming relationships and activities.

Why Clients Get Lost

It is very easy to lose touch with one's spirituality and centered sense of self. Although not an exhaustive list, the following are a few common reasons and experiences why this occurs.

First, many people have had negative experiences with organizations that are proponents of various forms of spirituality. Negative experiences may include abuse, condemnation, and the propagation of fear, guilt, or any ideology that attempts to restrict human potentials and growth—that is, spiritual violence. After having an aversive experience, people are wise to withdraw from that particular organization. Unfortunately, they also tend to withdraw from the idea of spirituality in general and, more specifically, the existence of loving, guiding spiritual energy. They tend to equate spirituality with judgment and oppression.

Another possible outcome of spiritual violence is that individuals disconnect from their inner wisdom and stay with the abusive spiritual practice, most likely as a way to gain acceptance and avoid rejection from significant others. Not unlike an abusive intimate relationship, these individuals are often traumatized and feel powerless. Again, they tend to equate spirituality with judgment and oppression; however, they continue to disregard their inner wisdom and tolerate the judgment.

A second common reason for becoming lost spiritually is fear. This includes not only fear of being violated spiritually by an organization but also fear of change. Many clients talk about fear associated with embracing their emerging awareness of spirituality, which may require them to live their lives differently. For many people, it feels like a *pull* that is interpreted with moral imperatives: to pray, to go to church, to stop drinking, to be a better person, and so on. The moralistic interpretation embedded in this feeling can be quite overwhelming and often triggers past negative feelings associated with organized religion. Consequently, they avoid the awareness that there may be something more to life—something spiritual.

A third reason that clients become lost spiritually is excessive rationalism, which occurs when empirical knowing and intellectual thought are held up as the only valid ways of attaining knowledge. Faith-based, experiential, and intuitive forms of knowing are seen as inadequate and unacceptable. This view is often accompanied by condescending views of faith and of any belief systems that can't be proven through the scientific method.

Clients also become lost spiritually because of the disorienting nature of living. Life can be assaultive: noise, environmental pollution, commutes, news of violence and fear, demands of jobs, financial pressures, pressures from others' needs, and so forth. Clients can even be assaulted by the pressures of their own needs. Many feel assaulted by the nagging awareness that there has to be something more meaningful than their current state of life.

Of course, there are also psychological reasons why clients become lost spiritually. The following discussion offers an integrative perspective on some important issues that contribute to clients losing touch with their inner wisdom and associated actualizing energy of their Real Self.

Role Modeling

Research suggests that parental modeling is one way that children learn how to manage their social-emotional lives (Bar-on, Maree, & Elias, 2007). Many clients were not supported during childhood in developing an inner-directed knowing and an ability to regulate themselves. Their parents may have lacked the skills related to helping them to develop a stable sense of self. Their parents quite simply may not have known how to be sensitive to the individual needs of their children. Consequently, clients didn't learn how to turn inward and to cultivate and value their own intuitive knowledge and personal power, which typically leads to the types of relational and psychological issues that send them into therapy. Thus they struggle with trusting themselves and knowing how to regulate their emotions as well as feel a grounded sense of self.

Invalidation

Sensitive parenting includes validating a child's experiences and unique emotional and cognitive reactions, rather than minimizing or disregarding them. Validation involves recognizing and affirming another person's feelings, thoughts and perceptions. Validation helps children develop congruence between their inner and outer worlds (Siegel & Hartzell, 2003). It provides a mirroring process of their experience that assists them with their identity development and self-regulation skills. When children are regularly validated they learn to recognize their feelings, identify who they are, and muster their internal resources. They are able to soothe themselves in the face of adversity and anxiety. Conversely, children who have their realities regularly invalidated tend to have difficulty trusting themselves, develop negative core beliefs, experience more symptoms of depression and anxiety in adulthood, and lack the ability to self-soothe when they feel anxious (Ford, Waller, & Mountford, 2011; Hong, Ilardi, & Lishner, 2011; Krause, Mendelson,

& Lynch, 2003; Yap, Allen, & Ladouceur, 2008). Linehan (1993a, 1993b) indicated that an invalidating family environment, especially for emotionally sensitive children, fails to help them learn to label and modulate emotional arousal, tolerate distress, and trust their own emotional responses or perceptions as valid interpretations of events. In short, chronic invalidation in childhood is one of the primary reasons that individuals enter therapy.

Consider the following example: Karl, a 51-year-old man, came to therapy struggling with depression, failed intimate relationships, and chronic anxiety. Low-level depression and anxiety were with him almost always; periodically these symptoms would increase to the point that he couldn't get out of bed all day. He grew up with a self-centered, alcoholic mother and an inconsistent father; his father was available if Karl succeeded at athletics but was distant the rest of the time. Karl's feelings and experiences were regularly invalidated; a strong implicit message from both parents was about the importance of maintaining an outer image of being a respectable family while ignoring the obvious problems within the family. Karl tried hard to gain his father's approval and avoid his mother's alcohol-induced anger.

Karl's intimate relationships in adulthood reflected a similar pattern: He was in relationships with volatile women who complained that he never seemed comfortable with himself; they never felt like the *real* Karl was present. When stressed, which was frequent, Karl would alternate between frantic attempts to get the approval of his partners and a sense of failure and resignation. Karl had all the telltale signs of chronic parental invalidation: a tendency to be a chameleon in his relationships with a tenuous sense of self, constant anxiety and insecurity, periodic depression, difficulty self-soothing, and low levels of personal power.

Roles

Every person engages in the interdependent process of being assigned a role or creating a niche in their family system. Children are assigned a role in their family based largely on an interaction between actual characteristics that children possess and projections from parents. Projections occur when parents *see* qualities in children that remind them of someone else (like their own parents) or of parts of themselves. The children then start to believe that they are this quality and act accordingly. These projections have the effect of creating a restricted role for children rather than encouraging them to become who they really are.

Other times, children look into their families and see a need. They perceive that it's up to them to step into a role. This tends to happen more frequently in families that are not functioning well, where the parents or caregivers are not willing or able to provide effective leadership. Research related to children who grow up in alcoholic and/or dysfunctional families (e.g., Alford, 1998; Black, 2001; Devine & Braithwaite, 1993; Veronie & Fruehstorfer, 2001) provides examples of these, at times, overlapping roles, which include:

- The Hero: the child who makes the family appear fine to outsiders.
- The Enabler/Caretaker: the child who takes care of others and cleans up their messes.
- The Scapegoat: the child who diverts attention away from family problems by becoming the focus of negative attention.
- The Lost Child: the child who is invisible and doesn't have needs.
- The Mascot: the child who distracts members from family problems through humor.
- The Parent: the child who provides leadership and guidance for the family.
- The Sacrificial Lamb: the child who endures abuse so that others will be spared.
- The Mediator/Placater: the child who tries to negotiate conflict between members.

How entrenched these roles become depends on the length of time the child is in the role, the degree of urgency and emotionality that motivates the role, and the degree of pervasiveness of the role. Specifically, when a child is in a role for longer periods of time, with higher levels of emotionality and urgency, and across different contexts, there is a higher likelihood that the child will continue this role into adulthood and that it will be rigid and difficult to change. When clients embrace a rigid role, their identity becomes based on the role rather than the natural, life-affirming possibilities of their Real Self.

Structural Family Difficulties

Every family has certain structures that provide the rules of relating among members (Minuchin, 1974; Minuchin & Fishman, 1981; Minuchin, Nichols, & Lee, 2007). Some family structures and associated rules tend to consistently lead to difficulties for children. In particular, the types of boundaries that exist within the family often predict the level of family functioning. Rigid boundaries between members allow for little affiliation and lead to disengaged relationships, which are characterized by emotional distance and lack of intimacy. Diffuse boundaries permit too much affiliation and lead to enmeshed relationships, which are characterized by a lack of separateness and autonomy. Healthy boundaries support affiliation and cohesion as well as independence and autonomy. Thus, healthy boundaries allow children to receive support from parents, and also give them a sense of individuality and autonomy.

The parental subsystem, also known as the *executive subsystem*, is the foundation of any family with children. The parental subsystem can include biological, adoptive, step, and foster parents as well as others filling parental roles. In healthy two-parent families, the parental subsystem is a stable alliance (Minuchin et al., 2007). The parents will disagree at times, but they typically provide a unified front and form a collaborative team to support each other with the various tasks of leading a family. The love, limits, and guidance that they provide are fair, reasonable, and age-appropriate. Research has consistently found that a strong parental bond is a fundamental feature of well-functioning families while a poorly functioning parental subsystem is associated with a variety of psychological and behavioral problems in children, teenagers, and adults (Chase, 2001; Teyber, 2000).

Single-parent families that function well also exhibit a clearly defined executive subsystem that provides leadership for the family. Although it is typical in single-parent families that some executive functions are shared with older children, friends, or extended relatives, an appropriate boundary still exists between children and adults, which allows children to feel secure and to know their place in the family. Children need to know that someone is in charge, there are limits to what is permissible, and their needs will be addressed and met.

Boundary problems in families typically result in some form of a *cross-generational coalition*. Cross-generational coalitions occur when the executive subsystem is weak and a parent has a stronger alliance with someone (usually a child) other than the other parent or designated member of the executive subsystem. These coalitions are often seen in families where a parent uses a child as a confidant or refers to the child as "my best friend." This cross-generational alliance, often referred to as *parentification of the child,* gives too much power to the child and typically creates a collusive contract between parent and child: The child will be the parent's confidant and share the parent's emotional burdens; in return, the parent won't play an authoritative role with the child. This dynamic leads to predictable problems for children, such as: struggles with authority and limits in other areas of life, anxiety due to feeling emotionally burdened, shame, and differentiation difficulties due to guilt associated with excessive emotional loyalty to the parent (Chase, 1999, 2001;

Jones & Wells, 1996; Peris, Goeke-Morey, Cummings, & Emery, 2008; Wells & Jones, 2000).

Commonly, children who are parentified have an exaggerated sense of self-importance, which covers up underlying feelings of inadequacy, a dynamic that has been referred to as the *imposter phenomenon* (Castro, Jones, & Mirasalimi, 2004). They are often privy to details about the parent's life or relationship(s), including the marriage. Children in these circumstances often feel emotionally responsible for the parent, which leads to feelings of being special or superior. However, because children can't consistently make life (e.g., relationships, finances, and addictions) better for their needy parent, they also feel burdened and inadequate; they simply do not have the experience, knowledge, or abilities to fix their parent's problems.

This grandiose sense of responsibility and power as well as underlying fears of inadequacy typically continue for these children into their adulthood. Alternating between extreme positions of arrogance (i.e., pseudo-confidence) and self-doubt, they are driven to succeed out of a fear of failure or inadequacy. Patterns of enmeshment and externally focused reactivity in their relationships also persist. They have learned to tune in and react to another person's pain rather than follow their own inner voice. The more rigidly they play the role of confidant, savior, or emotional support for another person, the more they can lose touch with who they truly are. The sustainable and unique potential of their Real Self becomes lost in their reactivity and flip-flop between self-doubt and overconfidence.

Consider the clinical case of Lee, a 35-year-old man who was dealing with emotional exhaustion and anxiety. The example captures elements of structural difficulties and problematic family roles. Lee grew up as the oldest in a family with parents who openly and loudly argued, sometimes violently. He remembered that as a 5-year-old, he would listen to horrendous fights between his parents and feel confused and terrified. Around this time, his father moved out, and his parents divorced. His mother's drinking increased, as did her depression. Lee's confusion and terror led to chronic feelings of insecurity and responsibility. He felt responsible for his mother's and his siblings' well-being. By age 9, he took over many parental responsibilities, such as cooking and bathing his younger siblings.

As an adult, he became a very successful attorney and worked exceedingly long hours. However, he was plagued by an "unending sense of responsibility and obligation," which led to fear-driven overworking. He feared that if he eased up his work schedule, his life would fall apart: He would let others down and would become financially destitute (he was actually quite wealthy). He knew that his fears were "irrational," but the fear-based reactions were initially too strong for him to change. Lee alternated between extremes of arrogance/superiority and inadequacy. He was far removed from the sustainable, balanced personal power of his Real Self.

Differentiation Difficulties

The differentiation process commonly creates psychological dilemmas for parents and children (Bowen, 1978; Carter & McGoldrick, 1999; Kerr & Bowen, 1988). The key dilemma for children is how to maintain connection with and approval of their parents while being true to themselves. The central issue for parents is how to support their children and allow them to separate and live their own lives. Parents must provide their children with a delicate balance between freedom that encourages their autonomy and guidance that provides support and direction. Young adults must walk the thin line between separating from parents, taking ownership for their own beliefs and choices, and maintaining connection to their families.

Some young adults deal with this balancing act by foregoing their own search process and accepting what parents or caregivers define for them. They remain *fused* with their parents and do not attain a separate sense of self. They foreclose on their identity search and blindly accept what has been told to them, without challenging or deciding for themselves (Johnson, Buboltz, et al., 2003). Thus, they become externally focused and disconnected from their Real Self.

Other young adults deal with the differentiation dilemma by re-actively *cutting off* from their families. They resist fusion by pushing against their parents. These individuals are also externally focused; they are simply reacting against the external demands of their families. They can be just as disconnected from their own sense of self as fused individuals; they cover up their lack of self with reactive identity choices related to relationships or lifestyle while espousing a façade of independence (Johnson & Buboltz, 2000; Johnson, Buboltz, et al., 2003).

The root of fusion and emotional cutoff as well as the intensity of their reactions are largely determined by the degree to which children are the recipients of their parents' projected anxiety (Miller, Anderson, & Keala, 2004). The most common form of parental projection occurs when children are triangulated into spousal conflict, which requires the child to choose sides between the parents (Williamson & Bray, 1988). Another common process occurs when parents project their own agendas onto the child. Examples include wanting a child to go to a certain school, practice a certain religion, or engage in a certain occupation, based largely on the parent's wishes or experiences rather than on what is truly best for the child. When children experience sustained or high levels of projected anxiety, they have trouble knowing how to regulate their own personal boundaries and tend to be overwhelmed by their own or others' emotions. They have trouble figuring out their own beliefs and lose touch with their core sense of self in the face of others' anxiety, especially that of their parents. To deal with this anxiety, they remain fused with their parents and/or reactively cut off (Johnson & Waldo, 1998).

Both fusion and cutoff result in poorly differentiated adults without a clear or stable sense of self, who tend to be highly anxious and to internalize the anxiety of others (Harvey, Curry, & Bray, 1991; Skowron & Friedlander, 1998; Skowron, Holmes, & Sabatelli, 2003; Tuason & Friedlander, 2000). They have difficulty self-soothing and also tend to alternate between extremes of closeness and distance in relationships. Specifically, they take on others' anxiety as their own or create distance to avoid being overwhelmed by the emotionality of significant others. Stated another way, poorly differentiated adults have trouble embracing the emotional middle ground and the appropriate boundaries needed for healthy relationships. The reactive aspects of differentiation difficulties, therefore, inhibit the development of an inner-directed sense of self, including personal integrity and inner wisdom.

Consider Casey, a 26-year-old woman who entered therapy for depression and anxiety. She reported having very low self-esteem and periodic panic attacks, especially related to autonomous activities. At the start of therapy, Casey lived with her single mother; her younger sister was away at college. The younger sister was vilified by their mother for leaving home, while Casey was praised by her mother for her loyalty. Casey was, for as long as she could remember, her mother's confidant and best friend. Her mother was hurt deeply by the divorce from Casey's father when Casey was 5 years old. Since then, Casey remembers she and her mother "being attached at the hip." At age 19, Casey had attempted to live separately from her mother. However, her mother convinced her that living away from home wasn't safe or cost effective. Her mother paid the fee to the landlord for prematurely terminating the lease, and Casey returned home after just a few weeks.

Casey felt responsible for her mother's emotional well-being. She reported that her mother had difficulty trusting others and that she was the "only one" who could really understand her mother. During the course of therapy she came to see how her fused relationship with her mother contributed to her overblown sense of responsibility, her underlying sense of inadequacy, and her difficulty with autonomy and separation. Instead of the natural, actualizing trajectory of her life, she was restricted by her mother's needs and projections. Because she was an extension of her mother, she had great difficulty in identifying who she really was and acting from an independent position. Therapy helped her to define herself more clearly and then find the courage and determination to alter her role with her mother.

Guilt

Guilt serves the purpose of encouraging people to reflect on the consequences of their words and actions. Children are thus socialized to be conscious of the standards set forth by their families and society. At its best, this process helps children internalize these lessons in a balanced way and build their own inner-directed sense of morality and personal integrity.

Unfortunately, guilt has some problems as a socializing agent. The most significant problem with guilt, particularly as a means of control used in parenting, is that it can inhibit the development of an inner-directed sense of integrity and interfere with the identity and differentiation process (Donatelli, Bybee, & Buka, 2007; Mandara & Pikes, 2008; Mayseless & Scharf, 2009; Rakow et al., 2009, 2011). In this way, guilt is an externally imposed energy that fosters depression and internalizing behaviors in children and keeps them stuck in old, developmentally inappropriate roles, especially when they are trying to assert a separate sense of self as teenagers and young adults.

When exposed to externally based guilt, children tend to feel disloyal if they express views or engage in behaviors that are deemed unacceptable by or threatening to their parents and other significant adults. Weiss (1993) refers to this as *separation guilt*. Young adults tend to deal with these feelings of disloyalty by reactively cutting off from parents or by ignoring and minimizing their own thoughts and choices. Either way, the development of their own sense of self and inner knowledge is inhibited and often replaced by ideas that others have for them or with reactivity (i.e., they are reacting against others' ideas rather than truly choosing their own). It is a very difficult choice for some young adults: (a) staying true to their developing sense of self and personal integrity, but giving up the love and approval of parents or significant others and living with feelings of guilt and disloyalty versus (b) gaining the approval of parents or others, but giving up their own core sense of self and living with feelings of inauthenticity and self-alienation.

Childhood Trauma

The consequences of childhood trauma tend to be far-reaching for individuals and their subsequent relationships. Traumatic childhood experiences typically result in increased rates of biological, emotional, and psychological disorders, including alcoholism, drug abuse, smoking, obesity and a variety of other health problems, sleep disturbances, impulse control issues, depression, anxiety, self-esteem issues, rigid and unhealthy thoughts and behaviors, emotional dysregulation, poor attachment, school failure and dropout, suicide, criminal activity, and a "deficient sense of coherent personal identity and competence" (Cloitre, Cohen, & Koenen, 2006; Courtois & Ford, 2009; Geffner & Tishelman, 2011; Tishelman & Geffner, 2011; van der Kolk, McFarlane, & Weisaeth, 1996; Wylie, 2010, p. 51). When "complex traumatic stress" (Courtois & Ford, 2009) occurs in children from various forms of maltreatment, they develop beliefs about the trauma based on their level of psychological and cognitive development. Consequently, children tend to think they are the cause of their own abuse and that they can control it by changing how they act. Thus children's beliefs about why traumatic experiences have occurred tend to be self-blaming, leading to rigid rules about how they must act to prevent, avoid, or change the abusive behavior (Weiss, 1993).

One fairly consistent effect of trauma is that it teaches children to tune in to external cues in their environment rather than in to their internal sense of self. They learn to read the environment for signs of danger, staying alert and vigilant to maintain their own or others' safety. Consequently, they lose touch with their own intuitive knowledge and inner-generated personal power and instead focus almost exclusively on external information and on fear-based attempts to control the environment around them.

Another unfortunate consequence of trauma is that it tends to be replicated throughout a person's life, although the type and intensity of the trauma may change over time. This happens for several reasons. First, the inflexible thoughts and behaviors, which are generated as children attempt to understand and cope with the anxiety of traumatic experiences, tend to be generalized to all areas of their lives and to be self-fulfilling in nature. Specifically, when individuals approach a new relationship with the same old rigid interpersonal style, others will usually react to their rigidity with a complementary response (Kiesler, 1996). Individuals also try to replicate familiar relational styles in an unconscious attempt to heal past trauma, disconfirm unhealthy beliefs, and increase behavioral flexibility (Weiss, 1993; Weiss & Sampson, 1986). By reenacting past trauma in current relationships, they hope better outcomes will occur than what occurred when they were children. Unfortunately, most of the time this repetition compulsion ends up retraumatizing all involved.

De-Selfing

Even when there was no obvious physical trauma in childhood, children can learn to *de-self* in their families of origin. Research has shown that "emotional abuse and neglect—the absence, failure, or distortion of the child's relationship to a primary caregiver—did as much, if not more, damage than actual physical abuse" (Cloitre et al., 2006; Wylie, 2010, p. 26). De-selfing occurs when children are told and shown they will not be lovable or acceptable unless they act in certain ways. They are not provided with the kind of parental guidance that supports ownership for their identity and choices. Rather, they are almost exclusively reacting to the demands of the external world by blindly accepting what they are told about themselves and the world or by reactively rebelling against those external demands. Either way, parts of them are rejected or split off from their consciousness and not integrated into their core sense of self.

Most often, children begin this troubling process by minimizing or denying parts of themselves that are deemed unacceptable by significant adults, such as emotionality, spontaneity, joy, playfulness, and intuitive knowing. Over time, children and adolescents lose touch with these important parts in an attempt to gain the love and approval of their parents. They trade the intuitive knowing of their inner wisdom for the conditional love of their parents or other adult figures, which can lead to a variety of problems, including eating disorders, perfectionism, self-criticism, depression, anxiety disorders, emotional dysregulation, and self-injurious behaviors (Teyber, 2000; van der Kolk et al., 1996; Wylie, 2010).

The flip side of this process occurs when children adopt a rebellious identity or role. Although a certain amount of testing and challenging the status quo is a natural and healthy part of psychosocial development, it can also become extreme and lead to enduring difficulties. Although it can be seen as an attempt to protect their identities from the soul-crushing consequences of de-selfing (Schwartz, 1995, 2001), many times, extreme rebellion is a sign that teenagers and young adults are losing touch with important parts of themselves, namely the parts that are viewed as being aligned with the societal mainstream: productivity, seriousness, honesty, and responsibility. Unfortunately, they also lose touch with their intuitive knowing and sense of what is life-affirming, often engaging in various forms of self-destructive behaviors: underachievement and school failure, substance abuse and addictions, criminal behavior, and self-injurious behaviors.

Compensatory Strategies

When individuals stop embracing their Real Self, for whatever reason, they replace their natural self-actualizing tendencies with compensatory strategies, usually in an attempt to adapt and accommodate to their environment. They trade their natural self for a compensatory self. Most often, they employ compensatory strategies to deal with trauma and the basic anxiety that is generated when attachment to and approval of parents or significant others is threatened. According to Karen Horney (1945, 1950), the three early compensatory solutions that children utilize to deal with difficult family situations, trauma, and basic anxiety are:

1. Moving toward others: approaching people to attempt to gain their love and approval.
2. Moving away from others: avoiding contact with others and their perceived demands.
3. Moving against others: attempting to control or master others and life's circumstances.

These childhood strategies tend to become patterned, automatic ways of relating and attempting to meet needs as adults.

Returning to the case example, Karl, will help illustrate this process. Karl's primary compensatory solution was to move toward others. He worked hard to read other people, especially his intimate partner, so he could meet her needs, gain her approval, and avoid her anger. As often happens to those who persistently use this strategy, his partner took Karl for granted, expected more and more, and was rarely completely satisfied with his efforts. Eventually, Karl would employ his next most used strategy: moving away from others. When he realized that he had been negating and disallowing his needs in an unsuccessful attempt to please his partner, he would become emotionally exhausted, depressed, and filled with self-deprecating thoughts. He would withdraw into himself and shut down his contact with others. His withdrawal was met with confusion and anger by significant others, especially his intimate partner. The angrier she became, the more Karl withdrew.

The complement to Karl was his partner, Julie. Julie also grew up in an alcoholic family. She was the *black sheep* of the family, the one who refused to play by the rules. She was the *truth-keeper* of her family, often commenting on the other members' denial and avoidance of the family dysfunction. Her primary compensatory strategy was moving against others. She was angry much of the time. She experienced Karl's moving toward relational style as disingenuous and superficial. He never seemed to be truly present with her. When he would withdraw, she experienced abandonment and rejection. Like Karl did, she would periodically collapse in depression, shame, and resignation. Eventually, she would return to a place of blaming Karl for her suffering and loneliness.

Karl's compensatory strategies triggered Julie's and vice versa. His attempts to please her were seen as disingenuous and his withdrawal was experienced as abandonment; both triggered her anger. Her anger triggered his reactive attempts to please her and his withdrawal; and around and around they went. Both felt somewhat more balanced outside of the relationship. Within it, they were locked in a repetitive, complementary cycle, which left each of them frustrated and disempowered. They were drowning in their compensatory strategies and restricted roles vis-à-vis each other. Their connection to their Real Self, which was already distant due to childhood experiences, faded even more within their relationship.

A Spiritual Perspective

Psychological dynamics, such as those described earlier, often lead to symptoms that motivate clients to enter mental health therapy. These psychological and relational symptoms can also be understood through a spiritual lens, as getting lost psychologically also has spiritual ramifications. The following are predictable consequences that tend to occur in clients who have lost touch with their Real Self and associated spirituality: reactive movement, excessive thinking and list-making, losing balance, incongruence, fighting against, fear, scarcity, losing perspective on suffering, existential vacuum, unbalanced responsibility, and alienation. The vignettes at the beginning of the chapter will be integrated in each section to highlight the various themes being addressed.

Reactive Movement

Along with being a reason for getting lost, reactivity is a marker that indicates clients have become lost spiritually. Life is chaotic and ripe for reactivity. Many clients go from one task or crisis to the next, and never get to a place of being proactive, only reactive. They have stopped listening to their intuitive voice telling them about balance and moderation. They don't read the signs of stress and burnout until their bodies start breaking down: backaches, extreme tension headaches (minor ones can be ignored or medicated), stress-related illness, and so forth. They can literally work themselves to death.

There is a time for activity and a time for quiet stillness, "spiritual stillness," as Marianne Williamson (2004) calls it. Spiritual stillness is a time when individuals see the beauty in nature, reflect on what is meaningful in life, and connect with their intuitive knowledge. For many individuals, spirituality is not something that only happens in a house of prayer or during worship. Opportunities to be awake to and embrace spirituality are available every moment, every day. Embracing spirituality requires clients to slow down and remember to be aware of its existence, and to accept the invitation to have it inform and touch their lives.

Shawn and Alicia are both compelling examples of reactive movement. Alicia could rarely stay still for very long. She was always distracting herself with tasks and activities as a way to avoid and manage her anxiety and the unhappy, conflicted, and unresolved aspects of her life. Shawn was a bundle of nervous activity; much of the time, he appeared unfocused and directionless. He was constantly in a reactive mode, responding to the unending crises in his life. Fortunately, for both of them, therapy as well as their personally defined, spiritual practices helped them connect with spiritual stillness and associated feelings of balance and clarity.

Thinking, Thinking, Thinking

A big part of losing touch with the Real Self and associated spirituality occurs when clients lose themselves in their thoughts. Most thinking-time is spent on what has happened and what will or should happen. As Eckhart Tolle (1999, 2005) pointed out, reality is always in the present. When clients spend the majority of their mental time in the past or future, they are living a life that is out of touch with reality—reality only exists *in the now*.

Thus, the fastest way to lose touch with the Real Self is to be excessively thinking about the past or the future. This type of thinking brings almost constant suffering. For many clients, their brains can trick them into thinking that they are okay if only they could change the past or if they could get or become something new or different. They simply can't change the past, no matter how much they focus their thoughts on it; and they suffer with their inability to change what has happened. And, if clients succeed at capturing a prized new condition, they soon discover that the satisfaction is short lived. They quickly experience the void that is created in the wake of attainment and begin the search again. They continue to feel a sense of lack—of something missing that is not here right now.

Many clients report that the fastest way to reconnect with the Real Self and associated spirituality is to have present moment awareness, regardless of the client's specific spiritual practices and beliefs. In other words, although most associated with Eastern spiritual traditions, clients with many different faiths and ideas of spirituality can enhance their practices through present moment awareness (Germer et al., 2005). Being present with their experience in the here and now tends to create a shift in consciousness. Instead of their consciousness being filled with what should have happened or what needs to happen, they are awake to what is happening. They shift from absence to abundance. The present moment is full of abundance whereas the past and future tend to be about wishing for what is not really here now. When clients have mindful awareness in the present moment they often remember and reclaim the wisdom and peace of their Real Self.

Again, Shawn and Alicia exhibited exemplary characteristics. Shawn often perseverated about his past military service while Alicia continually worried about tasks that needed to be completed. Both were overwhelmed by their continual thinking and worry. Both also utilized therapy and their personally defined spiritual practices as a way to ground themselves and have experiences of *being versus doing and thinking*. Shawn experienced a sense of calm and feelings of being centered while hiking in nature and during prayer. Alicia was able to notice her body and feel connected to a sense of being grounded when she used mindful breathing techniques. These experiences of *just being* and noticing a grounded sense of self were substantially different from their typical mind chatter and constant worry.

Tyranny of the List

Many people make lists of things they would like to accomplish or don't want to forget. At its best, list making is a cognitive support. It helps individuals remember important activities or tasks they can't complete at the moment. They can let go of the need to hold those thoughts in their minds; they can put them on paper and free up brain space for present activities. Unfortunately, instead of being supportive, lists can take on a life of their own and become life-detracting. For many, lists become a producer of anxiety and a reminder of personal inadequacy. This is what I call, the *tyranny of the list*.

Lists can become a tyrant, an oppressive agent. They can symbolize a sense of lack, that individuals and their life are inadequate in their current state. Lists can become a reminder of what needs to be done, changed, or fixed. Similar to excessive thinking about the past or future, clients sometimes struggle to feel okay until the items on a list are completed. Yet, lists rarely tend to be completed, and many times they grow. Or if they are completed, a new list is soon created. For many, the tyranny of the list never ceases, robbing clients of spontaneity and present moment awareness. Lists can rob them of feeling that they and their lives are fine, just as they are. They feel anxious and incomplete instead of full and whole. So, what could be a life-supporting tool becomes a detractor of their connection with their sense of fullness and adequacy.

Alicia, in particular, was a list-maker. She made lists of work, home, and personal tasks that needed to be completed. At times, her lists were helpful as a memory aid. However, most of the time her lists increased her anxiety because they were a constant reminder of what she needed to do. She was not okay just as she was. Her mindfulness practice, specifically, helped Alicia have the experience of nonjudgmentally noticing and accepting what was occurring in the present moment. Although her use of lists continued, her experience of being tyrannized by her lists reduced considerably.

Losing Balance

Balance is one of the most important aspects of successful living. The assaultive nature of life, which sends many clients into a reactive mode of operating in the world, also triggers feelings of discontent and unease. These feelings of unease lead to feelings of being out of balance with their natural state of being. They lose touch with their Real Self and feel outside of themselves. To deal with this, many clients resort to extremes. They work, exercise, eat, drink alcohol, self-harm, shop, engage in sex, and do just about anything to excess in order to feel better. Unfortunately, this only leads to greater feelings of being unbalanced.

Spiritual practice, in contrast, tends to invite and encourage clients to return to their bodies and to a sense of balance in their lives. Buddhist practice, in particular, tends to espouse *the middle path*, which focuses on moderation and balance. When clients remember to be awake to a life-affirming, personally defined spiritual practice, they often remember to breathe and return to their bodies. Their personal power is cultivated when they stay within themselves rather than being externally reactive. It is an extremely useful part of the process of health and healing when clients have some form of life-affirming spiritual practice that helps them regularly ground themselves and stay connected to a balanced sense of self.

A primary feeling for Alicia, in particular, was that her life was out of balance. She continually busied herself with external tasks, and also engaged in excessive shopping. (We defined it as a shopping addiction.) Although she experienced a temporary sense of being in control while she shopped at department stores, she began to realize that her shopping was a way to avoid unpleasant feelings and fill a strong sense of lacking. Her sense of control vanished as soon as she stopped shopping, which was followed by more feelings of being out of control and unbalanced. I often thought that one of the reasons Alicia was drawn to Taoism is the emphasis of that tradition on balance, which she increasingly embraced in her life.

Incongruence

When clients lose touch with their Real Self, they lose touch with their inner guide. Consequently, they can lose touch with a core sense of their own morality and personal integrity. When there is, at least periodically, incongruity between what clients say and what they do, others will have difficulty fully trusting them and their motives. Especially when life doesn't go their way, they can become self-centered; they may forget that how they act really matters and that their actions affect others.

A life-affirming spiritual practice helps clients remember to live in accordance with their higher self. Regular spiritual practice reminds them of what is important: relationships, family, and values such as honesty and compassion for others. A life-affirming spiritual practice helps clients foster these inner-directed values and convictions. When they are clear about who they are and what is important, success is not based on what happens to them but on how they conduct their lives. They realize that their actions impact others and can have a ripple effect in their lives and the world.

Therapy and his spiritual practice helped Shawn to develop a greater sense of personal congruence. He knew what kind of person, father figure, and intimate partner he wanted to be. But his past traumas made it difficult for him to consistently act in a manner that was in line with his stated values. At the start of therapy, Shawn had trouble managing his anger and often distanced himself from his girlfriend and her children. Over time, his group work at the VA Hospital and trauma work in therapy, as well as his increased sense of being loved and accepted by God, helped him to have a much more compassionate and insightful sense of himself. He developed skills that enabled him to live in accordance with his core values in a much more consistent fashion.

Fighting Against

When clients lose touch with their Real Self, they can lose contact with the meaning and flow of life. Instead of embracing the natural flow of their lives, they may fight against themselves and others.

Life can feel very hard to these individuals, like banging their heads against a wall. Unfortunately, rather than stepping back and returning to a centered sense of self, many clients continue to use the same old strategies that are working only moderately well, if at all.

As Joan Halifax (1993) pointed out, some Native Americans refer to God as the *energy-between-things*. This view of spirituality is supported by advances in quantum physics, which describe life as containing a complex web of energy that flows within and between all things and defines the experience of reality. There is a natural flow to life. When clients are centered and in touch with their life-affirming spiritual practice, their lives feel in-flow. When they act in accordance with the inner wisdom of their Real Self, they are happier, less anxious, and attain a rhythm to their lives that feels right. They tend to become awake and open to giving and receiving messages and experiences from others, often spontaneously.

When I first met Shawn he was fighting against almost everything: the government, the military, his parents, his girlfriend, and most importantly, himself. There was no flow in his life. Much of his fighting was a result of the childhood and combat traumas he experienced. As therapy slowly addressed his traumas, his level of trust increased, as did his openness to corrective experiences. His personal relationship with God emerged in the space of increased openness to receiving love, and it also further increased his trust and openness. As therapy progressed, Shawn developed a sense that life didn't have to be about just crisis and conflict. He began to believe that he was worthy of giving and receiving love and that he could let down his fight and attain a level of flow with life, rather than rail against it.

Fear

Fear is a major cause of becoming lost spiritually as well as a marker. Individuals who have lost touch with a larger perspective on life tend to worry a lot. They tend to think that life is more dangerous and more unmanageable than it truly is, staying in a state of fight or flight. Most of the time, they are fleeing. They are fleeing from relationships, challenges, new experiences, and the perceived threats that can be anywhere. Their fear not only restricts their actions and options but also robs them of joy, compassion, and love. They are so busy protecting themselves that they are not open to life-affirming relationships and experiences. Sometimes couched in intellectual thought, their decisions tend to be made based on avoidance of threats rather than what might be actualizing for them. Love is the guiding emotion of a life-affirming spiritual practice. Fear, on the other hand, is a thief that robs people of spontaneity, freedom, and joy.

At the start of therapy, both Alicia and Shawn were ruled by fear. He exhibited the fear-based symptoms of PTSD, while she was periodically debilitated by anxiety. For both of them, therapy helped reduce the symptoms of fear and anxiety and activated their internal resources to address their etiological issues. Their personally defined spiritual practices supported the process and goals of therapy by becoming essential aspects of their coping toolbox, which directly contributed to a reduction in their fear and anxiety. Therapy and their spiritual practice complemented each other in the attainment of their goals.

Scarcity

A life-affirming spiritual practice often brings *abundance thinking*. People who embrace their spiritual practice tend to feel like they are living a rich existence with relationships, activities, work, and meaning. They often feel a deep sense of gratitude for the blessings in their lives, which tends to bring more gifts and blessings. Catherine Ingram (2003) stated, "Gratitude is a precursor to delight. To be truly happy is to live in gratitude" (p. 171).

Individuals who have lost touch with gratitude tend to see themselves as never having enough. They can be fearful that they are not good enough and operate from the belief that when other people receive, it must be at their expense. Life becomes a competition to get whatever crumbs they can. This thinking, which I term the *scarcity model*, runs the show in families that have lost their way. In families where abuse and neglect are occurring, the children usually compete with each other for the limited resources and love that are available. Rather than support each other, family members demean or overpower each other in an attempt to meet their own needs. Children who grow up in families in which the scarcity model operates tend to have difficulty visualizing their potentialities or believing that they can make changes in their lives. Sadly, when the scarcity model operates, people act in ways that actually move them farther away from abundance and gratitude. Their existence can become defined by not having *enough*, and acting from this position brings more scarcity rather than less.

Shawn, in particular, was operating from a scarcity mindset. He and his girlfriend were struggling financially. However, the most difficult part was that he felt that he was owed something better in life, but that life would never get better. He was stuck in a place of scarcity and victimhood. He was angry at the government, his parents, and especially his father. His feelings of lack and anger consumed him and interfered with his ability to make positive changes. Therapy and his personally defined spiritual practice supported him in embracing a sense that he was a survivor, not just a victim. Correspondingly, his prayer life shifted from asking God to fix what was wrong in his life to thanking God for the positive changes that were occurring. Sometimes Shawn attributed the positive changes to God, while other times he described a sense that God was supporting him in making his own changes.

Losing Perspective on Suffering

Suffering is part of life. It is the first of the Buddha's Four Noble Truths. People who have some form of regular spiritual practice tend to have a much healthier perspective on suffering than those who do not. A regular spiritual practice encourages people to realize that suffering is not only unavoidable but also can bring great insights and growth. Every struggle and hardship can teach something about compassion. Hardships provide individuals with opportunities to experience parts of themselves and have a deeper understanding of the human condition.

Individuals who are removed from a larger perspective about life often see suffering as a terrible burden that has no purpose, which is where Shawn was at the start of therapy. Shawn alternately tried to excessively control his life in a futile attempt to avoid suffering and felt powerless in the face of his suffering. Either way, he was in pain and initially had few effective tools to deal with the pain. Again, his spiritual practice helped to shift his sense of being victimized by life. He began to connect to ideas of meaning that were larger than he had originally thought and experienced, which increased his sense of being grounded in his life.

Existential Vacuum/Sleepwalking

An existential vacuum occurs when individuals lack a sustainable sense of meaning. Clients attempt to fill this void of meaning in many different ways, some being quite life detracting: drugs, alcohol, sexual or relationship addictions, overworking, sport or activity addictions, and so forth. They compulsively race to fill the void of meaning and try to cover up the anxiety and discontent that it engenders. They define their lives and themselves through activities and avoid listening to and learning from the anxiety that is generated by the faint voice that reminds them there is more to life than they are realizing and that they are not living a fully alive and authentic existence.

In contrast, a personally defined spiritual practice supports meaning. When clients utilize their spiritual practice, they often become much clearer about why they are alive, how they impact the lives of those around them, and the many ways that they could be more impactful. In short, a life-affirming spiritual practice tends to bring a sense of purpose to life as well as passion and excitement for being alive. I have heard many clients say that their spiritual practice supports a change in their mindset: similar to shifting from sleepwalking to living life fully.

Both Alicia and Shawn reported this shift. They moved from just surviving the anxiety and reactivity of their lives to a sense of wonder about the possibilities in front of them. Shawn was able to go back to school and be successful in ways he had never dreamed were possible. Alicia created a much healthier work-life balance, including working less and attending yoga in addition to her mindfulness-based practice. Both took healthy risks and gained a level of freedom, meaning, and enjoyment in life that were remarkable.

Unbalanced Responsibility

Finding a balance between letting go and taking charge is often a central feature of healthy and successful living. Connection to a life-affirming spiritual practice seems to help individuals have insights into this balance, enabling them to neither under- nor overestimate the control that they have in their lives.

A client once told me about several dreams that she had, in which she was under a great deal of stress and dealing with dangerous circumstances. In one dream, she curled up in a ball in her closet, feeling powerless to influence the circumstances causing her fear. In another dream, she had superhuman powers; she was flying above the circumstances (a tidal wave), warning others of the impending danger. These dreams depict the two extremes of perception that individuals can have: too little or too much control. Both positions misjudge the degree of control that they have to influence the circumstances of their lives. Again, the ability to navigate in between these two extremes and achieve a balanced view of personal power is a key aspect to healthy living.

Shawn and Alicia characterized these extreme positions. Shawn felt largely powerless while Alicia tried to control everything in her life. With both of them I used the image of a small boat on a rough, wide-open sea to represent the struggle to find a healthy balance of responsibility and control. In the metaphor, life and all its conditions were the ocean currents, waves, and winds, which have the power to knock them around. The small boat, with a sail and rudder, represented them as individuals. They were no match for the waves during a storm. Yet, they had some ability to steer and to stay afloat. In calm seas, they could sail with intentionality and purpose, especially when they utilized the natural flow of the currents and winds. This metaphor fit with their evolving experiences with spirituality. Shawn and Alicia also used the Serenity Prayer, which they placed in prominent places in their homes, as a way to embrace this balance.

> God, grant me
> the serenity to accept the things I cannot change,
> the courage to change the things I can,
> and the wisdom to know the difference.

Alienation

Individuals who are disconnected from a larger perspective on life often see themselves as separate from other people and their world whereas spiritually grounded individuals tend to see themselves as interconnected with others. Understanding that they are connected with other people and things engenders compassion and ownership for their world and leads to a sense of being a steward, a *shepherd* of all that is around them. It leads to the understanding that their behaviors and thoughts truly matter. Relationships are also a key to supporting health, healing from trauma, and building structures that will support sustainable happiness. Not being in touch with a spiritual sense of interconnection, conversely, can lead to a disconnection from others and to feelings of alienation, fear, and discouragement.

Shawn, in particular, was discouraged and alienated in his life. He had little trust that others would have his best interest in mind. His personal relationship with God as well as with me and the members of his therapy group fostered feelings that he could start to value and trust others. He was able to take risks and allow his guard to drop, which facilitated positive relational experiences. His feelings of *belonging* in his life decreased his alienation and supported an adaptive spiral: The more he was open to others, the better he felt, and the more positive feedback he received.

In the next chapter, the discussion focuses on how therapists can assist clients with connecting with their inner wisdom through a personally defined spiritual practice. Practical steps for therapists are provided.

CHAPTER 5

SPIRITUAL HEALTH AND ABUNDANCE: PRACTICAL STEPS

There are many ways that a life-affirming spiritual practice can inform and support healthy living. Understanding client-defined spiritual beliefs and practices can be an important avenue for connecting with clients and useful for therapeutic change. The focus of this chapter is on practical steps for incorporating spirituality into therapy. In particular, clients' spiritual practice can be utilized to increase connection to clients' Real Self and to promote the development of personal integrity, which can be a guide in defining and achieving health and growth. There are several key steps involved in the process of integrating spirituality into a psychotherapeutic approach. These are:

spirituality in someones life should be healthy.

Step 1: Being open to client-defined spirituality
Step 2: Utilizing spirituality for resourcing
Step 3: Inviting spirituality to inform personal integrity
Step 4: Evaluating life structures
Step 5: Remembering and committing to spiritual practice

Again, it is essential for therapists to maintain a high level of spiritual-differentiation throughout these steps.

if not, could affect the clients trust in therapist.

Being Open to Client-Defined Spirituality

The first issue for therapists is to be comfortable with spirituality as a topic of discussion in therapy. For all the reasons discussed in Chapter 1, many therapists are uncomfortable with spirituality and often avoid it with clients. Some clients will avoid the discussion as well, often because they fear being judged, especially if they have specific spiritual beliefs and practices. Spirituality is a very personal issue. Each person has a unique history that shapes how he/she defines, experiences, and expresses a philosophical and/ or spiritual sense of the world.

Thus the first step in utilizing spirituality in therapy is to be sincerely interested in clients' spiritual beliefs and experiences, while maintaining a high level of spiritual-differentiation. The therapy is not about the therapist's spiritual experiences; the focus needs to be on exploring the clients' beliefs and practices. When therapists are open to learning about their clients' philosophical and spiritual views without projecting their own views onto their clients, they develop an understanding of their clients on a very deep and personal level.

Along with reactivity based on their own history, of the many reasons that therapists avoid approaching spirituality in therapy, they often report that they lack the competency and language to engage in the discussion with clients (Hickson et al., 2011). Accordingly, the most common question that I am asked at professional trainings on spiritually oriented therapy is how to talk to clients about spirituality. Therapists want specific examples of questions to ask. Although exhibiting an attitude of sincere interest in learning about clients' spiritual lives is more important than a specific set of skills and questions, having a few questions in mind often helps therapists increase their sense of competency and gets the conversation started. Some questions to ask clients are:

- Is spirituality important to you?
- How do you experience spirituality?
- What rituals or activities support your spirituality?
- What were you taught as a child about spirituality?
- Which, if any, of the definitions, values, and practices of spirituality that you were taught as a child fit for you today?

- Is there a distinction for you between organized religion and spirituality?
- When in your life, if ever, have you felt a *life-affirming* sense of spirituality?
- How does a life-affirming sense of spirituality emerge now in your life?

These questions can be asked of all clients, and each client will have unique reactions. Many people have had negative and judgment-filled experiences with organized religion; consequently, some are quite reactive to any conversation about spirituality. Other clients will be eager to discuss their beliefs and practices, while others will be uninterested in spirituality. Therapists should meet their clients exactly where they are with their current beliefs. It is important to honor clients and validate their experiences. Examples of clients in different places with spirituality are presented next.

Spiritually Interested Clients

For clients who readily want to discuss their spirituality, doing so significantly improves therapy outcomes (Smith et al., 2007; Swift et al., 2011; Worthington et al., 2011). For these clients, the focus should be on exploring how they define, experience, and access their spirituality. Questions can focus on the clients' unique, personal experiences. Therapists should avoid stereotypes and consider their clients as unique, even if they appear to espouse an identifiable faith or practice. It's important for therapists to remember, for instance, that if 100 people are sitting in the same church service, if asked, they will report 100 different internal experiences of the service.

Therapists need to allow their clients to teach them about their beliefs and unique experiences, regardless of their specific practices. Therapists should have a "beginner's mind" (Suzuki, 1973) that is open to new ideas. They shouldn't assume to know the answers.

Therapists need to be open to the opportunity to have their clients teach them about the many ways to know and experience spirituality. The therapist's stance should be one of interest and exploration of the specifics of their clients' beliefs and practices. If clients report that they have a personal relationship with God, for example, therapists can ask about the specifics of their prayer life and their experience of God. Much can be learned from how clients pray and practice their faith, including the specific words that they use.

Consider the case of Lana, a 42-year-old female who entered therapy for generalized anxiety related to an unsatisfying marriage, conflict with her adult daughter, and unfulfilling work. Her whole life Lana had tried to please others at her own expense. Recently, she had become increasingly unwilling to deny her needs so that others could be happy, which was creating conflict in her significant relationships. Other family members were used to her overfunctioning for them.

When asked about her spiritual beliefs, Lana talked for several sessions about her lifelong spiritual journey and how she came to her current beliefs and practices, which include a personal relationship with God. When I inquired more specifically about that relationship, she described an incident that occurred several weeks prior to starting therapy. She reported that she was walking in a nearby park on a lunch break from work when she was "knocked to her knees by God." God spoke to her and said that she needed to break out of her current life and help others who are experiencing oppression. She realized that she was feeling oppressed in her life and needed to "follow God's plan" for her by first working on herself. Since that experience with God, her prayer life was focused on asking God for continued guidance and the courage to make changes.

Initially Lana was sheepish when telling her story, fearing that I would judge her or not believe her. My attitude of genuine acceptance and interest was a catalyst for our therapeutic relationship (i.e., her trust in me increased dramatically), and for her life outside the therapy room. She noted that my care and support of her and of her spirituality gave her the confidence to trust herself and begin to make changes in her career and relationships. Her personally defined spirituality had been a central, guiding force in her life. Now, we could utilize it as part of the therapeutic process. To not incorporate her spirituality would have been missing a significant part of her life and a lost opportunity for her therapy.

Interestingly, when I discussed this case with a professional colleague, he asked me if I had considered that Lana may have had a psychotic break that day in the park. While it was a reasonable question to consider, his comments also highlighted the bias in the mental health field that tends to pathologize spiritual experiences, which is one reason that some clients avoid talking about their more profound spiritual experiences with therapists.

Spiritually Reactive Clients

Many people have experienced some form of spiritual violence, which is judgment, abuse, fear, guilt, and/or oppression in the context of spirituality. These experiences can often be characterized as traumatic for individuals and almost always produce reactivity. For some of these clients, their reactivity takes the form of a disavowal of the topic of spirituality, usually accompanied by harsh and critical judgments of spiritual types of people. They tend to equate spirituality with judgment, oppression, and small-mindedness, and are typically not interested in discussing spirituality. Some spiritually reactive clients make sharp distinctions between organized religion and spirituality, leading them to be open to some ideas and words but not to others. Other clients want a chance to process their experiences, including their traumas associated with spirituality. Again, it's vital for therapists to meet clients where they are rather than impose an agenda.

Consider the example of Alia, a 37-year-old Iranian American female who immigrated with her family to the United States when she was a teenager. Alia entered therapy due to being in a passionless marriage and confusion about her career and life path. When asked about her spirituality, she immediately reacted with detailed stories of her experiences with the Muslim faith in Iran, including times when she and members of her family experienced judgment and oppression in the name of religion. She also expressed anger about the discrimination that her family experienced in the United States due to their faith and ethnicity. For many sessions we talked about her spirituality and life journey, including traumas that she experienced in Iran and the United States as well as her evolving beliefs. She had both Muslim and Christian friends. Her beliefs had developed into a unique blend of Islam, Christianity, and her own ideas. She considered herself deeply spiritual, yet had strong feelings of hurt, confusion, and reactivity in relation to organized forms of faith.

Alia often indicated that it was a big relief to be able to process her traumatic and disparate experiences and feelings in therapy. As her feelings were heard and validated, her reactivity slowly reduced, and she experienced an increased sense of being more "settled and peaceful." She became more grounded in her beliefs and more resolved about her past traumas. What was most important to her was that I didn't judge her or try to convert her to any particular ideology. Instead, she could process the totality of her, at times, conflicting emotions about her negative as well as positive experiences with spirituality.

Spiritually Uninterested Clients

Some clients are not interested in discussing spirituality due to experiencing spiritual violence. Others have had very little direct experience with spirituality. Still others may not characterize their beliefs as spiritual, choosing to consider their reflections on life as rational, scientific, or philosophical. Even for clients who do not request that spirituality be addressed in therapy, a broad-based and inclusive view of spirituality can inform and support the therapeutic process. It tends to become an ally in the process.

With these clients it is important to not impose spiritual words or attributions. Rather, therapists need to listen for how clients talk about existential issues of meaning, values, mortality, and self-in-the-world. Their philosophical notions of existence often are related to the broad-based, spiritual themes that were presented in Chapter 2. The focus for therapists is on being open to how clients define, experience, and access whatever helps them stay connected to their core values and the inner wisdom of their Real Self, even if they don't identify these beliefs and practices as *spiritual.* Thus, even when clients don't talk explicitly about spirituality, the themes still tend to emerge in therapy.

The key for therapists, again, is to be open to and listen for the unique ways that clients make sense of their lives and derive meaning, while maintaining therapeutic spiritual-differentiation. Spiritual themes may emerge in nontraditional ways such as artistic expression, nature, stillness, awareness of breath, movement, relationships or encounters, images or symbols, physical sensations, coincidences, intuition, feelings of being in-flow, reflections on the cosmos, moments of clarity and interconnection, and connections to heart and heart-based experience. It is not important where or how philosophical and spiritual themes are accessed. What matters most is if the avenue of experiencing spirituality is life-affirming and supports personal integrity. Do the reflections and activities evoke feelings of love, peace, and clarity for clients? Do they help clients take perspective in ways that reduce fear and increase a sense of their connection in the world? Therapists can listen for and punctuate what makes clients feel alive, what makes their hearts sing.

Spiritual themes can also emerge in the therapy room: clarity, joy, perspective, wisdom, positive risk-taking, visions of health, ownership of a clear voice, and moments of authentic connection, to name a few. Helping clients define, experience, and access their own life-affirming spiritual beliefs and practices (even if they don't refer to them as spiritual) supports them in leading a discerning and intentional life and is a tremendous ally in the therapy process.

As an example, I worked with a client, Darla, who was 31 years old and was raised without organized religion or spiritual guidance from her family. She was not interested in talking about spirituality in therapy. She had grown up with an alcoholic single mother and her greatest struggles were with feelings of being undeserving of love and attention. One day she called late, with many apologies, and cancelled our session. At the next scheduled session, I asked her what was happening that she had to cancel. Darla indicated that she had gone horseback riding, something she loved but hadn't given herself permission to do in many years. Her initial expectation was that I would be disappointed and critical that she had canceled our appointment. Instead, I eagerly listened and watched her face light up as she described how her "heart opened up" while she was riding—like a "warm wind" blowing through her chest. She felt happy, peaceful, clear, and more confident than she had in recent memory. As we processed the experience, she indicated that it was a significant event for her; it reminded her of what "is possible" for her and who she "wants to be."

This event provided many gifts for Darla, and for her therapy. First, I was supportive of her horseback riding rather than being critical of her like her mother typically was. Her trust in me increased, and it provided a corrective emotional experience in that she realized she deserved support from others and happiness. Most important, the horseback riding was a grounding and defining experience: She could remember the feelings in her chest, use those feelings as a barometer of her own strength and wisdom, and could recreate those feelings, either mentally by remembering or physically by getting back on a horse. Those positive feelings were central to

Could this "spirituality" be like drugs? What if one day she doesn't feel this and then get depressed?

her knowing and striving for health, even as she processed difficult experiences in her past and current life.

Utilizing Spirituality for Resourcing

Resourcing occurs when clients employ internal strategies and/or engage in activities that support positive coping and functioning. Resourcing can also be conceptualized as intentional self-soothing. Spiritual resourcing, in particular, involves the use of clients' personally defined, life-affirming spiritual practice to intentionally ground themselves and to support self-soothing to deal with their symptoms as well as the inevitable anxiety inherent in life. Therapists can collaborate with clients to create a toolbox of coping strategies, including those that are associated with their spiritual practice. These spiritual strategies, which could include prayer, meditation, being in nature, mindfulness, and any form of life-affirming spirituality, are particularly helpful when clients are addressing trauma and emotionally overwhelming circumstances.

Dialectical Behavior Therapy (DBT) (Linehan, 1993b), for example, provides numerous practical strategies that therapists can use with clients to help them build resources, especially the use of mindfulness. Mindfulness is increasingly utilized by therapists from a variety of theoretical orientations to address anxiety, depression, and almost any form of emotional and psychological dysregulation. Research has shown broad-ranging positive effects of the three most common forms of mindfulness: (1) concentration practices, (2) open-field awareness, and (3) compassion and loving-kindness practices (Davis & Hayes, 2011; Siegel, 2011). Concentration practices emphasize focused attention on an object (e.g., a candle) or word (i.e., usually a mantra) as a way to promote feelings of groundedness and fullness; this form of practice is often best for clients just beginning to use mindfulness because it centers them and forms a foundation for practicing other skills. Open-field awareness, most

it's essentially calling on God's grace to help them

Pray + meditate

Relax + focus enough that one can focus on Present some find this easier to do if connected to spirituality associated with mindfulness per se, emphasizes the practice of clients nonjudgmentally noticing whatever they are thinking and experiencing each moment; this provides clients with a way to disidentify with the mind and its constant chatter. Thus, clients learn about the typical patterns of their thinking and how their mind increases suffering through unhelpful attachment to outcomes. Compassion and loving kindness practices, often called *metta*, emphasize helping clients to develop a loving attitude toward themselves and others.

When spiritual beliefs and practices are life-affirming, they tend to provide feelings of being centered and grounded, among other positive feelings, especially when clients are mindful in the present moment of their spiritual practice. Consider Kyle, a 32-year-old man, who entered therapy due to anxiety and dysregulation associated with childhood sexual abuse. He was sexually abused by a teenaged cousin when he was 6 years old, and was raped by an adult man at 12 years old. Kyle had started to have panic attacks associated with memories of the abuse, and was at risk of losing his job due to absenteeism. He had never told anyone about these experiences, until he told his wife just before initiating therapy. When he entered therapy, he was on high alert, showing signs of acute PTSD.

When asked about his spiritual beliefs, Kyle stated that he couldn't see how God could let his sexual abuse happen, but he, nonetheless, prayed regularly. When asked for specifics about his prayer life, he indicated that he often asked God to take away his feelings of shame and worthlessness associated with the sexual traumas. An important part of the therapy focused on resourcing, including a variety of self-care activities such as physical exercise and concentration-based mindfulness. After teaching him some basic mindfulness procedures, we discussed the idea of combining mindfulness with his prayer, that is, being very open and accepting in the moment while he prayed. We talked about the idea that he could visualize God's love entering his body and heart to provide healing and wisdom. He viewed this as the Holy Spirit coming into him.

The following session, Kyle reported that he had a better week. His anxiety, in particular, was reduced. He had more feelings of peace and of being grounded, which he attributed to the mindfulness and his connection with God. We spent many weeks processing his traumas and utilizing his evolving ideas about spirituality. He was increasingly convinced that there was a positive energy in the world he could tap into and that provided feelings of being centered and adequate in the moment. He commented that, "If God loves me, then I need to learn to love myself." Over time, he felt more and more self-compassionate and worthwhile.

Inviting Spirituality to Inform Personal Integrity

Another advantage for therapists of utilizing a client-defined, life-affirming spirituality is that it tends to inform their values and to support their personal integrity. As I have discussed, the essence of personal integrity is living life in accordance with what individuals know is right for them. Personal integrity is one's inner, moral compass. It is based on personal values, which have been forged through life experience. It represents an individual's core truth and convictions. Only when actions are solidly aligned with personal convictions do individuals tend to achieve the sense of wholeness that defines integrity. The inner knowing of the Real Self provides the substance of personal integrity. *Personal integrity represents the voice and consciousness of the Real Self.*

Oftentimes clients choose to not listen to this inner knowledge, however. They make decisions based on their fears or misgivings rather than from their Real Self. They desperately want to be liked and accepted, for example, so they trade in their inner wisdom for the hope of attaining approval from others. Then, they feel as if they are living their lives for other people, and ultimately they feel lost. They also can become so self-absorbed that they lose sight of the bigger picture. What really is lost is their connection to their personal integrity.

[handwritten margin note, left side:] i wanna love, "Just wanna see & accept"

[handwritten note, bottom:] Try to understand what happened to make your choices.

The good news is that personal integrity does not have to be lost forever. It can always be reclaimed. Clients can learn to clarify their values and courageously assert these values through their choices and behaviors. They can live a *value-driven life*. A value-driven life is about following one's inner-generated beliefs and moral compass. It is not about doing what others want. Neither is it about doing what others don't want. It is about doing what is right for the individual. A value-driven life is about taking ownership for life and choices. Only clients can take charge of their own life and happiness, including choosing partners and friends who will support their happiness. If they are waiting for others to change or for others to give them permission to change, they will suffer greatly. They must claim their own life. If their choices are based on the wisdom of their Real Self, it will be an expression of their personal integrity.

Some clients believe that a value-driven life can be selfish, that they need to consider others' feelings and needs, and not just their own. Clients do need to be sensitive to others, be aware of how their behavior affects others, and take responsibility for the consequences of their actions. When they listen to and follow their Real Self and personal integrity, they naturally make choices that are healthy and life-affirming for them and others. They don't tend to act in ways that are cruel, demeaning, or life-detracting to others. Despite fears to the contrary, when clients follow their personal integrity they don't suddenly become lazy, selfish, or criminal in their actions. When their Real Self leads the way, their personal integrity includes a core value related to being compassionate and sensitive to others.

I often tell my clients to *partner with health*. Their Real Self will be their voice of health, although not everyone may like their choices. However, when they act from a mindset of health and ownership for their lives rather than fear and attempting to please others, they will naturally make life-affirming decisions. So, how do clients know what is right? How do they know what is healthy? How do they cultivate their personal integrity and partner with health?

Any personal growth process, like therapy or a spiritual practice, which helps clients clarify their values and increase ownership for their identity and choices, can help them live a value-driven life. The key is that the activity is life-affirming and should support the awareness and development of their core values. A personally defined, life-affirming spiritual practice can inform and guide this process. Therapists need to listen for and invite clients to utilize the groundedness and wisdom associated with their spirituality. Clients can learn to listen for their intuitive knowledge, which may include quieting the external noise related to others trying to define them and quieting their internal fears and self-deprecating thoughts. Decisions and actions tend not to be successful or sustainable if they are based on fear.

Spiritual practice can help clients develop self-compassion and increase their intuitive knowing. This intuitive energy is an ally for therapists; it will assist clients in clarifying their core values and having the courage to act on their convictions. This invites their spiritual center to inform their actions in their day-to-day life as well as their major life decisions. How different their experiences would be if their lives were based on the state of mind that is achieved when they are meditating, praying, hiking, noticing their breath in the moment, or riding their horse. They would be living a spiritually informed, value-driven life that represents what is truest and best about their innermost being.

Evaluating Life Structures

When clients live a value-driven life, they become discerning of experiences. They awaken their senses to what is life-detracting and what is life-affirming, to what supports or detracts from their health. They start to value what is life-affirming and limit what is not. In this way, the therapy process and a spiritual practice help them to *define and live health.*

Therapists can help clients to define and partner with health by asking them to consider what they have learned thus far in their lives about what works for them, what brings meaning to their lives. When first directed to consider health in this way, many clients are so busy battling dysfunction and dealing with pain they can't easily do it. They have become lost and have forgotten to embrace what is good and life-affirming for them.

Health, broadly speaking, is defined as activities and experiences that clients know on an intuitive and heart-based level are affirming and meaningful for them. In fact, most often what constitutes health is what is meaningful. Meaning is what makes getting out of bed each morning truly possible. Life can't be just about various kinds of attainment, such as status or possessions. Life also can't be defined by the avoidance of what scares them. When clients stop chasing happiness through attainment of material possessions or running away in fear, they typically find what is meaningful.

The essence of a meaningful life is allowing one's personal integrity and Real Self to evaluate choices and dictate a life path. Most clients need to give their lives a good shaking, like shaking the dust out of a throw rug. The cream of their lives, seen through the eyes of their Real Self, will rise to the top of their consciousness and life-detracting experiences will feel empty, lifeless, and painful. Life-detracting experiences create a sense of incongruency and anxiety. When not living in accordance with the wisdom of their Real Self, clients experience a sense that they are not *fully inhabiting* their lives. Parts of them are excluded, removed from awareness, or blocked.

Life structures are the activities, relationships, and experiences that comprise one's life. Life structures can be categorized into six foundational areas: (1) physical, (2) relationships, (3) work and leisure activities, (4) financial, (5) community, and (6) spiritual/ philosophical. Right now, consider your clients across each of these

areas. Are they embracing health and what is life-affirming, or are they spinning their wheels and missing the mark?

Physical

How well are your clients caring for their body and supporting their physical health? What kind of exercise do they get—is it right for their body? How well do they identify and manage stress? Are they in touch with their emotions and their body? Do they eat when they are hungry? Or, do they become so task-focused that they forget to eat? Do they have some amounts of chronic or periodic pain: back or neck pain, headaches, stomach discomfort, and so forth? Do they ignore their body, only to experience intense discomfort occasionally? If your clients have physical ailments or pain, are their lifestyle choices exacerbating or healing their condition?

Physical health is about how well your clients care for their physical self, such as eating, sleeping, getting exercise, managing stress, and listening to their body. It is about understanding and respecting the natural rhythms of their being. A body will tell much about what it needs—food and rest, for example. A body can also tell which forms of exercise are best and what kinds of food and nutrients are needed. The key is to listen. Many clients are so busy following routines, completing externally based tasks, and reacting to crises that they forget to reflect internally. Therapists can encourage clients to assess each of the activities associated with their physical life to determine if it is life-affirming, and alter as needed.

Relationships

To what degree do your clients' relationships support their health and nourish their being? Do they feel controlled by others? Do they feel as if they need to be different to please others? Do they feel their energy being drained or replenished in their relationships? Do they have a need to change or control others? Do they like who they are in their relationships? Are they satisfied with the level of depth and meaning versus superficiality in their relationships? To what degree are they fully present in their relationships? To what degree do they trust that their significant others will be there for them if they need help or comfort?

Relationships include intimate partners, children, parents, extended family, friends, coworkers, and to a lesser degree, casual acquaintances. One of the most foundational human needs is social connection. The need is so strong that many clients desperately hold on to life-detracting relationships rather than face the terrifying possibility of being alone. For most people, the quality of their primary relationships is the strongest predictor of their sense of well-being. The more relationships are life-affirming, the better clients tend to feel about themselves and their lives. If the attachment and security of their primary relationships are compromised or fragile, they feel anxious, unsatisfied, incomplete, and untethered. Being seen, understood, accepted, and loved within significant relationships lead to a sense of meaning, purpose, self-esteem, and grounding in the world. Without life-affirming relationships, individuals tend to experience the world as orphans; they feel alone and lost.

Work and Leisure

Do your clients derive meaning and passion from their work and leisure activities? Or are they experiencing unemployment? If employed, is their work "just a job" or is it a calling? Do they dread going to work and have to drag themselves out of bed in the morning? Do they overwork? Do they use work as an escape from other areas of their lives? Do their leisure activities reflect their passions and core values? Are they satisfied with their balance between work and leisure activities?

This category includes paid work, volunteering, avocations, and leisure activities. Freud argued that love and work are the two essential ingredients for a meaningful life. Almost all of the clients that come into my clinical practice have issues with their primary relationships; most struggle with both relationships and work. For many people, work takes up the largest portion of their day-to-day lives. If it is not satisfying and meaningful, then they are spending the majority of their waking hours engaged in an activity that is not life-affirming. Their consciousness is likely filled with and reminded of what is lacking and unsatisfying. They likely feel listless and bored. By contrast, when clients' work and leisure activities are meaningful and congruent with their core values, they tend to feel alive and purposeful.

Financial

How do your clients view money? What feelings does money evoke in them—fear, joy, guilt, envy, inadequacy, dispassionate interest, and so forth? What role does money have in their day-to-day life? How much of their consciousness is filled with thoughts about money—not having enough, ways to make more, and so on? How well do they manage their money? Does their money work for them or do they work for their money?

The importance of reaching a place of peace and perspective related to finances can't be overstated. Much suffering in the world occurs due to money, most often related to feeling a sense of insecurity and lack. People will engage in morally reprehensible behavior when they don't have enough money to meet their basic needs. Even after basic needs are met, some people will take great risks and compromise their personal integrity in an attempt to obtain more money. People often are afraid of not having enough, long after they have plenty of money. Sometimes the more money people have, the less generous they become. Of course, not having enough money is a tremendous stress.

Money is something that should enhance your client's life rather than detract from it. Many clients work so hard to earn more money that they don't have enough time and energy to enjoy it. Others are simply trying to make enough money to survive. Shifts in perspective occur when clients think about money as a means to enhance life, align with and be an expression of core values, and support life-affirming activities. Money can provide security as well as options and choices. A sound financial foundation coupled with a healthy perspective on money provides the freedom to engage in soul-nourishing activities as well as freedom from the perpetual search for more and more.

Community

What are the primary social groups or organizations in which your clients function (e.g., schools, work, and community)? Do they like and respect the social organizations and community in which they live? To what degree do they identify with being part of their community? Do they feel as if they belong there? Have they found a life-affirming, meaningful, and helpful place in their social structures? Or, do they feel as if they are *just a visitor* in these structures?

This category deals with clients' sense of self vis-à-vis their social groups and larger community. Alfred Adler, a contemporary of Freud, posited that happiness and success in life are largely a function of social connectedness and finding a niche within one's primary social organizations, such as schools, workplaces, and communities. When clients lack a sense of connection with and useful place within their social structures, they are likely to become isolated and discouraged. By contrast, when clients take an active interest in the welfare of others within their community, what Adler termed *social interest*, they feel purposeful and positively connected to larger social goals. Research has provided support to Adler's assertions, identifying social connectedness and a sense of social interest as predictors of psychological adjustment and health in children and adults (Johnson, Smith, & Nelson, 2003).

Spiritual/Philosophical

What are your clients' beliefs about the meaning and purpose of their lives? To what degree are their spiritual beliefs and practices life-affirming? To what degree are their spiritual beliefs and practices based on love and abundance versus fear and scarcity? How do their spiritual beliefs and practices influence their behaviors and thoughts toward others? How much time do they spend reflecting on spiritual and philosophical questions? Do they avoid these types of questions about meaning and spiritual/philosophical worldviews?

This category deals with the ways in which clients make sense of their existence. Nearly everyone has some ideas and practices related to beliefs about existence, including agnostic and atheistic positions. Different spiritual and philosophical beliefs can have radically different outcomes related to how clients think about themselves and the world. For example, there are vast differences in beliefs about the degree to which life is governed by chance and randomness versus an intentional and purposeful force. Each conceptual position has ramifications related to the degree to which clients embrace ideas of free will and order in their lives. What matters most, in my view, is not the content of the beliefs, but the degree to which the beliefs are life-affirming. Generally speaking, spiritual views and practices that enhance feelings of love and compassion for self and others are more life-affirming while those that promote fear through a restrictive, moralistic vision tend to be more life-detracting.

Therapeutic Support for Evaluating Life Structures

An evaluation of life structures can be painful and reveal areas where clients are not embracing health. Realizing that certain life structures are not supporting health can lead to difficult questions and decisions. For example,

- To what degree are problematic life structures incompatible with your clients' personal integrity and vision of health?
- What keeps them holding on to life-detracting activities, relationships, or practices?
- What role is fear playing in their choice to maintain certain life structures?
- Can shifts occur to bring problematic life structures in line with their personal integrity and vision of health?
- Do they need to remove or reduce their participation in certain life structures or increase participation in others?

An important part of this evaluation process is to *not pathologize the underlying needs* across all these areas of life. The needs associated with meaningful work, satisfying intimate relationships, financial security, social connectedness, and philosophical/existential beliefs are not problematic; they are simply part of life. What is assessed closely is how clients are trying to meet their needs. Are the ways that they are attempting to meet their needs life-affirming and congruent with their core values? It typically is not sustainable to try to eliminate underlying needs; the focus needs to be on evaluating and modifying the methods and structures associated with meeting their needs.

This assessment process can be particularly difficult when clients' relationships are the focus. In this case, it's helpful when therapists encourage clients to embrace their personal vision of health and *invite others to join them in health*. In other words, therapists help clients to come from a place of personal integrity and to ask others to respond to them on that level. Clients should invite others to meet them and support their attempts to practice health in their lives. If others won't take the invitation and, instead, consistently try to restrict their health and what is life-affirming for them, the relationship itself will need to be reassessed. As a general and simplified rule, clients should be supported to embrace relationships and activities that are life-affirming and limit those that are life-detracting. Although it sounds simple, many clients choose to continue with life-detracting relationships and activities rather than deal with the fear and upheaval of major change.

Therapy can be a vital resource to assist clients with the evaluation process and the implementation of changes. Therapy can help clients to clarify their values and deepen their connection with their Real Self as well as provide support of courageous decision-making. Therapy can also assist clients' significant others by increasing their understanding and support for their life changes. A fear-based and controlling husband, for example, can be supported and challenged in marital therapy related to his fears and thoughts about his wife's changes. It may be possible for him to embrace her health rather than be threatened by the changes. If he can support her health, he can join her on the path. If not, they may need to make changes in the nature of their relationship.

Consider the case of Kendra, a 36-year-old woman, who entered therapy with complaints of depression, anxiety, and an unsatisfying marriage. Kendra had two middle-school aged children and worked full time in the financial industry. Although she was reasonably satisfied with her work and career, she was not fulfilled in her marriage. In her view, her husband was a "good father" to their kids, but overly passive in his life. She felt as if she had lost respect for him due to his passivity, and lost interest in him as an intimate partner. They hadn't been sexually intimate in several years. She had resigned herself to stay in a passionless marriage. Her husband was family; she couldn't see her life without him and didn't want to break up the family.

Six weeks before entering therapy, Kendra had an encounter with another (married) man at work. They had a very personal talk at a work function, which left her deeply affected. Shortly thereafter, they began communicating daily on the phone and by text. He seemed to understand her so well. They connected on levels that didn't seem possible with her husband. Although the relationship with the man had not become sexual, she was sexually attracted to him and felt deeply conflicted, confused, and unsettled.

Therapy with Kendra began with an exploration of the context of her life, including her childhood. She was raised in the LDS faith in a traditional, two-parent household where her father worked outside the home and was distant from the children. She began to make links between her distant relationship with her father and her mixed feelings about her husband. An emotionally distant husband felt like family on many levels, but triggered feelings of loss, sadness, and unmet needs for affection from her father.

Although she no longer attended church, Kendra believed in God and considered herself to be spiritual, which was primarily expressed in periodic "conversations" with God. I invited her to be mindfully aware of how she felt during her conversations with God. She reported that she tended to feel calmer and more peaceful after the conversations. We agreed that it would be useful to allow these peaceful and calm feelings to inform her values and decision-making. Over time, she indicated that her relationship with God was helping her "get clear" about her unmet needs, values, and options. She decided to end the emotional affair with the man at work and confront her feelings about her marriage directly with her husband, which led to a referral for marital therapy, along with continued individual therapy. Her spiritual practice was an important part of her therapy as it provided her with clarity about her issues, needs, and core values as well as the courage to be direct and honest with her husband. She was amazed at how much transformation occurred within her and within her marriage. Although not perfect, she and her husband decided to stay together, with both being committed to a more satisfying relationship.

Kendra's marriage could have gone either way. The important point is that therapy helped her utilize her spiritual practice to inform her personal integrity and evaluate her marriage. Prompted by an emotional affair, Kendra was given the opportunity to define her personal integrity and vision for her life. The process of addressing her feelings about her father and her husband and then directly confronting the state of her marriage was risky. She or her husband could have chosen to end the marriage. However, it was also risky to continue to live in a passionless yet safe marriage or to make choices that were not in alignment with her personal integrity.

Remembering and Committing to Spiritual Practice

The fifth step is for therapists to support clients to continue to utilize their personally defined spiritual beliefs and practices in sustainable ways. A client's spiritual practice can be accessed on a regular basis, possibly every moment if mindfulness is used. Clients simply have to remember to engage in their life-affirming spiritual practice. As I have said, most people experience spiritual truths as confirmatory rather than new information. Thus, they often need to remember what we already know.

Life-affirming spiritual practice will provide clients with a vehicle through which they can remember and experience what is healthy and positive in their lives. Unfortunately, it is easy to become reactively engaged in life and forget what truly matters. Clients may have a deeply spiritual experience one day and then quickly return to their familiar ways of engaging in the world the next, only to have another discreet experience that reminds them of what is available. This is why it is called *practice*. Therapists can encourage clients to practice regularly to become experts on their own spiritual lives.

There are many ways to engage in spiritual practice. What matters most is if the practice is life-affirming and *that* clients do it, not *how* they do it. Clients can engage in their spiritual practice through regularly scheduled activities as well as every moment through mindful awareness. They should be encouraged to practice whatever works for them. They can go horseback riding, go hiking, meditate, pray, go to church, do yoga, breathe, smile, enjoy the arts, connect to others with compassion and acceptance, and be mindful in their moment by moment activities.

In the next chapter, the discussion extends these five steps. For change to be sustainable, clients often need help from therapists to transcend a moralist self-evaluation by embracing their needs and parts of themselves that could be deemed unacceptable. Thus, clients need to integrate the shadow parts of their personality.

CHAPTER 6

INTEGRATING THE SHADOW

Chapter 5 focused on how clients' personally defined, life-affirming spiritual practice can support self-soothing as well as inform and nourish the development of their personal integrity. The activities and relationships that make up their lives can then be evaluated based on the vision and standards of their personal integrity. In this way personal integrity becomes a moral barometer and guiding voice in their lives.

As desirable as this is, if a moral code becomes restrictive and legalistic, a variety of psychological and spiritual problems can develop, including disconnection from the Real Self and other aspects of consciousness. Clients' conscious self-understanding becomes increasingly limited in the face of restrictive moral standards. Some of their needs and parts of their consciousness are deemed unacceptable, thus fostering the development of a *shadow* part of their personality—those emotions, needs, experiences, and parts they have difficulty acknowledging and incorporating (Johnson, 1993; Schultz & Schultz, 2009).

By remaining unaware of their shadow, clients feel protected from anxiety in the short term, but do so at great peril in the longer term. They are likely to act out their *shadow needs* in ways that contradict their personal integrity, causing harm to them and others. A sustainable moral vision needs to include all of who they are. All of their needs will seek expression and satisfaction, even ones that are seemingly inconsistent with their conscious understanding of who they would like to be. To be sustainable, their personal integrity must include a realistic and holistic understanding of *all parts* of their personality. Clients must be aware of and integrate their shadow. When accepted and assimilated, their shadow can become a great source of growth, creativity, and balance. Thus, the focus of this chapter is on the importance of therapists considering the theoretical and practical significance of their clients' shadow, including ways to increase balance and integration.

The Shadow

All individuals have standard ways of defining who they are, to themselves and others. They have a *personal story* that defines their perceptions of their history, current life, and future plans. They have *identity markers* (e.g., age, gender, race, ethnicity, marital status, family, friends, job title, significant life events, etc.) that they use to ground and define their sense of self in the world. Each day when they wake up, and periodically throughout the day, they remind themselves of their personal story and various identity markers. In this way, their conscious sense of self is reinstated and reaffirmed on an ongoing basis. This conscious view of self comprises what Jung (1971, 1981) referred to as the ego, the center of the consciousness. The ego is the totality of their conscious self; it is their mental story of who they are.

While the ego is their conscious sense of self, which is typically infused with ideas of who they think they should be, the shadow comprises all that individuals would like *not to be* (Johnson, 1993). The shadow includes all things they have difficulty accepting about themselves and what they find repulsive in others. Typically, individuals repress what they have learned to find unacceptable about themselves into the shadow of their awareness. They then tend to project their shadow characteristics, qualities, and attributes onto others. In other words, they deny ownership of certain needs, thoughts, behaviors, or traits and then disdainfully judge others who exhibit or represent those qualities. In fact, it is by exploring what annoys and scares clients about others that they are often first able to discover the existence of their shadow.

For instance, if clients were to define themselves as highly responsible and hardworking, behavior that they deem irresponsible would become part of their shadow. Consequently, they might not allow themselves to be playful or spontaneous and would likely react strongly to others they view as lazy, unmotivated, or carefree. Conversely, if they highly value their spontaneous and laidback persona, they may shy away from living on a schedule and may judge more structured people as *anal-retentive types*. If clients see themselves as people who take a logical approach to life, emotional aspects of living will likely be banished into their shadow. If they prefer to avoid conflict, then anger and assertive behaviors will become part of their shadow, and so on.

Interestingly, the shadow of individuals who see themselves in primarily self-deprecating ways contains positive thoughts about themselves. If clients view themselves as unworthy and inadequate, for example, more positive aspects of their self-concept would be banished into their shadow. Again, the shadow contains what the conscious view of self will not allow, support, or tolerate.

The shadow often presents itself in the form of characters in dreams (Jung, 1961). A number of years ago, I had a recurring dream that provides a humorous example of how to become aware of one's shadow. I call the dream *Dennis Rodman Won't Leave* and have recounted it many times in seminars and lectures.

The dream always starts with a knock at the front door of my home during the evening. My wife, young child (my second wasn't born yet), and I are going though our typical evening routine: giving my daughter a bath and getting her ready for bed. I answer the door and Dennis Rodman is standing there (Dennis was a famous basketball player and show-business personality known for wild and outrageous behavior, on and off the court). In my dream he is dressed outlandishly and is severely intoxicated due to drugs and alcohol. He pushes his way into my house and starts to act bizarrely. He yells, flails around, and crashes into furniture and walls. My wife and child are upstairs and don't know that someone has entered our home. I try frantically to calm him down and get him out of my house before he can scare or hurt my family. I keep telling him that he has to leave, to no avail. His behavior continues to escalate, getting louder and more out-of-control, before he passes out on the floor just as I wake up—usually in a cold sweat!

My life context during the time of this recurring dream is very telling. I was a newly hired assistant professor at a university and was focused on becoming tenured. I was working long hours at the university and at my private practice. We had recently had our first child and purchased our first home; consequently, I was feeling pressure to support my family financially and to succeed professionally. Our child was colicky and we weren't getting much sleep. When I wasn't working, I was home providing childcare and trying to support my exhausted and stressed wife. Even when I was working I was feeling guilty because I knew that my wife was likely dealing with a crying, colicky baby. I had very little free time, physically or psychologically. Clearly, I wasn't having much fun in my life. I often found myself resentful of friends and colleagues who didn't have children and had time to pursue self-oriented needs and interests. Although I feigned interest in and support of their adventures and exploits, I certainly didn't want to hear anything about anyone's wonderful yoga class or spiritually oriented trip to Peru!

Thankfully, I spoke with a colleague who helped me interpret my dream. What seems obvious to me now, but wasn't then, is that Dennis Rodman represented my shadow. He represented all that I was unable or unwilling to acknowledge in my life and myself: fun, spontaneity, carefree attitude, hedonism, and self-oriented gluttony. My consciousness was wrapped up in responsibility, control, achievement, and selfless giving. There was little room in my life for behaviors and experiences that didn't support my conscious, linear goals. As will be discussed throughout this chapter, this type of restricted sense of self is not sustainable. It will likely lead to judgment and resentment of self and others as well as acting in ways which contradict core values.

How Shadows Form

The process of developing a shadow part of the personality is inevitable. It is virtually impossible not to do so. Thankfully, the shadow is not always extreme and problematic. As a matter of fact, when clients become aware of and integrate their shadow, they feel a sense of sustainable wholeness and peace. However, their shadow will become problematic in their lives when their conscious sense of self becomes restricted beyond what is sustainable. In general, the more restricted the sense of self becomes, the larger the shadow grows. Clients' personal integrity must be large enough to include all of who they are, or their shadow will reactively expand and seek expression, oftentimes out of their conscious awareness. The following describe various aspects of how shadows form and grow.

Dichotomization of Experience

Individuals have a built-in tendency to categorize their experiences, to define them in ways that help them make sense of their world. Although plenty of gradation in categorization occurs, the tendency is to dichotomize experiences into what is good or bad. For the most part, this is an adaptive tendency. If individuals couldn't discriminate among various experiences, between what may be harmful or beneficial, for example, they would have great difficulty in their lives. Life would be much less safe and much more unpredictable.

As is, we live in a somewhat unpredictable and constantly changing world. Events happen periodically, if not regularly, that challenge our sense of safety and stability: a diagnosis of a serious illness, a job layoff, an automobile accident, a divorce, a destructive weather storm, a death, to name just a few. Even typical developmental changes, such as a child going off to school or an adult child getting married, raise awareness of the changeability of life.

When difficult and frightening events occur, individuals tend to feel an increased sense of urgency to categorize their experiences. They want to understand why events happened so they can gain some control of their circumstances and avoid being afraid and unpleasantly surprised in the future. They want to control and predict their world.

This tendency to dichotomize experiences into good and bad supports the development of the shadow, and as I discuss in the next section, plays a part in the development of one's self-concept. Through the socialization process, individuals learn to incorporate good experiences and behaviors into their conscious sense of who they want to be while bad ones are repressed into the shadow.

Idealized Self

To some extent, all individuals have been given messages from their parents and society about how to live life. Just as it is adaptive for them to categorize their experiences, it is adaptive for them to learn from their parents about the world and to maintain connection with them. Humans are not a species that can survive on their own. As young children, they need the protection, guidance, and support of their caregivers. Thus their need for connection with and approval from others, especially parents, is hardwired into their brains. In general, most people want to please their parents and avoid disapproval.

Throughout their lives and especially during childhood and adolescence, individuals receive messages from their parents and society about the world and what types of behaviors are acceptable and valued and what types are not. They learn that some of their behaviors are deemed bad while others are good. They come to learn that some of their behaviors bring approval from parents while others bring criticism and punishment. Thus, the need for connection and approval tends to lead to an insidious compromise: Individuals give up the vision and knowledge of their Real Self for the conditional love and approval of others.

In this context, they engage in the process of forming an identity, their self-concept. They begin to define *who they are* and *who they are not*. They learn that they must banish some of their needs and the parts of self that could endanger them or incur the wrath or disapproval of significant others, while they consciously embrace a sense of self that is based on these standards.

The dichotomy of acceptable and unacceptable behaviors thus becomes internalized and the *idealized self* is born and begins to grow. The idealized self is who individuals think they *should be* (Horney, 1950). It is who they think they need to be to gain the approval and acceptance of significant others. Even when the values and morals that are being internalized are positive and helpful, the process creates a restricted, conscious sense of self. To some extent, it is an inevitable aspect of the socialization process. Less acceptable aspects of oneself become repressed from consciousness. The conscious sense of self then becomes synonymous with one's internalized ideals, rather than the Real Self. The more that their conscious self becomes fused with their idealized self, the more of who individuals are gets shoved out of awareness and into the shadow of their personality. The narrower and more idealistic their conscious self becomes, the bigger their shadow becomes. And, the more individuals become alienated from the inner-generated, sustainable energy of their Real Self.

Sometimes, what becomes internalized is a reactive identity. That is, their conscious sense of self is formed in reaction to the internalization of standards and values that typically comprise the idealized self. In this situation, they adopt a persona of being bad. Prosocial values and morals are banished into their shadow, and their conscious sense of self is still restricted. Either way, the more restrictive their conscious sense of self is, the larger their shadow grows, thus leading to disconnection from their Real Self.

Restrictive Moral Visions

Humanity can be the most unpredictable and frightening aspect of existence. Collectively and individually, human beings are capable of a startlingly wide array of behaviors, from the wonderfully beautiful and creative to the horribly destructive and atrocious. Individuals can regularly be touched by genuine acts of love and kindness as well as be aghast by the horrific behavior of other individuals and groups of people.

Although the behaviors of others may scare them, the truly most unsettling awareness is that *each person is capable of all aspects of human behavior.* Individuals often like to believe that they are not capable of certain thoughts and actions. They want to believe that they would act differently if they were in the same situation as others—that they just couldn't possibly be capable of such things. They thus feel safe in their denial and righteousness, while pointing a judging finger at the behavior of others.

Awareness (albeit limited) of the collective human potential for *good and evil* as well as the unpredictability of the world create a great deal of anxiety and a corresponding need to feel safe. As has been discussed, social and moral codes of conduct tend to serve the purpose of regulating and socializing behavior based on the dichotomized view of good and bad. Behaviors that are deemed socially acceptable are reinforced and held as the ideal while unacceptable and unpredictable behaviors are vilified.

So, societies deal with unpredictable and unsettling behaviors by creating rules of conduct, which can become restrictive moral imperatives. Individuals also banish and negate some of their needs, especially the ones that will lead to disapproval from parents or remind them of their own potentials to engage in socially undesirable behaviors. However, restrictive moral visions and the corresponding attempts to negate needs do not work well in the long run. These strategies are simply not sustainable. All needs have a way of seeking expression, even if not directly. Needs can be banished for only so long before symptoms occur. Denial of needs will typically lead to judgment of self and others, frustration, and eventually depression or acting out.

There are many examples of this process that can be seen in the media on a regular basis. Although shocked, people are less and less surprised when they hear about individuals in positions that exemplify moral righteousness who act out in ways that contradict their stated morals and bring great harm to themselves and others. This occurs across faiths and cultures: Prominent figures who advocate morally righteous positions (e.g., politicians, civic leaders, law enforcement authorities, and church or spiritual leaders) are caught engaging in socially unacceptable behaviors, oftentimes the very behaviors that they proclaim as immoral or illegal.

Consider the following clinical examples, which represent several common outcomes of having ones' personal integrity too closely aligned with an idealized self and a restrictive moral code. John, a 47-year-old man, grew up in a church and family that preached a restrictive moral vision based on a dichotomized view of good and bad. Throughout childhood, his consciousness was largely filled with feelings of lack and inadequacy based on the moral standards he was being taught. In adulthood, he continued to be an approval seeker, especially with women and in his relationship with God, never feeling as if he reached the standard of acceptability. Thus, his spiritual template reflected similar interpersonal themes of shame, inadequacy, and self-deprecation. His prayer life, for example, was filled with apologies and asking God for the strength to change and address his inadequacies. He settled for a love-restricted marriage, often blaming himself for his wife's lack of interest in him. He did his best to negate or restrict many of his needs. His shadow and

his Real Self were almost totally out of his awareness. In addition
to constant feelings of dissatisfaction with his life and marriage, he
was chronically depressed and suffered with diffuse, chronic pain.
Through therapy he was able to stop internalizing shame and start
getting angry (a forbidden, shadow emotion) about what was happening in his life. The anger became a motivating energy, which
allowed him to take charge of his life and his happiness.

Sarah, a 22-year-old woman, also grew up in a church that
preached a restrictive moral vision. Unlike John, she received a great
deal of praise and often felt worthy of God's love. She knew very well
the rules of the church and the expectations of her parents and was
capable of meeting the standards. She excelled in all areas of her life:
school, church, friends, and family responsibilities. She was a shining
star of virtues. Her conscious sense of self was synonymous with her
idealized self: She was who she *should be*. During her college years,
however, she started to have experiences and thoughts that challenged
the dichotomized views of her upbringing. She began to realize that
she was expert at pleasing others, but ignorant of her own values and
needs. She became increasingly reactive to her parents' expectations
and eventually left the church. She began to abuse drugs and alcohol
and engage in sexually promiscuous behaviors. The more she acted
out, the more her parents withdrew their love and attention. She
also felt guilty about some of her behaviors. Sarah wasn't clear on the
standards for her behavior or the origins of her guilt: Was the guilt in
reaction to her parents' values or her own? She entered therapy after
a drug overdose almost killed her. She was confused, reactive, and
angry. Thankfully, she was also ready to take ownership for her life.
Like John, she was ready to reclaim her Real Self.

When Clients Marry Their Shadow

The quickest and most reliable way to learn about your clients'
shadow is by looking at their relationship history, especially their

spouse(s) or intimate partner(s). Based on their upbringing and past relationships, clients enter into their significant relationships with a certain sense of who they are, who they want to be, and who they want not to be. Characteristics and experiences that were deemed unacceptable have been repressed into their shadow, and then expressed through relationships. Clients will often unconsciously act out their unintegrated parts and experiences through their choice of intimate partners and the relational dance that develops over time.

Individuals typically find intimate partners who are like them in many ways (e.g., cultural background, values, and interests), but not like them in important other ways. They want to be able to relate to the other person but also want the person to expand them, to be different than they are. Thus, in addition to being attracted to others who feel similar and familiar to them, individuals tend to choose partners who possess characteristics they find admirable or even scary because they have trouble embracing those characteristics themselves. The unconscious hope is that they will be able to resolve their conflicts and integrate their shadow by being with someone who represents their unintegrated qualities and engages in some of their forbidden behaviors. Simply put, the answer to the question of what clients do with their unruly and unsightly shadow is that they repress it and then marry it.

This process can work well in some instances, but is disastrous in others. The difference between growthful and perpetually painful relationships and outcomes can be captured by two words: *acceptance* and *change*. Couples who experience their relationship as a place to grow and integrate their shadows tend to accept each other while other couples suffer greatly by their attempts to change each other. I'll start with situations when it works well, before discussing examples of how and why it goes poorly.

Generally speaking, when intimate relationships go well, a secure attachment exists between the partners (Greenberg & Goldman,

2008; Johnson, 1996; Johnson & Whiffen, 2003). The attachment is characterized by trust, care, respect, an ability to work through conflict, and mutual acceptance. To a large part, each partner feels known and accepted by the other. The relationship provides a secure base, from which each partner ventures out into the world, takes risks, and grows.

Like struggling couples, these individuals are drawn to each other, at least partially, because of each other's shadows. What is unfinished and underdeveloped in one, the other possesses to a greater extent. However, rather than trying to change the other as struggling couples often do, they maintain feelings of admiration and respect related to their differences. They can be role models for each other based on their mutual strengths. They each can learn new and more expansive and flexible ways of operating in and experiencing the world. Similarly, the secure base of the relationship provides a springboard to try out new behaviors and express various parts of themselves. For example, they can try out new careers or hobbies, possibly engage in creative outlets and relationships, or may intentionally expand their philosophical and spiritual beliefs and practices. This works best when they can trust that each will bring the energy of these experiences back into the relationship, for the benefit of both. Rather than being threatened by the other's growth and expansion, these partners are supportive and encouraging.

Obviously, this is easier said than done. Many couples struggle with these dynamics over the life span of their relationship. The struggles tend to focus on the fervent need to change their partners, which is often reflective of an unconscious need to change parts of their own personality, the parts that have been deemed unacceptable. Thus, rather than being supportive of the other, they are threatened by certain behaviors or traits, most often the ones that represent their own shadow. Each partner becomes identified with a restrictive role (e.g., the pure one, the emotional one, the unpredictable one, the angry one, the responsible one, etc.) within the relationship, and maybe also their life in general. As their conscious sense of self becomes restricted, they move away from the unifying and integrating energy of their Real Self. Projection and projective identification start to take over in their relationship. Specifically, each partner projects his or her repressed shadow onto the other. The other partner identifies with the projection and then acts from this restricted position.

The following are two clinical examples of this painful process; both represent couples who have lost touch with their Real Self, engaged in projective identification, and adopted restrictive, complementary roles based on their shadows. Each example revolves around the need for one or both partners to change, based on core relational themes, which occur commonly in individuals and couples who struggle with incorporating their shadows. Typical relational themes are highlighted, including control, trust, achievement, responsibility, purity, judgment, and emotional expression.

James and Judy

James, 36 years old, first entered therapy saying that his wife told him he must attend counseling and change, or she was leaving. He wasn't clear about what needed to be changed, other than she "wants me to be more motivated." James had a moderately high-paying job. He was comfortable and didn't want to expend much energy trying to become promoted or trying to find a higher paying new job. He preferred to spend his weekends relaxing or engaging in fun activities, rather than working on the house or other projects. He wished Judy could "learn to relax" and stop trying to control him.

Judy, 38 years old, was displeased about James' "complacency" in his career and in his life. She worked long hours and wanted to quit her job to have a baby. She was fearful that she couldn't count on James to "step up" and support them emotionally and financially when she stopped working outside the home. His laissez faire attitude activated deep-seated feelings of insecurity, anxiety, and judgment within her.

James grew up in a family where he felt ignored and neglected by both parents: His father traveled extensively and his mother worked long hours in a professional job. A core message that he internalized from his childhood (in reaction to his parents' overworking) was: "There are more important things in life than work." He didn't want to become like his parents, yet they were his primary role models. Thus, he worked hard enough to succeed moderately, but also vilified working "too hard." To some extent, his achievement needs were repressed into his shadow. He preferred to see himself as "mellow and easygoing." He was largely satisfied with Judy making most of the decisions in their life.

Judy grew up in a single-parent family. Her father left when she was young and her mother struggled to raise children and support the family financially. A core message that she internalized from childhood was: "If you want something done, you can count on only yourself." Trusting others, especially men, was difficult for her. She was a driven person, who had succeeded at everything throughout her life. Her primary strategies were to work hard and stay in control. She was regularly setting and achieving goals in her work and personal life. After working long hours during the week, her weekends were filled with chores, household projects, and preparation for the upcoming workweek. She often found herself feeling judgmental of James' mellow attitude. Now that she wanted to have a baby, she felt vulnerable and panicked about whether she could trust him to support her financially. Her needs for fun, spontaneity, and relaxation were banished into her shadow.

James and Judy were acting from restricted positions. He projected his shadow needs for achievement and control onto Judy, while she projected her shadow needs for fun and spontaneity onto James. They had the potential to support each other in finding healthy balance and perspective and to integrate their shadows. Instead, resentment and frustration festered and grew. Still, Judy was unconsciously attempting to incorporate her shadow by wanting to have a child and quit her job (a very risky venture for her psychologically). Through her actions, she was inviting James to help her integrate her shadow; however, she continued to utilize her familiar strategy of control as a way to manage her anxiety. The unresolved relational issues from each of their families of origin (e.g., neglect, loss, trust, and abandonment) were directly contributing to the maintenance of their shadows and their restricted positions in their marriage.

Katy and Don

Katy, 33 years old, and Don, 35 years old, entered marital therapy in crisis. Their 10-year marriage was hanging on by a thread. Both were saying they weren't sure whether they wanted to stay married. She had recently revealed that she had been having an affair for the past 6 months and wasn't at all clear if she wanted to end it. She felt as if she "couldn't be herself" in the marriage. She stated that she was able to be much more "free and comfortable" when she wasn't with Don. In her view, he was emotionally distant and psychologically stifling. He was always "so good, did the right things, and had the right answers." She felt as if she couldn't measure up to his high standards, no matter how hard she tried. Now, she had broken a shared rule (fidelity) and "would never be forgiven." Although she thought her relationship with Don may be over, she felt relieved the affair was out in the open, as were her feelings of dissatisfaction with her marriage. The one thing she was clear about was that she did not want to go back to business as usual; she couldn't go back to her life as it had been—no matter how much it hurt Don.

Don was shocked, hurt, and angry about the affair. He knew there had been distance in their relationship and was often irritated by Katy's "bouts of irrational emotion." He was also worried that she drank too much, at times. But he never expected her to break his trust in such a hurtful way. His usual intellectual style was breaking down; he was experiencing more emotions and pain than he could remember ever feeling. He had worked hard and followed the "rules," including his Christian faith; how could this happen? He wanted to file for divorce but also believed that they had to make sound decisions for the kids, ages 8 and 5.

Katy grew up in a large, "close-knit" family. Her father was a functional alcoholic. He drank alcohol every evening, but never missed work. When he drank, he would disengage from the family and become unapproachable. Periodically, her father and mother would get into heated verbal debates about his drinking. She remembers feeling powerless and afraid for her mother's safety during these arguments. Her primary role in her family was to make everyone laugh; she distracted them from the obvious tension and struggle. Her emotions were always on her sleeve. She was drawn to Don because of his "stability," which gave her a sense of comfort and security. However, over time she felt increasingly "trapped" by Don's stoicism and psychological distance. Her usual gregarious nature was more and more subdued in their relationship.

Don grew up in a family with three children; he was the oldest. His mother was an active alcoholic until she began attending AA meetings when Don was a teenager. He described his mother as chaotic, disorganized, and prone to crisis, especially during the years before she stopped drinking. His father was largely unavailable, except when Don participated in sporting events or succeeded in activities and academics. Don's father never missed one of his games. Consequently, Don excelled at athletics and everything else he tried, in an attempt to gain his father's attention and approval. He felt responsible for bringing positive attention to his family. He also looked after his younger siblings when his mother was impaired by alcohol and his father was unavailable. He learned to master his emotions and approach life from a rational perspective. He was initially attracted to Katy because of her ability to make him laugh and help him "lighten up." However, over the course of their marriage he had become increasingly displeased about her "emotional instability and irresponsibility."

Like James and Judy, Katy and Don had adopted restricted positions. Both had developed compensatory strategies from their families of origin. Her role as the family comedian, and his as the responsible one, had evolved into restricted roles in their marriage. He became "the Saint" while she became "the adolescent." She projected her shadow needs for safety and predictability onto Don, while he projected his shadow needs for emotionality and rebelliousness onto Katy. Katy had unconsciously attempted to integrate her shadow and *help them both* by having an affair. Initially, she felt more alive and was consequently unwilling to let go of the affair. However, her behavior was outside her own personal integrity and was not sustainable. But the pain of the affair gave them the motivation to learn and grow. The affair was an opportunity to understand the depth of their shadows and how they became lost from their Real Self. Thus, they had an opportunity to resolve core relational dynamics from their childhoods, take ownership for their lives, and reclaim their Real Self.

Integration

The process of integrating the shadow is lifelong. The shadow will always exist as a repository of what is deemed unacceptable or is unfinished and underdeveloped in one's personality and life. However, clients can become more centered and whole by understanding and embracing their shadow. The integration process tends to include two continually repeating steps: (1) awareness and (2) ownership.

Awareness

The content of one's consciousness is constantly changing; it ebbs and flows based on internal and external factors. Individuals are constantly bombarded by demands of their life contexts as well as their internal thoughts and needs. Experiences and needs are categorized and judged, with some being deemed less acceptable or worthy than others. As the conscious sense of self and corresponding behavioral options become restricted, the shadow grows. To counteract this restrictive process, clients need to become aware of the existence of their shadow. They must become aware of all of who they are and of all their various needs. Thus, the first step in the process of integrating the shadow is increasing clients' self-awareness.

As I have said, a good place to start is by looking at their relationships. Therapists can ask questions of their clients about the various people in their lives: intimate partners, family, friends, co-workers, and so forth. Which individuals evoke strong emotions in them? Who rubs them the wrong way? Who scares them? Are they in a restricted role in any of these relationships? Therapists can ask them to visualize a person in their mind who activates strong feelings within them and ponder: What feelings are arising in them? What does this person represent to them? What does this person do that they don't allow for themselves? It is likely that they are projecting some of their shadow onto this other person—or any person with whom they have intense, judgmental feelings. It may also be that they are the recipient of this person's projections.

At this point, the goal is simply to increase clients' awareness of when they become emotionally activated. It's helpful to have them notice their discordant feelings about this person, especially their desire for the person to change in certain ways. When activated, they can be encouraged to pause and experience the feelings rather than banishing or acting on them. They can learn to listen to what their fearful, angry, or judgmental voice is saying, including what the voice might be saying about them.

Clients can learn the most by considering how this person is acting out an underdeveloped or unfinished part of them. Therapists can help clients become aware of what rules or restrictions may be defining what is allowable for them as it relates to this person. It may be that they are negating or restricting certain needs, which this person acts out more freely. Any person who evokes a strong response in clients provides an opportunity to learn about their underexpressed needs.

Don't Pathologize Needs; Needs Just Are

The important thing is that clients become aware of their needs and how they are trying to get their needs met. If they are unaware of their needs or vilify them, the needs will still attempt to seek expression and attainment. Being unaware of needs is a recipe for clients to act out their shadow in ways they may regret. Awareness, on the other hand, leads to choice. They can, therefore, be much more intentional about how and when to meet their needs.

Ownership

Once clients' awareness begins to increase, the next step is ownership: taking responsibility for their needs. Again, a handy way to increase ownership is to have clients look at other people for whom they have judgmental feelings. Once they become aware of who activates them, they should then turn their attention back to themselves, to their needs and their lives. What can they learn about themselves from this other person? What do they think might happen if they were to incorporate the very characteristics of this person that generate their judgmental feelings? How would their life be different if they didn't pathologize those needs? What would happen if they took ownership for all of who they are? Do any fears emerge as they ponder this?

Rather than being victimized or offended by the disowned characteristics, clients can be encouraged by therapists to incorporate them as their own. They can imagine utilizing the energy of those *unacceptable* characteristics for their own life. One technique that therapists can use is to have clients mentally and emotionally picture the denied characteristics and then visualize owning them in a way that stays true to their integrity. For example, if they are offended by another person's "laziness and immaturity," they are most likely not meeting their needs for relaxation, fun, and spontaneity. The other person's laziness can teach them about their unmet needs as well as their tendency to overwork. They don't have to meet their relaxation and enjoyment needs the same way the other person does; they can choose how they will meet their needs. However, they also need to make sure that their personal integrity is not being hampered by a restrictive moral vision.

Another example would be when it is difficult for clients to tolerate someone who acts in a brash or demanding manner with others. It would be helpful to first have them notice their discomfort with this person, and consider how they have dealt with this discomfort. Have they avoided this person or even tried to change him/her in the past? If instead they are able to embrace the energy of this person, they will learn how they can become more whole and integrated. Maybe they don't need to be brasher, but they can probably use the strength and assertiveness of this energy.

When clients regularly practice this type of awareness and ownership, they typically become thankful for those who annoy, frustrate, or scare them, because clients eventually understand that they (others) will become their teachers. Clients can learn about what they are avoiding and need to incorporate into their own life. They will be thankful for the awareness that these teachers live within them, in their shadow. They will learn that they can be assertive or spontaneous or any other denied characteristic and they can do it in a way that is congruent with their personal integrity. They can meet their needs and be true to their convictions.

Many individuals, when they allow themselves to imagine a life driven by their needs in this way, have fears about losing control and engaging in immoral or self-centered behaviors. Typically, their fears focus on becoming lazy or hedonistic. For example, they picture that they might lie around the house all day, eating chocolates.

Maybe they would allow themselves to become addicted to sex or drugs, and so forth. In most cases, their fears are unfounded, and contribute to the development of unintegrated shadows. In other words, because of these fears, individuals tend to banish these needs and work hard to avoid activating their unwanted potentials. In contrast to their fears, most people make balanced life choices, especially when they are based on self-awareness and the wisdom of their Real Self.

To illustrate this integration process, consider the following clinical example. Ramon, a 35-year-old man, grew up as an only child in a middle-class, Christian family. His parents were intellectuals who expressed a strong religious faith and stressed nonviolence and caring for others. A strong interpersonal theme in his family was avoidance of conflict. Disagreements were rare. Being gracious and accommodating to others were prized values in his family.

As an adult, Ramon viewed himself as a caring "good guy." He never wanted to be the center of attention or seen as too needy. He married a woman who grew up in a chaotic, alcoholic family. She was regularly upset emotionally and was drawn to Ramon's stability. He was drawn to her ability to be open with her emotions, since he felt detached from his own. Over time, Ramon and his wife focused on raising their four children; their marriage became stale and lifeless, although neither would acknowledge it initially.

Ramon entered therapy due to a series of events. He had started to experience debilitating depression, which was impacting his work performance. He had just received a poor evaluation at work. He also admitted that he had been frequenting strip clubs, although he indicated he didn't know why he was going. In therapy, Ramon was able to recognize how many of his needs were being negated and repressed into his shadow. All of his expansive characteristics and needs, including assertiveness and sexuality, had been denied and vilified. His restrictive moral vision of conflict avoidance and accommodation were squeezing the life out of him and his marriage. He was being a "good guy," but was now acting out his shadow in ways that were contradicting his integrity. His depression was a sign that he was not living his life based on his Real Self. Rather, he was desperately trying to live up to his idealized vision.

Thankfully, his self-awareness began to increase. He reported dreams in which characters were engaged in bold and repugnant behavior that he would never consciously allow for himself. These characters represented his shadow. He began to see how he was living as a restricted self, and not a whole self. He began to recognize his tendency to avoid conflict and accommodate others, to the exclusion of his own needs and wants, which led to his shadow acting out in ways far beyond his personal integrity. He stopped going to strip clubs, but was able to express those forbidden needs in ways that were more in line with his personal integrity, such as exercise, work achievement, and increased sexuality with his wife. He began to listen to the voice and feel the presence of his Real Self.

In addition to individual therapy, Ramon and his wife went into marital counseling, where they were able to grow and learn through the crisis as a couple. Although she was hurt and scared by his deceit and actions related to the strip clubs (which reminded her of her father), she also felt relieved and empowered by the honesty. Over time, they both began to reclaim the disowned and denied parts of their personalities. Consequently, they each felt more alive and engaged in their marriage and their lives.

This example illustrates the power of awareness and ownership. An awareness of who clients think they must be (the idealized self) and who they don't want to be (the shadow) allow the Real Self to emerge into consciousness. The shadow will continue to seek expression, a process that represents the Real Self's unconscious attempt to become whole, especially in the face of narrow and restrictive visions. Although it may show itself in ways that are unsustainable and outside of clients' personal integrity, *health is trying to emerge.* When their consciousness fills with the presence of their Real Self, they make choices that are congruent with their personal integrity and incorporate all aspects of who they are. They thus claim their lives and feel a sense of balance and congruency.

Therapists can help clients to evaluate the degree to which their spiritual beliefs and practices are life-affirming and promote a moral code that supports a wide and sustainable sense of personal integrity. A central focus with clients, then, is supporting them in living a *value-driven life*, one that takes into account all of their needs. A value-driven life is based on awareness and choice. Behaviors are chosen based on internal values and needs rather than externally imposed rules. If they look deeply, clients will often find that their values include responsibility, caring for others, and accomplishing goals, as well as fun, freedom, and pleasure. Finding a healthy balance of their various needs takes much intentionality; when clients are able to do so, their lives feel like their own. When their lives are based on a sustainable sense of personal integrity, they will feel a sense of wholeness, integration, and personal power. I often tell clients that, rather than living a *self-centered life*, they can live a *Real Self-centered life!*

SELF AND NO-SELF

Throughout this book, I have referred to the idea of a core self, the Real Self. I have also discussed other parts of the personality: the idealized self, the shadow, the ego, and so forth. These conceptions of self have been developed largely within a Western psychological frame of reference. In fact, much of Western psychotherapy practice tends to focus on identifying and building a person's conception of self. For example, therapists regularly focus on exploring and improving their clients' self-concept and self-esteem. The central aspect of increasing differentiation, a likely therapy goal, is the development of a separate sense of self and associated psychological boundaries within relationships.

Other paradigms, including some philosophical and spiritually based points of view, challenge the notion of a separate self, and sometimes, the idea of the existence of a self at all. From these perspectives, the psychological focus on the development of the self can be problematic. In short, self-focus either perpetuates an individual's difficulties by supporting a false or distorted view of self and separateness or becomes the problem because it supports self-centeredness.

The differences between Western psychological and spiritual/philosophical views of the self can generate difficulties for therapists when trying to integrate these worldviews. Before entering into the summative and integrative discussion presented in Chapter 8, it is important for therapists to consider various spiritual and philosophical views of the self, especially ones that seem to contradict traditional therapy models. In this chapter, the dilemmas inherent in these views as well as an integrated model are presented. Rather than being antagonistic, psychological and spiritual views can support and complement each other in therapy. The Real Self, which is the spiritual center, is again the unifying concept.

No-Self

How do your clients view what defines and designates who they are? To what degree do they see themselves as separate from everything else? Is their sense of self derived from physical or psychological boundaries between them and others? How do they understand differences in the way they act in different situations and contexts? Could it be that they have various parts to their personality that emerge in different contexts? What role does consciousness play in their definition of self?

Eastern Philosophical Perspectives

Eastern philosophical thought is extremely vast and broad. Although significant differences exist among Eastern paradigms, and even within Buddhist traditions, there is a common theme related to ideas of *no-self.* In fact, ideas of no-self are most associated with Eastern philosophies and religions. Whereas Western thinking tends to focus on each individual as a distinct self, Eastern philosophy, and Buddhism in particular, views the idea of a separate self as a false belief and as a delusion.

A central part of the wisdom of the Buddha's enlightenment focuses on the ideas of interconnection and *anatman,* the Sanskrit word meaning non-self. These concepts illustrate the idea that there is no independent existence that is separable from everything else. Everything in the world is interconnected. Individuals are part of a vast web of particles and energy that intermingle with everyone and everything. Any action that is made occurs within a larger context and affects all parts of that context, even if not obviously. In other words, when action occurs, it ripples out like a drop of water in a pond, although the effects may be subtle and difficult to perceive. And it isn't just actions. Thoughts also occur within and affect this larger energy field.

In Buddhism, the idea that all things are interconnected is sometimes referred to as *dependent origination*, or the Buddhist law of Conditionality. This principle has three major parts. First, all things come into existence as a result of conditions, not just in isolation. Second, a whole thing exists based on the interaction of its parts, again not in isolation. Third, all things remain in existence only as they interact with everything else that is or could be related to them. Thus, nothing exists as an independent entity.

Dependent origination implies that interconnectedness occurs not only spatially, but temporally. Events that have happened in the past set in motion certain conditions, options, and expectations. For example, ancestors have deeply influenced individuals' lives, even if they have never met them in person. Ancestors' choices and experiences, years before individuals were born, have influenced the circumstances of their lives in many ways, including genetically, financially, educationally, geographically, and relationally. Many philosophers, especially Eastern ones (e.g., Dalai Lama, 2005) argue that historical and current life circumstances and conditions are far more powerful than most people tend to believe, quite possibly even more powerful than free will. The options that individuals have freedom to choose from are really quite limited, due to the behaviors of many others and the conditions that these behaviors and circumstances have created. Thus, even though their brains trick them into believing they have a tremendous amount of free will, individuals' capacity to choose is extremely limited.

Another related aspect of non-self is the Buddhist concept of *sunyata*, emptiness of self. This tends to be understood as emptiness of a separate self. But this concept also represents the idea that we are empty, that we truly have no self. Thus, not only are all things interconnected, but they possess no intrinsic identity (Adyashanti, 2006).

From this perspective, all that exists is experience in the moment; present moment consciousness is all there is (Parsons, 2007). What individuals perceive as their self is a false construction. It is their constructed self that they affirm by reminding themselves of the various labels that they use to define a self. The most common forms of self-identification include possessions, job title, social and financial status, physical attributes and appearance, achievements and accomplishments, abilities, relationship status and history, and various belief systems. These self-identifications, or ego-identifications (Tolle, 2005), as they are sometimes called, are not really who they are but are labels and mental constructions.

Scientific discoveries at the atomic and subatomic levels have provided support and credibility to ideas of no-self by revealing that all things are mostly empty (Chopra & Mlodinow, 2011; Dalai Lama, 2005; Lederman & Hill, 2011). What seems solid, including one's body and hard objects, are actually almost completely empty space. Physicists have demonstrated that great distances occur between atoms in relation to their size and that atoms contain almost nothing, except empty space. What creates the sense of solidity and separation among things is more like an energy field than an actual solid substance.

Thus, from a Buddhist (and quantum physics) perspective, the idea that individuals are separate and distinct is an illusion, and is also an incorrect and dangerous delusion. It fosters a mindset of objectification of people and things, which leads to unhealthy attachments to some things and disregard for other things, rather than an understanding that they are part of all things. Unfortunately, this mindset also supports the assumption that individuals can act with limited consequence to their larger context.

A relevant example, which a friend pointed out to me, is how driving in a car can provide a basic lesson on interconnection. The actions and decisions of all drivers affect the safety and well-being of many people. If one person acts, intentionally or by accident, in a careless manner while driving a car, the consequences can be severe and far-reaching. A serious car accident can change not only the lives of the drivers and passengers but also of the bystanders, emergency responders, family members, friends, and even of the people who read about the tragedy in the newspaper the next morning. The effects can ripple far beyond what we normally consider. We truly are part of an interconnected web that is well beyond our normal comprehension.

Existential Perspectives

As with Eastern philosophy, *existentialism* represents the ideas of various thinkers rather than a unified paradigm. I will not attempt to summarize the variety of systems of thought associated with existentialism. However, some unification around the idea of no-self can be formulated.

Unlike Buddhism, which embraces interconnectedness, existentialists tend to view each person as separate, often alienated, and ultimately responsible for his or her own existence. However, similar to Buddhism, the sense of self (i.e., ego) is primarily seen as a false self. Individuals' typical belief system about who they are is viewed as a compensatory creation. It exists in reaction to a largely unconscious sense that they inherently lack meaning and permanence (Loy, 1996).

Specifically, many people have a chronic fear of death as well as a discomfort and struggle with meaninglessness, which create constant low-level anxiety and periodic panic (Yalom, 2009). Anxiety associated with the precariousness of life and the inevitability of death motivates people to create a compensatory identity. Thus, existential anxiety is the root of self-deception. When individuals believe that they actually are the various labels that they use to define themselves, they are in a state of denial and are distracting themselves from the inevitability of death and their struggles with attaining authentic meaning in their lives.

From this perspective, the primary danger occurs from believing that a false, constructed self is a true self. One's view of self, with its various identity markers, needs to be deconstructed. That is, a self-identity needs to be examined, and self-deception needs to be removed. So, although existentialism doesn't directly say that individuals are empty and have no self, like Buddhism does, it harkens to a similar point: People are prone to self-deception and the tendency to create a false sense of self, which compensates for the chronic, low-level awareness of impermanence and foundational meaninglessness and groundlessness.

Christian Perspectives

Although not widely known for espousing views of no-self, Christianity provides several ideas relevant to the discussion. Most notably, there is a focus on selflessness versus selfishness and God's plans versus individual plans. Again, whereas Western psychotherapy tends to address each individual's wants and needs, Christianity tends to see this self-focus as missing the bigger picture and potentially quite problematic; consequently, some Christians espouse the avoidance of mental health therapy.

A strong Christian belief is the notion that individuals are prone to selfish thoughts, desires, and behaviors. Too much self-focus, even in therapy, can lead to selfishness and disregard for others. This message proposes that the path to growth and salvation includes giving up selfish tendencies and living a life based on a higher purpose (Warren, 2003).

This perspective has, at times, led to a disavowal of the physical body and self-oriented striving as well as a devaluing of material possessions. The body is seen as the repository of unhelpful urges and sensations, which need to be contained. Material possessions, which are based on self-needs, are seen as an unsustainable attempt to replace the sense of lack that is created in the absence of embracing God. Similar to the existential view, self-oriented thoughts and behaviors are understood to be compensatory. While existentialism would propose that individuals are compensating for a lack of meaning and the fear of their inevitable death, Christianity attributes the lack of meaning and fear specifically to a disconnection from God's love and guidance.

From this perspective, people need to replace their individual wants and plans with God's plans for them. Individual plans will be inherently selfish and lacking perspective. Thus, individual plans are doomed to be a struggle and unsatisfying over time. Getting clear about God's plans provides the guiding focus and direction across all areas of life. The main idea is that life will work much better when choices and actions are congruent with God and a larger spiritual perspective on one's life.

Multicultural Perspectives

Multiculturalism, which includes views on gender and ethnic diversity, has largely been embraced as an essential paradigm for contemporary psychology. However, Western psychotherapy has historically taken an excessively individualistic and male-centric approach to understanding and intervening in clients' lives (Christopher & Smith, 2006; Worell & Remer, 2003). The need to conceptualize clients' issues from a more systemic and culturally sensitive perspective as well as to consider and adapt therapy to match client preferences and cultural backgrounds is increasingly being viewed as necessary to providing effective mental health therapy (Enns & Byars-Winston, 2010; Smith, Rodríguez, & Bernal, 2011; Swift et al., 2011). Although there are various components and movements within the multicultural field, in this discussion I will focus narrowly on the aspects most related to no-self.

As I have stated, Western psychology has traditionally given greater importance to individual self-development than to interpersonal relatedness and context. The focus has tended to be on developing a separate self, which includes punctuating the development of autonomy and independence as markers of health and maturity. A relational focus, which is more associated with females than males, has tended to be pathologized and viewed as less mature than characteristics such as separateness and autonomy (Comstock et al., 2008; Worell & Remer, 2003). Thankfully, gender-sensitive models for conceptualizing human development have challenged this pathologizing view of a relational orientation (American Psychological Association, 2007; Enns & Byars-Winston, 2010).

In addition, interpersonal neurobiological and contemporary relational theories have proposed that the self develops in an interpersonal context (e.g., Siegel, 2012). How individuals define themselves is inextricably linked to what is mirrored to them through countless relational experiences, especially with parents and other family members. Their very idea of who they are and what they can expect from the world is formed in relationships. Their relationships become internalized as templates or blueprints of self, others, and self vis-à-vis others, which they carry with them throughout their lives. So, there is no self without others. The conception of self doesn't develop or exist in isolation.

Along with gender-oriented models, ideas of individuality and togetherness must be considered from an ethnic diversity perspective. Concepts of the self have been challenged as less relevant in some non-Western cultures (Christopher & Smith, 2006; Johnson & Smith, 2011). The construct of self holds different meanings, values, and visions across cultures. For example, some non-Western cultures have a much more group-oriented consciousness than is typically understood in Western societies. The emphasis in group-oriented cultures tends to be on cooperation and socially oriented values as opposed to competition and individualistic values. In group-oriented cultures the self often doesn't exist conceptually as a separate entity. Consciousness of self is always in relation to family (including ancestors), community, geography, and culture.

An Integration of Self and No-Self

What is the nature of the self? How can individuals have a self and have no-self at the same time? Is the experience of self inherently compensatory, simply trying to fill a void or a sense of lack? Does connecting to a core sense of self have to mean a disconnection from God or a larger spiritual energy? Is self-focus synonymous with selfishness? Is a self-conception incompatible with a social and relational consciousness? How is the discussion of self and no-self relevant for therapists?

Transcending Self

It will be helpful to continue the discussion by reviewing some of the concepts of self that have been mentioned thus far. Specifically, I define the core of all people, their very essence, as the Real Self. As the seat of their spiritual potential and a deep pool of inner wisdom, the Real Self contains not only individual knowledge, but also taps into the ancestral wisdom of the collective unconscious, as described by Jung. Furthermore, the essence and life breath of the Real Self is God's life breath. It is the Holy Spirit, or spiritual energy, within. And spiritual energy is not just within people; it is within everything. It is what binds everyone and everything together.

Every other state of consciousness, outside the Real Self, is compensatory. One's consciousness can be distracted by and filled with many forms of mentalization and self-identification. Individuals' minds can be consumed by endless thoughts and mental noise. For example, they can believe that their ego-driven, personal story and self-identifications are real, that they truly are their occupations, socioeconomic status, material possessions, and so forth. They can also lose themselves in the consciousness of their idealized self—who they think they should be, if they are to be acceptable and adequate to themselves and/or others. Simply put, their consciousness can be so wrapped up in their ego and ego ideal that they come to believe that this is who they are, which creates a false and deluded sense of self.

The Buddhist and existential views of no-self can first and foremost be understood as *no ego or idealized self.* These compensatory states of consciousness need to be deconstructed; they are a false and fragile self. They keep individuals stuck in a consciousness of separateness and underlying fear. Individuals need to be helped to empty themselves of these self-identifications and experience the fullness and energy of their Real Self. It may sound like an oxymoron—emptying oneself as a way to experience fullness. However, by emptying oneself of ego-based identifications and idealizations, individuals open themselves to the fullness of their Real Self and corresponding spiritual energy.

The Real Self is filled with spiritual energy. When individuals connect with this energy, they become calm, centered, and clear. Spiritual energy flows through them, as it does all things. It is the interconnecting force. It allows their consciousness to be able to see and experience the interconnection between all things. When they are awake to spiritual energy, they are filled with God's life breath— they are not alone.

When individuals make decisions and take action from the consciousness of their Real Self, they are inherently unselfish. They are *self in relation* to all else. The boundary between self and all else melts away. Thus, contrary to the fears of selfishness and being self-centered, when individuals connect with the spiritual energy that emanates from their Real Self, they are compassionate with others and considerate in their actions. Individual plans and wishes are connected to the wisdom of spiritual energy. For example, they do not forsake God's plans for their individual plans, as some Christians fear. That happens only when they are not connected to their Real Self and, therefore, their plans are ego-driven. *Turning inward to the Real Self and spiritual energy is connecting with God.* They connect with their *soul's intentions,* which are God's intentions for them. Their lives become in-flow with the life-affirming spiritual energy within and around them.

When individuals are removed from their Real Self, it is like being naked in the world. They tend to be fearful and alone. Their compensatory self and ego-identifications can quiet the fear, but for only so long. Most people have a vague sense that there is more to life than what their ego tells them; there is more to who they are than they consciously know. Eventually, they awaken and begin to realize that their ego-driven views of self are false and fragile.

So, why do individuals give up the clarity and centeredness of their Real Self for an unsustainable compensatory self? The primary reasons for losing touch with the Real Self, as were discussed earlier, are fear and reactivity. Life is full of fear, and the ego is a magnet for it. Fear drives the ego to create a false self. The ego is bolstered by compensatory behaviors, like achieving social status and amassing possessions, which run rampant when individuals are insecure and anxious. Fear drives them to act reactively rather than thoughtfully. However, the fear-driven ego will soften and recede in the face of a life-affirming spiritual practice.

As the Real Self is reclaimed and spiritual energy emerges, fear and ego identifications dissipate. In its place, individuals experience a sense of presence within them and around them. They often report having a feeling of being at home in their bodies and deeply connected to their own being. And at the same time, they experience a connection with everyone and everything around them. Thus, they can have a self and no-self at the same time. They have a sense of *self* (Real Self) and of *no-self* (interconnection), simultaneously. Ideas of separateness drop away. Their consciousness embraces spiritual energy as the presence within them and within all things as well as an interconnecting energy. Their breath is the breath and energy within and among all things. Their breath is God's life breath. It is the Holy Spirit, their Buddha nature. It flows through and among all things.

Helping Clients Reclaim Their Real Self

First and foremost, it is important that therapists do not become emotionally reactive to any words that clients may use related to spirituality: God, spiritual energy, divine source, Holy Spirit, and so forth. They are just words used to convey an experience, a connection with something larger than oneself. When therapists have a high level of spiritual-differentiation and are nonreactive to the words clients use, they tend to accept and learn from their clients' experiences, which creates space for a spiritual perspective to be utilized in therapy. This often facilitates a deep, trusting therapeutic connection.

It is often helpful to therapists when they can conceptualize the process of clients' reclaiming their Real Self as well as the formation of their spiritual identity as a developmental one, which evolves over time (e.g., Allport, 1950; Erikson, 1963, 1968; Fowler, 1981, 1991, 1996; Marcia, 1966, 1980; Rizzuto, 1979). In childhood, clients (as we all do) begin the process of defining a self, looking to parents and siblings primarily, to see and understand who they are through others' eyes. Clients learn about their wants as well as their likes and dislikes. They learn what is acceptable to others, what brings approval, and what brings scorn. Thus the formation of the ego, ego ideal, and shadow is well underway.

The process expands and intensifies during adolescence as clients become deeply influenced by friends and societal views of what is cool or hip. Their realization of their idealized self increases; they learn more about what is acceptable, even as they don't always fit well into this mold. They struggle to be true to themselves and be accepted by family, friends, and society. The shadow continues to grow as a way to deal with the mismatch between who they are and who they want to be; it grows as the repository of unacceptable emotions, experiences, and parts of themselves.

In the struggle to define a self in the face of familial, cultural, and societal expectations and ideas of who they should be, the ego takes hold. Clients develop a personal story of who they are, complete with ever expanding ideas of what that means. They pick up self-labels, ego-identifications. These serve the purpose of creating a self, albeit somewhat false and misguided, which keeps them afloat in the world. They use their ego-driven view of self as a structure and scaffolding in the face of meaninglessness and groundlessness. Many clients simply do not have the psychological and spiritual maturity to be aware of their ego-driven views of self, much less to deconstruct these views. The Buddhist-based adage, *you can't lose your self until you have a self*, is very relevant during this stage of development.

Most clients begin adulthood with a strongly entrenched personal story and sense of *I, me,* and *mine*, including some ideas of spirituality. Boundaries tend to be a primary issue for clients at this stage. They tend to struggle to define themselves in relation to others, either over- or underemphasizing separateness of self. Some of their identity includes the Real Self, but most of it is ego-driven and compensatory. The degree to which they have experienced life challenges, such as loss, trauma, and unhealthy role models, is often predictive of how disconnected they are from their Real Self. The more they utilize compensatory behaviors and ego-driven views of self, the more lost from their Real Self they tend to be.

Thus, clients venture forth into adulthood with their toolbox of compensatory strategies and a corresponding cognitive map of who they are and what to expect from the world. The process of defining and implementing a self continues: educational and employment choices, relationships, and various life experiences, including spiritual ones. Many clients are simply struggling to survive in their lives, financially and psychologically. To some extent, fear is the motivating force that drives them to continue the compensatory patterns in their lives. For some, these patterns and strategies predominate for the rest of their lives.

Even while fear and an ego-driven view of self are largely in charge, *health is trying to emerge*. Health is the force and intentions of the Real Self. It is how clients would live their lives if they were led by their Real Self rather than driven by fear and compensation. It is the wisdom and energy that is trying to help them resolve the blocks in their lives, which cloud their vision and keep the presence of their Real Self out of their awareness.

Somewhere in adulthood, some clients become increasingly aware that their ego-based view of self and their well-worn compensatory strategies are not sustainable or all of who they are. They may start to have more frequent glimpses of their Real Self or some other connection with spirituality that sparks an awakening within them. They also may have experiences that humble them and overwhelm their usual protective strategies and view of self. The usefulness of their personal, ego-based identity begins to run its course.

For many clients, this awakening happens around mid-life. There is a reconsideration of how they have defined who they are and their lives. Clients in this stage can become reactive against the institutions of their lives, such as their relationships and career choices. Although this can be a tumultuous time, the underlying impetus is the Real Self emerging. Health is trying to emerge into consciousness.

This is a time for clients to try out new behaviors and experiences and to be open to the possibilities of life. It is often described by clients as an attempt to be more honest and real with themselves and others in their lives. This can be quite threatening to the clients and their relationships, especially when it is coupled with a lack of awareness. If clients are unconscious to the underlying intentions of their Real Self, as many people are, their behaviors will be more like reactive flailing rather than thoughtful action. In this case, marriages, friendships, and careers can sometimes become sacrificial lambs. In some situations this is necessary, while in many others it is unnecessary and quite unfortunate.

Some clients engage in this mid-life process in dramatic fashion while others are more subtle in their approach. Either way, it is important for therapists to help clients realize what underlying intentions and questions are emerging. What core questions are being asked and acted out? What issues or dynamics are trying to be resolved? What is the definition of health that is emerging? What are the honesty and integrity that underlie the impulses, behaviors, and needs?

Again, it's important for therapists to remember that even clients' impulsive and seemingly unproductive behaviors are being motivated largely by a need to resolve past blockages and to reclaim their Real Self. One key to successfully utilizing the momentum and intentions of this process is to help clients utilize the wisdom and perspective of their life-affirming, spiritual practice. Accessing the wisdom of their Real Self through a personally chosen spiritual practice provides the guiding vision they need to harness the underlying motivations. Difficult choices may have to be made as they reconsider the activities and relationships in their lives. Sustainable decisions about what is life-affirming versus life-detracting can be made only by their Real Self. Otherwise, they will likely continue to make reactive and unenlightened choices.

It is imperative for therapists to become aware of what is really emerging for their clients. Many times it is not the surface choice (e.g., whether to stay with a job or relationship) that truly matters, but a deeper need to resolve what is unfinished and unresolved in their lives. It is vital for therapists to remember that *health is trying to emerge.* Therapists can help clients to utilize the underlying energy and intentions to heal, grow, and more fully inhabit their lives. Therapists can assist them to utilize their Real Self and spiritual practice to ground themselves in their body and to attain clarity and wisdom about what health means for them.

The following example provides an illustration of this entire process. Donna grew up in the Rocky Mountain West, on a farm. Her parents were traditional in their gender roles and Christian in their religious beliefs. She had an idyllic childhood in many ways. She was close to her family, including her older brother and younger sister. She remembers being happy and content in her home and school life throughout her childhood. She has fond memories of playing in the barn with her siblings and riding the tractor with her father. The expectations of her were clear, and she was able to meet those expectations most of the time. Verbal expressions of love and appreciation were rare in her family, but she knew she was loved by both parents.

The first signs of difficulty began to emerge during adolescence when she would express points of view that were contrary to her parents' views. She was startled on several occasions with the intensity of her parents' reactions to her thoughts and questions. She quickly learned that differences in opinion, especially about religion, were perceived by her parents as threatening and rebellious. Thus, she became adept at suppressing her feelings and needs that she thought might offend or create discomfort for others. She became a master at conflict avoidance while denying parts of herself. Her questions and concerns about her parents' religious views remained largely unaddressed and avoided.

By the time she went off to college (a one-hour drive from home), she had never had a serious intimate relationship or even dated. She was sheltered and largely living her life through the eyes of her idealized self. In her mind, being a "good Christian" meant waiting for the right man before dating or engaging in sexual intimacy. She got good grades, worked a part-time job, and went home almost every weekend. Her primary compensatory strategies continued to be conflict avoidance and suppression of almost all of her self-oriented needs. Her shadow was far out of her awareness.

Shortly after receiving her undergraduate degree, she began a graduate program in the human services field. Her parents were openly critical of this; they didn't see the point of graduate school. They wanted her to get married and return to live near home. She began to feel a great amount of pressure to live up to the idealized vision of a traditional marriage and family life.

During this time, she met Derrick. He also grew up in a farming family. He was divorced, which was contrary to her family's values, but seemed to be "someone her parents would like." Derrick charmed her with promises of support and love. Shortly after meeting him, she invited him to meet her parents. He convinced her parents that he loved Donna and wanted to be her husband. The parents approved, and they were married within 3 months.

Soon after they were married, Donna found out she was pregnant. Unfortunately, almost as soon as the ring was on her finger, Derrick began to treat her with disrespect and disregard. He started drinking heavily, staying out all night, and acting in controlling and demeaning ways toward her. She went to her doctor's visits for her pregnancy without him. He frequently lost or quit his jobs and was unemployed much of the time.

Donna hid the truth of her marriage and her feelings about it from her family and friends. She didn't want to disappoint or worry them. She became increasingly isolated in her pain and shame. She had stopped attending church, largely based on Derrick's criticism of her attendance, which led to further isolation. She continued with her usual compensatory behaviors of conflict avoidance and suppression of her needs, even in the face of Derrick's hurtful behavior and her great pain. Derrick was the epitome of who she didn't want or allow herself to be. In very bold and painful ways, he acted out her shadow.

In some ways, she can thank Derrick. His behavior was so outrageous that she was eventually prompted to action, which ignited her differentiation and growth process. His mistreatment of her became a catalyst for health to emerge within her. If he had been just moderately disregardful, she likely would have put up with it indefinitely. However, his indifference and disregard were also extended toward their baby daughter, which triggered something for her. Although she wasn't feeling entitled to much kindness from him, when he rejected their daughter, she became more empowered.

It started slowly, but built in strength—her connection to her Real Self. Donna went from living in accordance with her parents' wishes to living with Derrick's indifference. But her strategies of conflict avoidance and need-suppression were running their course; they simply couldn't quell the growing dissatisfaction within her. She couldn't stand it anymore. Encouraged by friends who began to question how Derrick treated her, she started to see a therapist. In fits and starts, she began to reclaim her Real Self.

The voice within her reminded her of her worth. Her Real Self spoke with increasing clarity about her truth—what was life-affirming versus life-detracting in her life. She was finding her voice and starting to speak it out loud. First, she began setting boundaries with Derrick, and demanding that he treat her and their daughter with more respect. When he didn't, she found the courage to tell her family about her marriage and her unhappiness.

Initially, her parents told her to try harder and lectured her about not giving up. Her therapist helped her express herself clearly to her parents, and for the first time, assertively disagree with their advice. Over time, they expressed their sorrow about her failing marriage and validated her experience. With her parents' blessing and her newfound strength, she eventually left Derrick.

She finished graduate school and found employment that utilized her skills and passions. With some successes under her belt, she continued to find her voice with her parents. Their support was vital to her, but their judgment of her was at times oppressive. She needed to continue with her differentiation process and stake out her own life. Over time, she was able to maintain a strong connection with them while also being more able to differ with them and assert her independence when appropriate. Although her life was not perfect, for the first time she was living her own life rather than someone else's.

At this point, Donna had challenged her attachment to her idealized self and had moved down the path of differentiation and ownership for her life. She had defined a self in her relationships and had strong and more frequent experiences of her Real Self. Her awareness and utilization of her shadow had increased, mostly in the form of strong convictions, clear boundaries, and assertiveness.

Interestingly, the religious and spiritual questions from her adolescence started to resurface, but in a more mature way. At this time in her life, what did she believe about her faith? How could her spiritual beliefs and practices play a greater role in her life and growth? These types of questions began to emerge in her therapy.

She began to be open to various forms of spirituality, including her Christian roots. The experience was qualitatively different from when she was a child, however. Her faith matured and developed. She discovered a sense of presence in herself and her life. She had moved to a place where she was conscious of how her Real Self was aligned with her spirituality. She began to live a value-driven life, where she was in charge. Her spiritual practice nourished and informed her life and her decisions.

As happens for many clients, the very painful struggles in Donna's life became the catalyst for her growth. Her marriage, as miserable as it was, prompted her to search for her Real Self. Health was always trying to emerge but had been largely unconscious. Her Real Self was always there, waiting to be remembered and reclaimed.

Because of her unhappy marriage, she learned to assert herself not only with Derrick but also with her parents, friends, and co-workers. The core questions that she was unconsciously attempting to resolve rose to the forefront of her awareness. Questions such as: Who am I? Can I have needs? Am I entitled to a voice? If I assert myself, will I be rejected? As health emerged, she resolved these core questions and reclaimed her Real Self.

Therapy helped Donna a great deal on this journey, as it can for many people. Spiritually oriented therapy, in particular, can assist clients with this developmental process by helping them reclaim their Real Self, identify and connect with a personally defined, life-affirming spiritual practice, and utilize their struggles to embrace health as it emerges in their lives. This process will be expanded upon in the next chapter, where the emphasis will be on how therapists can further utilize client-defined spirituality to identify and support health as it emerges in their clients.

CHAPTER 8

How Spiritually Oriented Therapy Helps

There are an extraordinary number of different therapy models that are available, with each one claiming to have solutions. Over the past few decades, therapy approaches have been increasingly put to the test and held accountable for claims of effectiveness. Along with assessing the general and specific effectiveness of psychological approaches with a variety of issues, researchers have attempted to understand the factors that account for client change across therapy models or approaches (Duncan, Miller, Wampold, & Hubble, 2010).

This research has shown some interesting and encouraging results. First, psychotherapy in general is largely effective at helping people with a variety of symptoms and issues (Hubble, Duncan, Miller, & Wampold, 2010). Meta-analyses have revealed that clients in treatment are better off than 80% of those who do not have the benefit of therapy (Lambert & Ogles, 2004; Wampold, 2007, 2010). In short, therapy works for the vast majority of clients.

Second, the focus in the field on identifying specific therapy approaches for specific types of clients and client issues has proven to be largely misguided. Wampold (2001, 2005) reported that differences among therapy models account for only 1% of the variance of outcome. Orlinsky (2010) summarized the current state of therapy research by stating that the treatment-specific model that

> . . . assumes that treatment is basically a process of applying psychological techniques to emotional and behavioral disorders, that therapeutic efficacy inheres in the procedures used, that there is a set of optimal procedures for use in

treating each disorder, that patients are "carriers" of diagnosable disorders and are more or less cooperative recipients of treatment, and that therapists are more or less discerning diagnosticians and are more or less skillful at administering the optimal procedures for each diagnosed disorder . . . does not fit very well with 6 decades of accumulated research findings and therefore does not serve very well as a paradigm for psychotherapy. (p. xxi)

Thus, it seems that specific interventions have some effect on therapy outcomes, but not nearly to the degree that was originally expected by researchers who have focused on developing empirically validated treatment protocols (Hubble et al., 2010; Norcross, 2010).

Third, certain factors common across therapy approaches account for most of the change that occurs in therapy. Additionally, the common therapy factors have an interactive effect rather than work in isolation. The most potent factors accounting for client change in therapy are (Duncan et al., 2010):

(a) **Client and extratherapeutic factors**, which include clients' readiness for change, strengths, resources, level of functioning before treatment, existing social supports, socioeconomic status, personal motivations, life events, and other factors independent of treatment (Bohart & Tallman, 2010). Specifically, "It is the client's self-healing capacities and resources that are responsible for resolution of problems and for change in everyday life and in any form of psychotherapy" (Bohart & Tallman, 1999).

(b) **Models and techniques**, which are much less about the specific model used and much more about how models and techniques provide therapists and clients with culturally acceptable explanations for existing problems as well as healing rituals that instill structure and positive expectations for change (Anderson, Lunnen, & Ogles, 2010). Thus, when therapists have allegiance to a therapy model, it provides the therapy with structure and conceptual scaffolding that support clients' hope and expectations for successful outcomes.

(c) **Therapeutic relationship/alliance**, which focuses on a strong partnership between client and therapist to achieve the client's goals. A strong client-therapist relationship is consistently found to be one of the best predictors of outcome (Norcross, 2010; Norcross & Lambert, 2011; Norcross & Wampold, 2011b; Wampold, 2010).

(d) **Therapist factors**, which focus on the person of the therapist, are "the most robust predictor of outcome of any factor ever studied" (Hubble et al., 2010). In other words, some therapists are much more effective than others and more readily use the common factors to achieve better outcomes (Wampold, 2005).

Spiritually oriented therapy is not different from effective therapy in general, in that it utilizes the same common factors to attain successful outcomes. The primary goal of therapy needs to be doing what works with clients. Spiritually oriented therapy incorporates spirituality for therapeutic value by inviting clients to explore their definitions of and experiences with spirituality and philosophical ideas of existence. The focus is on acknowledging and embracing clients' beliefs and practices, especially those that bring feelings of centeredness as well as wisdom and clarity of perspective. In short, spiritually oriented therapy intentionally invites clients to utilize their personally defined, life-affirming spiritual practice within the context of effective therapy to notice and access the inner wisdom and clarity of their Real Self.

In this chapter, I discuss key themes and aspects related to how therapy can support healing and growth, and the ways in which a life-affirming, spiritual practice can aid and facilitate the psychotherapeutic process. The emphasis is on how therapists can incorporate client-defined spirituality into therapy that utilizes the common factors to help clients reclaim their Real Self.

A Collaborative Team

What are the key elements of a strong and productive client-therapist relationship? Why and how does the therapeutic alliance assist clients with finding their own inner wisdom and connecting to their Real Self? How does clients' spirituality relate to the client-therapist relationship?

For many years, I have given students in my "Introduction to Counseling" classes the opportunity to attend counseling sessions with a therapist of their choice and then write a paper about the experience. It has been an amazing privilege and an extraordinary learning opportunity for me to read over 1,000 of these papers. Over and over students write about the importance of the relationship with their therapist. Students consistently equate success in therapy with how well their therapist does across several key points and questions. For example, does their therapist show sincere interest in them? Do they feel genuinely cared for by their therapist? Does their therapist listen accurately and nonjudgmentally? Does their therapist understand their concerns? Are they and their therapist able to form a shared understanding of the goals and direction of therapy? What happens when there are challenges to their therapeutic relationship?

In support and confirmation of these student views, research has concluded that, generally speaking, if the therapeutic relationship goes well, the therapy goes well (Norcross, 2010; Norcross & Lambert, 2011; Swift et al., 2011). The complex nature of this relationship boils down to some key elements: trust, respect, nonjudgmental acceptance, accurate empathy, positive regard, therapist congruence/genuineness, clear expectations of the professional relationship and of boundaries, match between therapist conceptual intentionality and client needs, feedback between client and therapist, shared focus and goals, shared motivation for progress, appropriate therapist self-disclosure, encouragement of risk-taking, management of countertransference, appropriate relational interpretations, and ability to work through challenges to the relationship (Elliott, Bohart, Watson, & Greenberg, 2011; Farber & Doolin, 2011; Hayes, Gelso, & Hummel, 2011; Horvath, Del Re, Fluckiger, & Symonds, 2011; Kolden, Klein, Wang, & Austin, 2011; Norcross & Wampold, 2011a; Safran, Muran, & Eubanks-Carter, 2011; Tryon & Winograd, 2011). When these key elements are in place, the relationship is healing, facilitative, and allows for an environment where other important factors can have an impact (e.g., interventions and client self-healing capacities).

The essence of a productive therapeutic alliance revolves around the ability of the client and therapist to form a team to collaboratively address issues and concerns that are important to both. This collaborative team, which I call *Level One Therapeutic Alliance*, is foundational to success in therapy. A healthy and productive client-therapist relationship is a safe place where clients can quiet down and look inward, look and listen to their Real Self. They are able, for example, to reflect on their conflicted and painful feelings and begin to make sense of their needs and difficult and confusing experiences. A strong therapeutic alliance provides the kind of attunement and validation that were missing in many clients' childhood and family experiences.

The therapeutic relationship creates a transitional space where clients can explore parts of themselves and try out new behaviors as they prepare to try them out with others in their lives. Thus, it also provides an experiential model of how to have an authentic relationship with another person. Ideally, the therapeutic relationship offers an invitation for clients (and therapists) to embrace their Real Self and to have a genuine encounter. This deceptively simple process sets the stage for how much and how quickly therapy will be helpful to clients. It sets the trajectory for the entire change process.

Spiritually oriented therapy also focuses on developing a strong therapeutic alliance. Just as individualizing treatment to match clients' needs and preferences in general is important (Norcross & Wampold, 2011a; Swift et al., 2011), when therapists address client-defined spirituality, outcomes in therapy improve (Smith et al., 2007; Worthington et al., 2011). When clients believe that their therapist is genuinely and nonjudgmentally interested in their spiritual beliefs and practices, the therapeutic relationship tends to become much stronger. Clients usually feel connected with their therapist in a foundational and deeply personal way.

Self-Awareness

Self-awareness is a foundational aspect of how therapy helps in general and of how it assists people specifically in rediscovering their Real Self. As I have discussed previously, life tends to come at clients in an assaultive fashion, knocking them off center and away from their Real Self and from their spiritual grounding. As they move away from the guidance of their Real Self, they are likely to become reactive and lose touch with their core sense of personal integrity.

Unfortunately, it is common for clients to operate from a reactive position, acting with little reflection or awareness of the emotions, thoughts, and agendas that impact their moods and behaviors. Once they become reactive, they can act in ways that they may regret: expressing anger inappropriately, getting caught up in other people's dramas, responding to or initiating excessive flirtation with others, and so forth. At some point, clients are likely to step back and question their motives and choices, and sometimes realize that they need to fix a mess that they inadvertently created. So, how do clients stop acting reactively? A big part of the answer is self-awareness.

Many clients have been taught to not be self-centered or self-absorbed. They have received messages about not focusing too much on their own needs and about engaging in activity-oriented ways of operating in the world. In other words, they are taught to define themselves by what they do rather than by who they are, by *doing* rather than *being*. The problem, of course, is that they move away from listening to the grounding energy and intuitive knowing of their Real Self.

A funny, yet true, example of this occurred to me during the first year of my doctoral training. I was very happy to be in my graduate program and extremely busy with all the various tasks. On any given day, I was taking classes, working with clients at the university counseling center, teaching undergraduate classes, studying, and working as a research assistant. Some days I would get so busy and task-focused that I would *forget* to go to the bathroom. One day while teaching a large class, I suddenly became painfully aware that I hadn't relieved my bladder in many hours. I became literally bent over with pain and urgency. I had been ignoring my body and all internal cues until I couldn't wait one more moment! I had to excuse myself and hurry down the hall to the bathroom. It was not only embarrassing but also startling in terms of the degree that I was out of touch with my body and inner experience, focusing almost exclusively on the external world and tasks. And it happened on more than one occasion.

While most aspects of life encourage clients to be externally focused, self-awareness is about tuning in and listening to one's inner experience, including emotions, thoughts, and body sensations. Therapy provides an opportunity for clients to slow down and turn their awareness inward. This will likely include approaching and investigating anxiety and uncomfortable feelings. Anxious feelings will be a teacher if clients listen to what those feelings are saying rather than blindly reacting to them, ignoring them, or acting on them, which can increase their ability to thoughtfully choose, not just react.

All behavior serves a purpose and represents an attempt to meet needs. This simple, yet profound, statement reminds therapists that all behavior, including seemingly odd and dysfunctional behavior, is purposeful, even if clients are not fully conscious of the purpose. In fact, most clients are not very conscious of the emotions and needs that underlie much of their behavior. Everyone has basic needs for love and belonging, for example. Unfortunately, the need for love (or any need), can prompt clients into reactive attempts to attain connection with others, such as caretaking, accommodating, placating, pursuing, and controlling, to name a few.

A very important point to remember is that needs per se are not problematic! *It is how clients attempt to meet their needs that can lead to difficulties.* Therapy is a place where clients can be guided inward, to explore and normalize their needs and to understand the various ways they have been trying to meet them. By understanding that their behavior is an attempt to meet a need, clients tend to feel less pathologized and more empowered in their attempts to find healthy ways to meet their needs. For example, it is not wrong or bad to want to be loved. However, when clients attempt to meet their needs for love and belonging in unhealthy ways, it can bring great suffering to them and others. Simply put, therapy provides a place where clients can increase their awareness of their needs and can find healthy ways to meet those needs.

Similarly, before changing an *unwanted* behavior, it is advisable to understand what the behavior has been trying to accomplish. For example, if a man has been distancing in his relationships, although hurtful and infuriating to his partner, it is quite likely that the distancing behavior has been serving a protective purpose, possibly protecting him from rejection or criticism. Unfortunately, the *protective* behavior ends up bringing more rejection and criticism as his partner becomes increasingly impatient and annoyed with the distancing behavior. Thus, therapy helps increase awareness of the needs, emotions, and anxiety that may underlie and motivate specific behaviors.

All clients have certain emotions that are easier for them to access than others. And they have shadow parts of their personality, which contain denied or disowned characteristics, emotions, or experiences. The emotions that drive reactive behaviors are both complex and conflicted; clients often have good reasons for avoiding them. The emotions cannot easily be acknowledged, understood, or integrated.

For some clients, anger and frustration are the first emotions that they experience, while sadness and shame are less accessible and exiled into their shadow. They may readily blame others and externalize their emotions, especially if sadness, loss, or shame is activated. Simply put, clients who are *anger-sadness-shame* types (Teyber, 2000) are more comfortable expressing anger than they are acknowledging the underlying hurt. They are *externalizers*. They tend to blame others and to look externally for sources of their discomfort.

Conversely, people who are *sadness-anger-guilt* types are *internalizers* (Teyber, 2000). They are more comfortable turning anger inward and blaming themselves than blaming others. When they do get in touch with and express their anger, guilt is activated and triggers them back into disempowered sadness. This is an underlying dynamic of depression and chronic sadness (dysthymia) for many clients.

Thus, for many clients, conflicted and painful emotions tend to be pushed out of awareness into their shadow. They live within a muted and truncated range of emotions, consisting of the most acceptable and easily accessible ones. Deviations from the emotional range are regulated by rigid rules and harsh beliefs. For example, "crying is a sign of weakness," "anger is dangerous and unacceptable," and "I will lose control if I get in touch with my long-avoided pain." Therapy provides a space where clients can engage with and express thoughts and emotions that are more difficult for them to access. Therapy provides them with a chance to break the rules that limit their ability to be more emotionally free. It offers a place for them to become more aware of and integrate the shadow parts of their personality.

Spiritually oriented therapy, in particular, invites clients to increase their awareness of how their spiritual beliefs and practices can be useful to them and the therapy process. When spiritual beliefs and practices are life-affirming, they tend to provide opportunities for clients to feel centered and grounded. Client-defined spiritual practice (e.g., church services, prayer, meditation, hiking in nature, physical exercise, creative arts, etc.), especially when combined with present moment awareness, often increases their connection with their inner life of emotions, thoughts, and felt-sense of their body. This not only provides resourcing for clients, but also access to their inner experience and intuition.

A common technique that I use to help clients increase self-awareness is a mindfulness-oriented body scan (e.g., Brach, 2003), which can be combined with other reflective practices such as prayer and meditation, to match the client's beliefs and needs. In other words, I use mindfulness as a trans-spiritual activity, which can be combined with clients' personally defined practice. The mindfulness-oriented body scan starts by having clients bring their awareness to their breathing, and then center their awareness on their body and any sensations they may experience. I assist clients (or teach them how to do it on their own) to go through each part of their body and invite and notice any feelings and sensations. Along with grounding themselves to a greater degree in their bodies and learning from their emotions and experience, they often describe a sense of *spiritual stillness*, which then opens their consciousness to the wisdom and clarity of their Real Self.

Spiritually oriented therapy also invites clients to utilize their spiritual practice to clarify their values and their personal integrity. In other words, it helps clients live a *value-driven life*. Again, a value-driven life is about following one's inner-generated beliefs and moral compass. Spiritually oriented therapy helps clients take greater ownership for their values and life choices. If their choices are based on the wisdom of their Real Self, clients will likely feel a greater sense of congruence and integrity.

Insight

Many clients have very little insight into the sources of their difficulties. Clients often avoid thinking about painful memories and minimize the impact of past experiences on their current life. Yet, they may periodically feel, for example, anxious, depressed, angry, lonely, unlovable, inadequate, and unworthy. Therapy provides a forum to understand the various forces, past and present, which impact their patterned thoughts, moods, and behaviors.

Where and how do clients develop beliefs about themselves and about what they can expect from others? For the most part, the answer is that they learn who they are and what to expect from others from their significant relationships, past and present. Significant relationships typically include: (a) past experiences with family members growing up, (b) past experiences with intimate partners, friends, and others, (c) current experiences with members of their family of origin, and (d) current experiences with intimate partners, children, friends, and others, including therapists. One of the ways therapy is helpful is when it facilitates insight into the links between these various relational systems and experiences.

Linking fosters insight into the patterns and themes that occur across relationships in a client's life. Often, clients first learn about who they are in their families. In their families, they: (a) have significant relational experiences, some of which can be traumatic, (b) play certain roles (e.g., caretaker, pleaser, rebel, etc.), and (c) learn how to protect themselves relationally (e.g., to be a *good boy/girl*). These experiences, roles, and protective strategies tend to then be replicated or reacted against in relationships outside of the family, often beyond their conscious awareness. Many clients feel a sense of relief when they begin to understand the reasons why they feel and act the way they do.

Insight helps clients put the pieces of their lives together in their minds, to reclaim *lost* parts of their relational history. Trauma, in particular, is associated with gaps in memory. Therapy provides a space where clients can make connections between events and develop a *coherent narrative* of their life story. Insight helps provide a conceptual framework that they can use to make sense of themselves and their lives. Thus, when therapists facilitate insight through linking and accurate interpretations of clients' interpersonal dynamics, clients achieve higher levels of success in therapy (Crits-Christoph & Gibbons, 2002; Norcross, 2010).

In addition to clients' interpersonal dynamics, spiritually oriented therapy focuses on helping clients develop a coherent narrative of their spiritual identity and journey. Clients can gain a deeper understanding of the events and experiences that have shaped their spiritual beliefs, values, practices, identity, and reactivity. Oftentimes, clients' spiritual beliefs reflect themes that are part of their relational templates. For example, if clients have issues with trust due to abuse from a parent, their feelings about developing a trusting relationship with a higher power may be affected. They may yearn for the spiritual connection and/or react strongly against it. Spiritual violence, in particular, tends to create spiritual templates that are embedded with reactivity and restricted views as well as an underlying longing for connection and healing.

Whatever their life and spiritual journey may have been, therapists can help clients by increasing their understanding of the roots of their spiritual beliefs as well as the patterned ways of responding to current triggers. Thus, insight is an important part of the therapeutic process that can help clients develop greater awareness of the etiology of their relational and spiritual templates, heal from and integrate spiritual violence, and take greater ownership for their spiritual beliefs and practices.

Reexperiencing Relational Dynamics

As helpful as insight can be, clients often need something more to assist them to overcome patterned feelings, thoughts, and behaviors. Lasting change tends to occur on an experiential level. In other words, clients often need to *experience* change, in addition to developing an understanding of why they react the way they do. Where can clients experience change? One very likely and important place is with a therapist.

Again, relationships, especially with parents and significant others, teach clients about themselves and what they can expect from others. Clients bring their relational expectations and styles into therapy. To greater or lesser degrees, they transfer expectations of how they have been treated in the past onto their therapist. They also tend to use the same interpersonal strategies (i.e., caretaking, accommodating, externalizing anger, distancing, etc.) with their therapist that they use in other areas of their lives. And, therapists bring their own expectations and strategies into the process. (Hopefully the therapist has engaged in some meaningful exploration in therapy of his/her own relational templates and corresponding issues.) When the client-therapist relationship reaches the level that the dynamics that are occurring between them can be usefully and intentionally processed, they are operating on what I call *Level Two Therapeutic Alliance*.

Although these dynamics occur in all therapeutic relationships to some degree, some psychological approaches (e.g., cognitive-behavioral, behavioral) do not typically value or recognize these dynamics as useful to the therapy process. In these cases, client and therapist consciously or unconsciously choose to not notice or address these dynamics. Or, they get acted out by clients and therapists in ways that can become detrimental to progress in therapy. At the very least, therapists that don't usefully address the dynamics between themselves and clients are missing the wonderful and typically profound opportunities for experiential change that a Level Two Therapeutic Alliance generates.

So, how is the re-enacting of relational dynamics therapeutic? When therapists are able to intuitively or intentionally respond to clients in ways that challenge their problematic relational beliefs and expectations, a *corrective emotional experience* can occur. That is, as therapists respond in ways that challenge clients' unhealthy expectations, clients begin to experience healing related to their original wounds (i.e., the experiences that created their problematic expectations in the first place). Clients then have an opportunity to experientially disconfirm their erroneous expectations of themselves and others. This typically leads to greater freedom of choice; clients are less likely to respond in automatic and rigid ways in an attempt to protect themselves. They are then often able to generalize the experience with their therapist to others.

A scenario that some clients unconsciously experience with their therapists, for example, is an expectation that their therapist will be critical or rejecting, largely based on their past experiences with their parents and/or significant others. Clients with these issues will eventually *test* their therapist to see if their therapist will respond in ways that are similar to these important others. They may even try to bait their therapist into a critical response, for example, by being critical or rejecting of their therapist. When clients and their therapists can usefully talk about these dynamics and the underlying motivations, healing and growth tend to occur (Crits-Christoph & Gibbons, 2002).

The essence of *testing* is about healing on an experiential level (Weiss, 1993). All clients have a Real Self that wants to heal and to embrace health. When they are out of touch with their Real Self, their attempts to test and heal often become a *repetition of familiar and fear-based experiences.* Conversely, as therapists respond correctively to their testing behaviors, clients regain some connection with their Real Self. They start to understand that they don't have to blindly act out old patterns; they can instead take intentional risks to embrace the life-affirming aspects of their relationship with their therapist. They experientially learn, for example, that not all women will be rejecting and that not all men will be critical or cross their boundaries, and so forth. This experiential learning softens the rigidity of their beliefs and their protective strategies. As the strength of their pathogenic beliefs and fear-based inner voices recede, the voice of their Real Self naturally emerges.

This corrective re-experiencing of relational dynamics can be mirrored and supported by inclusion of clients' personally defined spiritual beliefs and practices. Sometimes clients will project their relational conflicts onto their conceptions of spirituality or a higher power, which tends to lead to some amount of testing. Among a variety of client-specific ways it can manifest, testing often emerges in a flip-flop between denying/rejecting and accepting/embracing a loving higher power. Therapists can assist clients by nonjudgmentally helping them process their evolving relationship with spirituality, in whatever form envisioned by clients. As clients feel that they are understood and their spiritual/philosophical frameworks are respected and valued by therapists, they are more likely to take risks within the therapeutic setting.

In addition, a life-affirming spiritual practice tends to provide opportunities for clients to have corrective experiences. The feelings of peace, centeredness, clarity, and belonging/connectedness that a life-affirming practice tends to bring are antithetical and corrective to clients' symptomatic feelings of anxiety, depression, fear, and alienation. Thus, not only are clients correctively re-experiencing relational dynamics with their therapist, but also with their spiritual practice. Therapists can support this process by passing client-specific relational tests, processing clients' evolving, developmental spiritual identity, and encouraging clients to utilize their life-affirming spiritual practice as a way to correct core relational wounds and conflicts. Clients then learn to not only trust their relationship with their therapist, but to also trust themselves and the support of their spiritual practice.

New Relationship With the Real Self

A positive and corrective therapeutic relationship, which may involve a corrective and supportive relationship with spirituality, supports clients in developing a new relationship with their Real Self. As an Internal Family Systems (IFS) therapy colleague of mine said recently, the primary goal of therapy is to help clients be led by their core Self, their Real Self. How does therapy help the Real Self lead the way? An integration of various theoretical approaches, especially IFS therapy (Schwartz, 2001), provides a useful framework to further understand this process.

Various contemporary models are based on the idea that the personality is made up of multiple parts (e.g., Noricks, 2011; Schwartz, 2001; Watkins & Watkins, 1997). In IFS language (discussed in detail in Chapter 3), there are *managers, exiles, firefighters*, and the core *Self*. For most clients, their conscious sense of themselves is as a manager: They define themselves by their actions and their attempts to control their world. Many clients spend the majority of their time surviving, planning, organizing, mastering, and striving; this is their basic sense of who they are. Once in a while (the frequency and intensity typically depends upon the level of unresolved trauma in their background), they become aware of some painful and disavowed emotions or memories that are normally exiled out of awareness (e.g., shame, hurt, self-criticism, anger, dependency, etc.). When these intolerable emotions or memories are accessed, their firefighters often jump in to protect them from these painful feelings. Firefighters may include addictions, dissociation, rage, withdrawal, and other strategies designed to quickly return their painful emotions and memories to their place of exile, that is, out of conscious awareness. Then, their managers can regain control and return them to a task-focused way of operating.

Thus, for many clients, their consciousness is filled with their managers, and to a lesser extent, their exiles and firefighters. They often have only a faint awareness of the existence of their core self, their Real Self. Therapy is productive when it helps clients *remember* to access their Real Self and when it fosters a new relationship among the various parts of their personality.

Specifically, the Real Self is accessed by remembering and noticing its existence: moments when clients feel calm, centered, connected, competent, capable, clear, and courageous. This is a place where spiritually oriented therapy can be of great assistance. Spiritually oriented therapy encourages clients to utilize their life-affirming spiritual practice to resource and connect with feelings of being calm, centered, and so forth. Clients can also experience and access spirituality during sessions. For example, I find that helping clients to attend to their breathing in the present moment is often the quickest way to begin to reconnect with their Real Self. Quieting down the external and internal noise allows clients to listen to their intuitive knowing and to be filled with a sense of spiritual presence. Therapists can support this process by inviting their clients to turn inward and attend to their hearts and to utilize their reflective and spiritual practice. Over time, what emerges are ever-stronger glimpses and clarity about what is life-affirming and growthful.

Each part of the personality serves a purpose, but the Real Self needs to guide the way, to be the leader. Exiles need to be heard, for example. Painful memories and emotions need to be expressed. This is often referred to as *inner child work*, when clients have experienced trauma in childhood (i.e., verbal, physical, or sexual abuse; or neglect). The inner child needs to be seen and heard or it will become increasingly frantic in its attempts to be noticed. These frantic attempts can include uncomfortable feelings leaking out at inopportune times and their consciousness being flooded with painful images, dreams, and physical sensations, to name a few. Rather than clients' firefighters automatically jumping in with their oftentimes destructive protective strategies, therapy can help them learn to pause, what Tara Brach (2003) refers to as *the sacred pause*. By pausing right after being emotionally activated, clients can then notice and access their Real Self and have their Real Self develop a healing relationship with the other parts, including the exiled inner child. Their Real Self can thank the firefighters for bringing the situation and associated need to protect to their awareness, and then ask the firefighters to step back while their Real Self takes over.

Typically, facilitating a relationship between exiles and the Real Self involves allowing exiles to speak while clients are consciously operating from their Real Self. An analogy to this process is a parent listening to and comforting an upset child. I often have clients engage in some mindful breathing to bring their Real Self to their conscious awareness, then visualize their inner child in a state of pain. Then, the Real Self asks the visualized child what he or she is feeling, wants to say, and needs. The Real Self listens, comforts, and soothes the child, rather than exiling him or her. In some cases where the inner child is not trusting of the Real Self, it is most helpful to just compassionately notice the child's pain without offering parental comfort. Over time, the exiles gain trust in the Real Self and become less reactive as they feel heard and their feelings are validated and integrated.

Again, a personally defined spiritual practice can support this process and provide access to soothing energy for clients. The Real Self and associated spiritual practice can provide *self-validation* and *self-soothing* to exiles and leadership to the internal system, which is crucial for clients as they heal from trauma and regain a sense of balance and personal power. In this way, the relationship between their Real Self and their exiles begins to resemble the relationship between therapist and client, and the relationship between client and personally defined, life-affirming spiritual practice. All three relationships are based on validation, love, respect, guidance, nurturance, and empowerment.

When clients learn to access their various parts in healing ways, their Real Self leads more and more of the time. Their managers still keep them task-focused, but the fear-based motivations are softened and the joy of the tasks can be experienced. Their exiles still alert them to pain and unresolved experiences, but they are much less frantic; their exiles are feeling validated and soothed. There is also a greater freedom of emotional expression. Their firefighters still alert them to times when they feel vulnerable and need protection, but the urgency and destructiveness of their alerts are reduced and they more readily step back and allow their Real Self to handle the situation; their firefighters trust that their Real Self is capable of addressing their concerns. In general, life-detracting behaviors are replaced with life-affirming choices based on the wisdom and guidance of their Real Self and associated spiritual practice.

Embracing Inner Health

Inner health is always trying to emerge. The Real Self is always trying to help. Therapy is most effective when the process encourages clients to recognize the voice of health and their own self-healing capacities (Bohart & Tallman, 2010). Therapy assists most when it utilizes clients' strengths, calls upon and facilitates their capacities, and utilizes their struggles as opportunities to learn, grow, and become more whole.

Health often emerges in clients' consciousness through emotions, thoughts, and behaviors that they first experience as an impulse. Clients might experience, for example, an impulse to connect with an intimate partner or to engage in some form of addictive behavior. Neither of these impulses is problematic per se. Impulses reflect an attempt to meet a need or resolve a conflicted issue. Specifically, the need to connect with an intimate partner could reflect an underlying sense of loneliness and a desire to be loved and accepted. The addictive behavior could be a repetition compulsion related to unresolved past trauma. That is, clients can be driven to engage in behavior in an unconscious attempt to heal and resolve experiences where they have become emotionally stuck. In this way even seemingly *bad* or unproductive behavior is often an attempt (albeit largely unconsciously) to heal and grow.

Consider the example of John, a 45-year-old married man who entered therapy after his sexual addiction was revealed. He was meeting women on the Internet and engaging in sexual liaisons, after which he experienced excruciating shame and guilt. Yet, he was unable to control his impulses or change his behavior. When she found out, his wife was horrified by his behavior, viewing his actions as a personal attack on her as well as moral weakness in him. His impulse had to be bad or wrong, right?

Shortly after starting therapy, John revealed that he had experienced repeated sexual abuse from a teenage male babysitter when he was 6 to 8 years old. Although causing great harm, his sexual addiction and underlying impulse could now be understood as an attempt to repeat and fix his unexpressed and shame-based trauma history. Health was trying to emerge through the impulse to engage in addictive behavior.

Therapy provides clients with a place to explore the underlying needs and motivations of an impulse, rather than blindly act in automatic and patterned ways. Once underlying needs and motivations are understood, this insight can be put into action through self-awareness. In John's case, his insight allowed him to develop a greater understanding of why he was acting in these ways and what was really at stake—he could work consciously to heal his unresolved sexual abuse history or keep traumatizing himself and others through his addiction. His behaviors needed to change, while the underlying impulse needed to be honored. When he was able to become aware of his impulse in the moment, he could pause rather than act mindlessly and automatically. He was able to experience the impulse, and then pause and connect to his Real Self. His Real Self provided the wisdom into what could effectively and responsibly meet his underlying needs without addictive behavior. He also developed a mindfulness-based spiritual practice that supported his ability to pause and embrace healthful energy in his life. He began to equate his increasing awareness of present moment peace and wisdom with a deep sense of spirituality.

John's story provides a wonderful example of the power of the health impulse. Health is always trying to emerge into consciousness, even in seemingly odd or problematic ways. Struggle can remind clients (and therapists) that something isn't right. Therapy can provide an opportunity to view and re-experience the struggles as an attempt to define oneself, heal unresolved issues, become more whole, and meet needs in healthy ways.

Embracing Relationship Health

Although the therapeutic relationship provides an experiential model for a healthy relationship, the client-therapist relationship is a transitional one. And, although it should be an authentic relationship based upon genuine caring, it is also a relationship that is ethically and clinically limited by professional boundaries. Thus, clients need to transfer the learning and experiences from their therapists to other significant relationships in their lives. Healthy relationships are where lasting change occurs: with therapists, with one's Real Self, with life-affirming spirituality, and with significant others. As therapy assists clients in remembering and reconnecting with their Real Self and associated personally defined spiritual practice, clients naturally become more discerning between life-affirming and life-detracting relationships and experiences. Their Real Self provides the barometer and guide in this journey while their spiritual practice can support the development of their personal integrity.

Therapy provides a place where clients can notice how they feel and ask a variety of questions about the various relationships in their lives. For example, do they like how they feel and who they are when they are in their relationships? To what degree are their relationships life-affirming or life-detracting? Do they feel a sense of personal integrity vis-à-vis their relationships? What are their experiences telling them about what is right for them and who they want to be?

As they evaluate their relationships based on the inner knowing of their Real Self and associated spiritual practice, they become increasingly clear about what is life-affirming for them and the ways in which they need to grow. With their Real Self in charge, they will naturally begin to notice and value what is healthy and life-affirming. They will also find more effective ways to meet their needs and address their underlying impulses to heal and grow. Clients can internalize the healthy aspects of their relationship with their therapist and choose life-affirming relationships, where their souls can be nourished and sustained.

Utilizing Spiritually Oriented Therapy

One of the most potent predictors of change in therapy is the client. Clients have the most power to change their lives and to embrace health; and spiritually oriented therapy provides an avenue to support their growth. The following is an example of a client that utilized the power of spiritually oriented therapy to reclaim her Real Self, transfer her emerging health into sustainable relationships, and transform her life.

Joan entered therapy when she was 38 years old, suffering from debilitating bouts of depression. She was unhappily married with two kids. Her husband did his best to stop her from having friends outside the family. She was isolated, disempowered, and self-hating.

The first, and central, aspect of Joan's therapy was forming an authentic and healthy relationship with me, her therapist. This was not easily accomplished. She did not readily trust others, especially men, and her self-criticism often prevented her from believing that she was worthy of another person's attention and care. Slowly, we formed a therapeutic team, which became the *sacred space* where she could process her enormous pain and gain the support she needed to risk taking ownership for her life.

Joan began to reveal a history of horrific physical and sexual abuse at the hands of various relatives, including her father. Insights related to the abuse and other dynamics in her family of origin helped her understand why she developed such low self-esteem and tended to protect herself by distancing and self-punishment. These insights also made her difficulties with trust, including with me, make a lot more sense to her. She began to test me to see if I would be there for her, or if I would abandon or abuse her, as others in her life had done. Over time, Joan and I collaboratively addressed her transferred expectations that I would abandon and hurt her, which led to numerous corrective emotional experiences.

Insights that linked her past experiences with current relationships also led to increases in her self-awareness. Typically, she felt "numb" when she was triggered emotionally. Over time, she began to experience her emotions and became much more aware of her inner experience. She began to realize that she would "flash" to a memory of abuse from her childhood, right before she went numb. Slowly, she was able to pause before she "tuned out." She was able to "stay in her body" for longer periods of time.

She also started to have experiences of being calm and centered, moments that included feelings of clarity and peace. I often invited her to notice these moments and to understand their importance for her healing and growth. She began to be interested in various forms of spirituality. She joined a church, where people were openly inviting to her. Her prayer life brought more moments of peace and support. She indicated that on several occasions when mindfully praying, she experienced the "Holy Spirit" filling her with feelings of acceptance and love. She began to intentionally access spiritual energy regularly through prayer and mindful breathing, which increased her sense of a loving and guiding presence in her life. She reasoned that if she could be loved and accepted by God, then she must be worthy of being treated better than how she was treated as a child and how her husband treated her. Thus, her spiritual practice helped to experientially and cognitively correct her conflicted relational template and associated pathogenic beliefs.

Joan became increasingly in touch with her Real Self. She had more frequent mental and physical sensations of her "true self" emerging. The impulses that emanated from her Real Self were about creativity, exploration, and freedom. She had dreams and visions of herself as a butterfly emerging from a cocoon. Joan wanted to express herself in ways she had never allowed herself before. She became aware that she wanted to go to college. She wanted friends. She wanted to pursue creative arts. And she wanted her husband to support her in her growth and healing.

Unfortunately, he was threatened by her changes and tried to suppress her emerging health. Again and again, she tried to reason with him and include him in her process. Eventually, she realized that she would not be able to be healthy if she stayed in the marriage. Despite being nearly incapacitated with fear, she maintained connection with her Real Self and drew strength from her spiritual practice, which provided her with the guidance and courage to proceed on her path of health. After a difficult and painful divorce process, Joan emerged with her integrity intact. She had refused to engage in conflict-drama with her ex-husband. She pushed for a fair and reasonable settlement, despite his attempts to sabotage her efforts.

Although rocky times occurred, Joan's self-esteem continued to improve. She continued to take risks by pushing herself to meet people and to build upon her life-affirming friendships that had formed over the past year. Much to her surprise, she met a man who really wanted to know and support her. She tested him repeatedly. Her Real Self knew what she really wanted and deserved in a relationship. She eventually opened her heart to his genuine kindness and love, leading to many corrective experiences.

Joan was breaking all of her childhood rules. She was listening to her Real Self. She was accessing spiritual energy, which nourished her soul. And she embraced the health of her life-affirming relationships. She truly blossomed with the support of therapy, guidance of her Real Self, support and encouragement from healthy relationships, and nourishment of her spiritual practice.

Final Thoughts

Therapy was a vital and vibrant aspect of personal growth and healing for Joan, as it can be for many people. Therapy assists clients on multiple levels, most foundationally by providing a relationship that supports all the elements of the change process. Therapy is most helpful when it is in line with clients' inner wisdom and supports their impulses for health and healing. In short, therapy is most effective when the process encourages clients to notice and activate their Real Self as a guiding force. Once their Real Self is accessed, they naturally become more discerning in their lives. They evaluate their life structures and determine the ways they need to grow and the changes they need to make. Real Self-defined spiritual practice, which supports life-affirming choices and activities, is an invaluable part of the process. For many clients, spiritual energy provides a healing and growthful presence, which reminds them of who they truly are and of their potentialities for being. Therapy that supports engagement with their Real Self and utilizes personally defined experiences with spirituality provides clients with tremendous opportunities for empowerment and for attaining sustainable health.

To ethically and competently utilize this approach, therapists must maintain high levels of spiritual-differentiation. Therapists need to spend time reflecting on their own spiritual identity and journey, especially on events and experiences that were emotionally intrusive and fostered strong beliefs and reactivity. These experiences will likely have a profound impact on therapists' ability to work with spiritual issues in therapy. When therapists are emotionally reactive, they run the risk of projecting their biases on clients. Spiritual-differentiation allows therapists to be genuinely interested in hearing about clients' spiritual experiences, beliefs, and practices without becoming emotionally reactive and imposing their own views onto clients. When therapists exhibit high levels of spiritual-differentiation, they can utilize clients' spiritual beliefs and practices not only for resourcing, but also as an ally in the entire therapy process. The next chapter will address differentiation, including ways therapists can increase their spiritual-differentiation, in greater detail.

CHAPTER 9

SPIRITUAL-DIFFERENTIATION

Differentiation of self (Bowen, 1976, 1978; Kerr & Bowen, 1988) is a multifaceted concept that can be used by therapists to assess the psychological health of individuals, including clients and themselves. It can also be used as a comprehensive, integrative concept to understand the spiritual identity process. The essence of differentiation is the development of a system of beliefs and values that is forged through personal experience and exploration. Individuals define who they are through a process of exploring their world and learning about others' beliefs and values (most notably parents), and then determining what fits best for them, which leads to ownership for oneself across a variety of identity dimensions, including spirituality.

Allport (1950) provided a simplistic summary of the identity process specifically related to spiritual faith development. This process, which is discussed in more depth in Chapter 3, proceeds through three steps: (1) believing what has been taught about faith, (2) doubting what has been taught about faith, and (3) dealing with the ambiguity of what has been taught by fluctuating between faith and doubt. The successful process leads to a mature, well-differentiated faith, which is characterized by a system of personal spiritual beliefs that is owned, yet also flexible enough to accommodate and integrate new information.

In addition to Allport, a variety of developmental theories (e.g., Erikson, 1963, 1968; Fowler, 1981, 1991, 1996; Genia, 1995; Marcia, 1966, 1980; Oser & Scarlett, 1991; Piaget, 1965; Rizzuto, 1979; Spero, 1992) provide ways of understanding the process of spiritual identity formation and attainment. In my view, these theories point to a developmental path for individuals that can be conceptualized as the differentiation process, in general and specifically related to spirituality. Thus, differentiation is an umbrella concept that can be used as a way to understand individuals' level of psychological health as well as their spiritual journey and identity development.

Spirituality is a subject that requires high levels of self-awareness and psychological maturity from therapists, which are captured by the concept of spiritual-differentiation. For therapists to be able to work competently and ethically with spiritual issues in therapy, it is essential for them to have engaged in their own personal therapy or any personal growth process that supports reflection on the development of their spiritual beliefs and practices and leads to high levels of spiritual-differentiation. This allows therapists to facilitate discussions of client-defined spirituality without therapist reactivity. To this end, the present chapter includes a discussion of the identity and differentiation process and characteristics of varying levels of differentiation, with an emphasis on spiritual development. It concludes with a focus on how therapists can increase their own spiritual-differentiation.

The Identity and Differentiation Process

The differentiation process starts for almost everyone in a family system, be it biological, nuclear, extended, blended, adopted, foster, or some other kind of residential group. Within the family, each young child begins a process of attaching to and separating from caregivers (usually parents), which is the central dynamic of the differentiation process. Parents experience a mirror process of attachment to and separation from children, largely based on the developmental needs of their children. In other words, healthy development occurs when parents and children form a solid attachment bond and also maintain enough psychological space between them to allow children to develop independence and autonomy, both psychologically and physically (McGoldrick, Carter, & Garcia-Preto, 2010).

The differentiation process is a lifelong journey for children and parents, with research indicating that high levels of differentiation aren't typically achieved until adult children are 30 to 40 years of age (Johnson & DelCampo, 1995; McGoldrick et al., 2010). The emphasis during infancy is on forming a strong attachment bond; infants are completely dependent upon their parents to care for all their basic needs. As children grow, they quickly begin to express their needs for self-reliance and autonomy, in addition to attachment with parents. Effectively managing this delicate balance requires sensitive parenting. Parents must read their children and respond with parenting that alternately, and sometimes simultaneously, provides love and support as well as opportunities for the child to develop autonomy and mastery (Siegel & Hartzell, 2003). In order to develop a healthy sense of self and their abilities, children need many opportunities to wrestle with tasks that are frustrating while feeling support, rather than overinvolvement, from their parents. This dialectical balance of connection with and separation from parents continues unabated throughout childhood, with children typically requiring more independence as they age.

The push-pull of this experience comes to a head during a variety of developmental stages, with adolescence and young adulthood having the potential to become a family battleground. Young adults typically press for high levels of independence and autonomy from parents, propelled by their need to form a separate sense of self and identity, intimate peer relationships, and independence related to work and finances. They are forming opinions and acting upon choices related to values, ideologies (including spirituality), lifestyles, relationships, and careers with varying levels of parental involvement. Some young adult children want more parental involvement in this process while others want less. At this stage, parents are engaged in a balancing act that requires them to encourage autonomy in their young adult children while also being available for mentoring.

Many parents find it excruciatingly difficult to support their children if they perceive that they are making poor choices. This is one place where projection rears its dysfunctional head. In fact, projection is a main culprit when the differentiation process goes poorly (Johnson, Schamuhn, Nelson, & Buboltz, 2012; Kerr & Bowen, 1988; McGoldrick et al., 2010). Projection typically occurs when parents act as if their children are extensions of themselves; either consciously or unconsciously, the parents live through their children. In other words, whatever is unresolved for parents is projected onto the children. For example, if a parent was unable to attain a certain life goal or occupation because of pressure from his or her own parents or due to life circumstances, that parent may demand that his or her children attain that specific goal or occupation. Similarly, if a parent was forced into a certain occupation (e.g., a woman forced to be a nurse when she wanted to be a medical doctor), the parent may demand that her children avoid that specific occupation (i.e., a nurse).

In addition to career choices, this kind of process can occur related to all aspects of identity development and lifestyle (Jenkins, Buboltz, Schwartz, & Johnson, 2005; Johnson, Buboltz, et al., 2003), such as spiritual practices, choice of intimate partners, thoughts about having children, and decisions about where to live (Marcia, 1980). All parents have hopes and wishes for their children. The more those hopes and dreams are based upon the parents' own unresolved issues, the more problems are likely to develop. In situations with high levels of projection, children need to react to not only their own struggles and competing agendas, they must also contend with the psychically intrusive quality of their parents' unresolved desires and agendas. Consequently, children often become flooded with indecision and identity-based questions: "Do my parents approve of my choices related to lifestyle, marriage, children, spiritual practices, education, occupation . . . ?" Parents can also be consumed by complementary questions and thoughts: "I love my children, but their choices make me angry and worried. I know it's their life, but how can I support them when they are making the wrong choices?" Children often must choose between doing what they think their parents will approve of versus doing what they think will make themselves happy; either way, they are reacting to the psychically intrusive forces of their parents' agendas.

I once worked with a family in which the mother had been forced by her mother to attend a certain university. When she had children, she all but refused to allow her own daughter to attend that same university ("You can go anywhere except to *that* school"). Of course, her daughter made the emotionally charged choice and went to the forbidden university! Then, the mother had to decide if she was going to reactively withdraw her emotional and financial support of her daughter. Or, the mother could let her daughter make her own choices, which would require that the mother work through her unresolved issues with her own mother.

The consequences of difficulties with the differentiation process were discussed in Chapter 4 and are fairly predictable. To summarize, one consequence is that young adult children remain *fused* with their parents. In this case, young adults do not engage in their own identity process; rather, they adopt the identity markers (e.g., education, career, relationships, spiritual practices, etc.) that their parents define for them (Johnson, Buboltz, et al., 2003). They tend to become externally focused and disconnected from their own inner wisdom; they don't want to risk parental disapproval by asserting their own ideas and needs. Another typical consequence is *emotional cutoff*. In this case, young adults reactively remove themselves from their parents' influences (e.g., reject their parents' spiritual beliefs and practices), which are seen as too toxic or threatening to their emerging identity. Lack of parental mentoring and support as well as high levels of reactivity are aspects of cutoffs, which tend to make thoughtful decision-making and the attainment of life goals less likely (Buboltz, Johnson, & Woller, 2003; Johnson & Buboltz, 2000; Johnson et al., 2012; Skowron & Dendy, 2004).

An unsettling aspect of differentiation difficulties is that it tends to be passed down through the generations, in what is called the *multigenerational transmission process* (Kerr & Bowen, 1988; McGoldrick et al., 2010). Specifically, the differentiation level of parents is passed down to their children through projection and role modeling (Johnson, Thorngren, & Smith, 2001; Miller et al., 2004).

Thankfully, the differentiation process generally goes relatively well. In this case, parents and young adults find a dynamic balance of connection and separation, of support and autonomy, and of mentoring without too much projection. Young adults define their identity (including spiritual identity) and take ownership of their lives without cutting off contact from their parents and families. Parents remain involved in their adult children's lives, yet don't define their lives solely through their children. Both generations are able to utilize the process to define who they are, clarify their boundaries, and further their development rather than remaining stuck in developmentally inappropriate roles.

There are thinkers who believe that, as a species, humans are moving to higher levels of psychological and spiritual functioning (e.g., Wilber, 1996, 2000). Among these is David Schnarch, who asserts that *differentiation is an evolutionary goal of the human species* (Schnarch, 2004). Specifically, the process of dealing with the differentiation dilemma, that is, needing others and needing autonomy, is a primary vehicle through which people grow psychologically, intellectually, emotionally, and spiritually. Being connected to others often provides some amount of security as well as some amount of emotional intrusiveness. Individuals can utilize the security as well as the intrusion to grow and further their differentiation. Both conditions are optimal for growth, and the balance between them is the key. The security of relationships provides a foundational springboard to take risks while emotional intrusions force individuals to define and clarify themselves. In other words, the differentiation dilemma provides individuals with opportunities to define and assert themselves *within* their relationships. The alternatives to healthy differentiation are being alienated from significant relationships or suffering the *soul crushing* consequences of allowing others to define who they are and what they believe.

Characteristics of Well-Differentiated Individuals

Healthy differentiation is about finding one's own voice, the Real Self, within the context of relationships. It's about defining oneself without cutting off contact with others. Although differentiation levels can change based on context and circumstance, when the differentiation process goes well, individuals are able to embrace their Real Self and attain high levels of psychological, relational, and spiritual health, which is associated with a predictable set of characteristics, including the following.

Connection and Separation: Healthy Boundaries

Poorly differentiated clients tend to have difficulties with boundaries (Johnson & Stone, 2009; Johnson & Waldo, 1998; Kerr & Bowen, 1988). If someone else is upset, they internalize that stress, which is a hallmark of fused relationships. Conversely, individuals with low levels of differentiation may avoid connections with others (i.e., they cut off from relationships) as a way of managing stress and the possibility of fusion.

Well-differentiated individuals, on the other hand, are able to connect with others without losing themselves, which is an extremely important characteristic for therapists, especially when dealing with clients' spiritual issues. First and foremost, well-differentiated individuals can psychologically separate themselves from their parents without disengaging from them. They are able to find *emotional middle ground* between the extremes of fusion and cutoff.

In addition to their parents, highly differentiated individuals have relationships with friends, intimate partners, and their own children that are characterized by emotional middle ground and healthy boundaries. Boundaries define where they end and where others begin, psychologically speaking. Boundaries regulate the amount of reactivity within relationships, with looser boundaries tending to lead to higher levels of reactivity (Buboltz et al., 2003; Johnson & Buboltz, 2000; Skowron & Dendy, 2004).

Boundaries are rarely defined solely by physical distance, but by psychological perception and emotional experience. Individuals who have cut off from their parents, for example, are often distant physically but not psychologically. The distance is a reactive attempt to deal with unresolved fusion (Johnson & Waldo, 1998). In other words, the individual has not attained healthy levels of psychological separation; the distance is a pseudo attempt at differentiation. In these instances, individuals tend to reactively cut off from fused relationships with parents and then enter into fused relationships with intimate peers (Johnson et al., 2001; Rosen, Bartle-Haring, & Stith, 2001).

Healthy boundaries, conversely, support intimate contact with others and a separate sense of self. Healthy boundaries allow individuals, including therapists, to be in close contact with other people without fears of being engulfed, overwhelmed, or eclipsed. Again, this is vital when dealing with spiritual issues in therapy. Thus, healthy boundaries are like a gift that therapists can give to their clients. When therapists have healthy boundaries clients are able to be close and share their spiritual beliefs without fear that their personal beliefs and practices will be trampled. Much of the subsequent discussion in this chapter will focus on the consequences of healthy and unhealthy interpersonal boundaries.

Low Levels of Emotional Reactivity

Emotional reactivity occurs when individuals respond to environmental stimuli with emotional flooding, emotional lability, or hypersensitivity (Skowron & Dendy, 2004; Skowron & Freidlander, 1998). In other words, they become so activated by external stimuli that they become overwhelmed. To cope with this, they react in ways that are excessive and based more on the external stimuli than on their internal awareness. They lose touch with their Real Self and move into an externally reactive mode. One example would be reacting strongly to stimuli on television, such as a political figure. A person could be sitting calmly one moment, and then when a despised political figure appears on the television, the person instantly begins yelling profanities. The person is now in an emotionally reactive state. Although yelling may be unlikely to occur in therapy, emotional reactivity is a very real possibility when dealing with spiritual issues, for therapists and clients.

Although reactivity largely depends on specific stimuli and contexts, some people exhibit greater levels of reactivity across a variety of contexts than do others (Buboltz et al., 2003). Some people are more susceptible to being overwhelmed by external stimuli, especially others' anxiety, and thus react more strongly. The primary root of high levels of emotional reactivity is poor boundaries (Johnson & Buboltz, 2000). When individuals have poor boundaries, they become easily activated by external stimuli and can't easily regulate their emotional responses. Thus, reactivity tends to lead to interpersonal defensiveness. Reactive individuals become quickly activated and feel the need to defend their positions or *correct* others. Other people often feel as if they are walking on eggshells when interacting with reactive individuals, making healthy communication difficult.

Highly differentiated individuals, however, have appropriate boundaries and therefore do not become as easily activated. This allows them to be in close proximity to external stimuli, such as another person's aroused emotional state, without becoming overwhelmed. They can be near another person's anxiety and pain, for example, without claiming it as their own. They can hear feedback without becoming defensive. *They can be fully present with others without losing themselves.* This balance is an essential aspect of most healthy intimate relationships. It is also a vital characteristic for effective therapists, especially related to spirituality. It allows therapists to be fully present with a client as they describe their spiritual journey, beliefs, and practices, even if they differ significantly from the therapists' beliefs and experiences.

Balanced Ownership of Responsibility

Most people under- or overestimate their ability to affect their world and relationships. Many believe that their happiness depends upon another person changing. As Michael Kerr (1988) stated, "Many supposed attempts at self-definition are really attempts to get others to change or to pry oneself loose from emotionally intense situations" (p. 46). In general, our clients suffer when they perceive they have no ability to change their lives. They also suffer if they continuously try to change others and control their world. Differentiated individuals, by contrast, are more able to find a healthy balance between these two extremes. The healthy boundaries associated with high levels of differentiation allow individuals to know the limits of their responsibility and control.

I often tell clients that there are two primary ways for change to occur: (1) love and (2) duress. Loving relationships provide a secure base that allows them to experience intimacy, care, and strong attachments. This foundation provides a springboard for risk-taking and growth. Relationships also typically provide some amount of emotional coercion and duress. Other people are commenting on them and attempting to influence their thoughts and choices. Differentiating and successfully changing under duress commonly proceeds through a three-step process:

1. Clients point at a dynamic in their life that they don't like and say, "No, I don't want *that* anymore!"
2. They turn their finger from pointing externally back toward themselves and say, "*I* don't want to *do that* anymore."

3. They have the courage to make changes and act on their convictions.

In the first step, clients become aware of a dynamic that is not working for them. It is important for them to objectify and label the dynamic so they know what they are addressing, so they see it when it emerges in their lives. The difference between the first and second step is startling for most clients. When they point their finger back toward themselves, they move from a blaming and/or disempowered victim stance, to a place of ownership and personal power. They more clearly see their role in the dynamics in their lives, and they become more empowered.

Unfortunately, many clients stop at the first step. They get so close to change, then back off and return to the same old patterns, because they are hoping that others will change. In fact, their initial awareness and momentum becomes another attempt to influence others. Instead of pointing at themselves, they point at others and demand that they change. Or, they start to own their values and lives, but fearfully choose not to act on their convictions. Either way, they return to a state of disempowerment.

Well-differentiated individuals are more able to find the balance of what they are and are not responsible for in their lives. When they define what isn't working in their lives, the power primarily rests with their ability to choose how they act, rather than waiting for others to change. They realize how they act matters. They have power to affect their own as well as others' lives, while also realizing that their ability to change others is quite limited.

Therapists deal with this paradox every day. They are in the business of helping clients change, yet have very little control over their clients' actual choices. Although therapists may care deeply about their clients, their clients are the ones who must act on their convictions and live with the consequences of their choices. Clients, like everyone, must eventually take responsibility for their own lives and choices (including spiritual beliefs and practices) and not let others dictate to them and define who they are; the consequences are too severe.

Balance of Thoughts and Emotions

Individuals who have struggled with the differentiation process tend to internalize the stress around them, which leads to excessive emotionality and dysregulation (Johnson & Buboltz, 2000; Skowron & Dendy, 2004; Skowron et al., 2003). Their emotions overwhelm their rational thought processes. They become prone to impulsive, reactive decisions. Other individuals tend to cope with situational anxiety and fears of fusion by distancing from their emotions, being excessively stoic. They become alienated from the emotional aspects of themselves and tend to project their denied emotions onto their partners.

Stoic and emotional types tend to find each other and form a collusive partnership. They are drawn to the other person, who displays what they believe they don't have. Each plays out the denied parts of the other, sometimes in extreme fashion. Then they try to change their partner to be more like them, which, of course, creates a great deal of frustration for both. Their styles are flip sides of the same undifferentiated coin. The extremes of excessive emotionality and stoicism mirror the relational patterns of fusion and cutoff. Thus, both positions are associated with low levels of differentiation (Skowron, 2000; Skowron & Friedlander, 1998).

Individuals with higher levels of differentiation, by contrast, are able to separate thoughts from emotions (Skowron & Dendy, 2004). They have the ability to experience strong emotions without being flooded or overwhelmed by those emotions. They feel deeply, but don't lose their ability to think rationally. Individuals with high levels of differentiation, then, have the ability to experience strong affect as well as to shift into calm, logical reasoning when circumstances dictate.

Inner-Generated Convictions

Although everyone has access to their Real Self, when there are struggles with the differentiation process, individuals tend to be externally focused and reactive (Johnson & Buboltz, 2000; Johnson, Buboltz, et al., 2003). They tend to make decisions based on their perceptions of others' judgment of their decisions rather than on the inner wisdom of their Real Self. They tend to alternate between accepting and acting upon what they think will gain approval and reactively pushing against their need for approval by actively choosing behaviors that will bring disapproval. This is what one client referred to as the "rebel without a cause" part of his personality. Either way, the development of their Real Self becomes inhibited.

Individuals with high levels of differentiation have an *inner compass* that guides them in their lives and their decision-making, what in the differentiation literature is called a strong *I Position* (Skowron & Friedlander, 1998). Of course, this inner compass is their Real Self. Through a healthy differentiation process, their Real Self is developed and emerges into awareness. They engage in an experiential search process that defines who they are: their values, beliefs, vocations, joys, passions, dislikes, and what makes their soul sing. They do not blindly accept the identity markers that others preach, nor do they reject them reactively. They take in the wisdom of others as well as experience life for themselves. Through the differentiation process, they define their beliefs, find their voice, and connect to the wisdom of their Real Self, all of which is reflected in their spiritual identity development.

Ability to Self-Soothe

The differentiation process includes learning to tolerate the fear and frustration associated with developing autonomy and mastery in the world. When it goes well, the process begins with a secure bond between child and parent, which allows children to imagine a caring and supportive parent even when that parent is not physically present, a process that can be reflected in one's spiritual development (Rizzuto, 1979). This ability to borrow ego strength from a parent (or higher power) sets the stage for the development of self-soothing skills. As the differentiation process continues, a clear sense of self emerges, including confidence in one's abilities to manage the anxieties of life.

Individuals with low levels of differentiation lack self-soothing skills and, therefore, have difficulty experiencing intense emotions without becoming flooded or shutting down (Skowron & Friedlander, 1998). They utilize a variety of strategies to compensate for this difficulty, including internalizing and externalizing blame. Internalizers attempt to regain some sense of inner calm by blaming or hurting themselves. Externalizers attempt to regain inner calm by blaming, hurting, or focusing on others. Either way, they are activated by anxiety and become reactive. They lack the ability to tolerate anxiety and various uncomfortable emotions without engaging in behaviors that are costly to their psychological and relational health.

Although all people become activated by stress and anxiety to some extent, well-differentiated individuals are able to maintain their sense of self in the face of anxiety (Miller et al., 2004). They are able to self-soothe. They exhibit the ability to experience their emotions without shutting down or acting out, on others or themselves. Even when anxious, they experience their emotions and then are able to return to a centered sense of self. They rarely lose touch with their Real Self for long. As has been discussed, a life-affirming spiritual practice can support self-soothing and increase confidence to handle setbacks and inevitable anxiety.

Direct Communication

The reactivity and poor boundaries associated with individuals who have struggled with the differentiation process make direct communication less likely. In general, their relationships are characterized by high levels of drama. Fusion, by nature, lacks psychological separateness and leads to reactivity and interpersonal drama (Skowron & Friedlander, 1998; Skowron & Schmitt, 2003). Fusion invariably requires the inclusion of a third person into relational dynamics. In other words, poorly differentiated individuals lack the ability to handle interpersonal stress without venting that stress and attempting to stabilize their relationships by including others in their relational dynamics.

Similarly, when individuals haven't been able to define who they are or deal with fusion without reactively cutting off, they tend to struggle with this throughout their lives. They tend to shut down or include others in their relationships, especially when anxiety increases. If they were recipients of parental projection in childhood, especially *triangulation*, they tend to repeat the same patterns in adulthood and with their own children and intimate partners (Johnson & Nelson, 1998; Skowron, 2000). They tend to include their children in their marital conflicts, which makes it difficult for their children to get close to one parent without the other parent being threatened (Bray, Harvey, & Williamson, 1987).

Well-differentiated individuals, with their healthy boundaries and low levels of reactivity, rarely engage in gossip and triangulation. They can tolerate others' pain and relational anxiety without becoming reactive and threatened. They don't need to involve others or shut down. They have the confidence to deal with their relationships directly and the ability to self-soothe without triangulating others in their interpersonal dynamics. They realize that, in most cases, it is far more effective to deal directly with someone than it is to complain and attempt to get others on their side.

Adult-to-Adult Relationships With Parents

For most people, the first 20 or so years of life are about finding their way within a particular family system. Parents tend to be very large figures that dominate life and decision-making. Parents seem bigger than life, with their ideas being the benchmarks against which an identity is forged, including a spiritual identity. As individuals age, they define and assert themselves; however, many people never achieve a sense of personal power in relation to their parents. They continue to *see their parents through a child's eyes.*

Part of the differentiation process is coming to terms with the good news and bad news about one's parents and family of origin. Each family has its strengths and weaknesses. In most cases, parents do as well as they can considering their upbringings and life circumstances. Each new generation has the ability to become aware of the consequences of growing up in a particular family situation. This awareness can be translated into higher levels of differentiation than the previous generation, through ownership of one's life. Eventually, individuals need to understand the ways in which their families have shaped their lives and then transcend those familiar patterns and roles and connect with their own wisdom, vision, and personal power (Bray et al., 1987; Williamson, 1981).

The degree to which individuals are able to view their parents as equals tends to be contingent upon cultural factors (McGoldrick et al., 2010). Some cultures do not have a conceptual framework for this that wouldn't be considered disrespectful. However, as they evolve psychologically, most people are able to eventually understand the basic humanity of their parents. When this happens, they no longer cower in relation to their parents or attribute omnipotent characteristics to them (Bray et al., 1987).

As they own their personal power and inner-generated sense of self, they begin to relate to their parents with a shared and compassionate understanding of the existential dilemmas of living. Parents are travelers, as we all are, trying to create meaning, find their way, and deal with the uncertainties of living life and the certainty of facing death. Healthy differentiation allows individuals to see their parents through compassionate and accepting eyes as they more fully take responsibility for their lives. Differentiation allows them to truly *choose* to be with their parents, sharing time and experiences, rather than acting out of obligation or powerlessness (Bray et al., 1987). Similarly, individuals can choose their own spiritual beliefs and practices rather than adopting their parents' spiritual paths out of obligation or fear.

Personal Authority

Personal authority relates to the belief that individuals have the right and ability to meet their needs (Bray et al., 1987; Bray, Williamson, & Malone, 1986; Johnson & Nelson, 1998). It is a sense of personal efficacy. Many people refer to it as *personal power*. It isn't power to control, dominate, or manipulate others. It is power in one's own life. At its core, personal authority is about taking responsibility for one's own life and choices.

When the differentiation process goes poorly, individuals are busy reacting to others, be it to please or to rebel (Jenkins et al., 2005; Johnson, Buboltz, et al., 2003). They lose touch with their inner compass. Their relational (and spiritual) consciousness is caught up with controlling others or reacting to being controlled by others. Either position is undifferentiated and alienated from their Real Self. Tying their self-worth to their ability to change another person is unwise and precarious. Conversely, allowing others to control them is equally soul crushing. Either way, their personal power lies outside of their consciousness and they suffer.

Well-differentiated individuals have a strong sense of personal authority. They do not need others to take responsibility for their lives. And they freely choose to be in relationships, not out of obligation or fear. They know they have the ability to get their needs met across many areas in their lives. They know who they are and are not afraid to embrace their personal power. This sense of efficacy in the world is the culmination of the differentiation process, which has supported life learning and ownership for one's choices. A healthy differentiation process leads to clarity about what is life-affirming and confidence and courage to act on those convictions, all of which is directly related to a healthy spiritual identity process.

Personal Integrity

Poorly differentiated individuals often struggle to know what is meaningful to them. They do not have a consistent sense of the organizing themes in their lives. Or, the themes seem superficial and based on interpersonal drama rather than based on personal ownership. Their sense of personal consciousness is largely externally based. They are busy playing roles that have been prescribed to them or they are reacting against these roles. Their lives are not their own. They lack connection to an inner compass.

Individuals with high levels of differentiation have all the ingredients for a strong, life-affirming sense of personal integrity (Schnarch, 2004). The differentiation process has forged inner-generated convictions. These convictions have developed from a balanced place of connection with others and healthy boundaries. Well-differentiated individuals are not simply reacting to others, but are proactive in their beliefs and choices. They experience the emotionality of life without losing touch with their rational thought processes. They have the ability to self-soothe and manage the anxieties inherent in living. All of which has forged a strong sense of confidence in their beliefs and abilities. Thus, their behaviors and choices are congruent with their inner-generated convictions.

When individuals act in ways that are in accordance with their values and core beliefs, they act from their personal integrity. As Schnarch (2004) says, they courageously *hold on to themselves*, even risking disapproval and rejection from others. The opinions and approval of others may change, but one's personal integrity will be a consistent guidepost. *Personal integrity represents the voice and consciousness of the Real Self* and can be supported and enhanced through a life-affirming spiritual practice.

Increasing Differentiation

Differentiation is a developmental process, but it can also be intentional. As children, individuals have a limited view of normalcy. They often assume, no matter how crazy their families may be, that they are normal. They have very limited reference points against which to judge their experiences. They mostly just react to the psychological energies and emotional entanglements of their families of origin. Their developmental needs and capabilities interact with the emotional and psychological climate of their family context. Thus, their attempts to define themselves are mostly reactive rather than intentional.

As they age, individuals see more examples of different kinds of families and family interactions, and their view of normalcy expands. They develop a more consistent ability to reflect on and define relationship dynamics, rather than just react to them. As teenagers, they typically categorize and objectify their parents, but they don't yet possess the emotional maturity or psychological distance to understand them as real people. They tend to see them as caricatures, which is a way to deal with the psychological intrusion that parents represent.

As young adults, individuals typically have enough emotional distance from their parents to begin to define who they are in relation to their families in intentional and proactive ways. This tends to be a slow process, with many opportunities to define who they are or suffer the consequences of not doing so. Differentiation, then, is not an event that happens just once, although profound opportunities and defining moments may occur periodically. The process of increasing differentiation is more like an unfolding of awareness, which provides opportunities to seize ownership of one's life. The process becomes more conscious and intentional for most people as adults (Johnson & DelCampo, 1995; McGoldrick et al., 2010).

Bowen's (1976, 1978) original thinking about the ability to increase differentiation was quite pessimistic. The belief was that individuals are about as differentiated as their parents, and without atypical effort, raising their level was not often achieved. Most contemporary differentiation theorists, however, are more optimistic about the chances of intentionally increasing differentiation levels, with the focus on increasing client self-awareness and ownership for life choices. Therapists from a variety of theoretical orientations can help clients increase their differentiation, with the aforementioned indices being markers and overall goals of psychological health for therapists to utilize.

Consider the following clinical example. At the time she entered therapy, Sasha, a second-generation Russian American, was 49 years old. Her presenting issues were depression and anxiety related to a break up of her marriage. Her husband had moved out and initiated divorce shortly after they launched their only child, about three months before she started therapy. Sasha had experienced a number of challenging circumstances while growing up. Her father died when she was 12 years old, leaving her with an alcoholic and sometimes violent mother. Her primary role in her family was as her mother's caregiver and confidant. She became expert at trying to proactively managing her mother's moods and behaviors. Sasha lived away from home for a brief time when she entered an in-state university. However, her feelings of responsibility for her mother and her guilt related to "abandoning" her led to poor grades and a withdrawal from college, which exemplified her complicated differentiation process. Her mother suddenly died when Sasha was 23 years old. She managed to support herself financially, but entered into a series of relationships with chaotic and emotionally unavailable men. Eventually she married her husband, who was more stable, yet again emotionally distant. After the birth of their son, she threw herself into parenting, defining herself almost exclusively through that role.

Therapy with Sasha initially focused on increasing her coping skills to manage the immediate loss and upheaval of her marriage ending. Over time, we began to explore the links between her childhood and the patterns of her intimate relationships. Deeper levels of loss and anxiety emerged as we experientially processed the cognitive and emotional aspects of the nodal experiences of her childhood, including her father's death and her mother's instability. Increased insight and awareness as well as experiential processing (primarily Internal Family Systems therapy) provided her with a new sense of herself and a desire to try healthier behaviors with others.

Sasha increasingly exhibited markers of increased differentiation and connection with her Real Self. She started to recognize how her unmet needs for love and care had led to compensatory behaviors of overfunctioning and criticism and blaming with her ex-husband and son. Sasha learned to self-soothe by embracing her emotionally traumatized parts and connecting with a foundational sense of herself, her Real Self. Thus, her emotional reactivity decreased and a felt sense of her core self increased. She began practicing healthier boundaries with her friends, and eventually with a new boyfriend. Instead of automatically overfunctioning with others, she developed a stronger understanding of her own emotions, wants, and needs and an increased sense of her right and ability to meet her needs. Her connection with her personal authority and personal integrity increased, leading her to return to school to pursue her undergraduate degree. By the end of therapy, Sasha remarked that although she hadn't chosen divorce, she felt blessed by the events that subsequently transpired; she felt the most free and empowered that she had in her entire life.

Now let's consider another example that is more specifically related to spiritual-differentiation. Clarissa was a 34-year-old woman who was raised in a family that she described as espousing "new age spiritual beliefs." Her family interwove ideas of regard for all things and interconnection, along with Pagan rituals and a communal living arrangement. Clarissa was the oldest of six children and was often responsible for caring for her siblings. She experienced her upbringing as chaotic and unpredictable, describing her father as needy and her mother as unavailable. Her parents were unsupportive of her attempts at differentiation. When she was a teenager, they vocally criticized her intentions to move away from home to attend college. Although Clarissa internalized her parents' projections and lost confidence in her ability to move away from home, she didn't want to give up on her dreams; so she enrolled in a local community college. She soon became overwhelmed by the demands of her family while taking classes, however, and dropped out of school.

Clarissa longed for stability and support, which she found in her devoutly Christian husband. Their marriage allowed her to move out of her parents' home (although she felt guilty about leaving her siblings) and provided an alternative to her parents' spiritual beliefs, which she was emotionally rebelling against. Instead, she wholeheartedly embraced her husband's faith. However, soon after her first child was born, Clarissa started to feel trapped in her marriage and his faith. Although she loved her husband and had been enjoying the structure of his beliefs and practices, she felt unfulfilled, anxious, and depressed, which is why she entered therapy.

When therapy began, it was clear that Clarissa did not know who she was. She had been in a reactive state throughout her entire life, which left her disconnected from her Real Self. In childhood, she reacted to her parents' spiritual beliefs as well as the chaos and needs of her family, adopting a caregiver role. In her marriage, she reacted to her husband's spiritual beliefs and tried to internalize them. She was reactively, but not intentionally, attempting an identity exploration process.

The essence of therapy with Clarissa was increasing her self-awareness and the intentionality of her identity development, including her spiritual identity. It became evident that she was ready to grow and try new things; she used the stability of her marriage to explore life. She went back to college and started to investigate other forms of spirituality. She became a voracious reader of spiritual books, embraced the creative arts, joined a yoga class, and attended a women's bible study group. She was developing an ability to be discerning of what types of spiritual practices felt life-affirming for her and which ones didn't. She got into heated debates with her husband about spirituality, using him as a place to practice finding her voice and defining herself. For the most part, he was open to her exploration process. Her marriage could have gone either way, but due to his relative flexibility and their shared value related to the importance of family, she *chose* to stay in the marriage while she continued to explore her spiritual journey and life path. She focused on intentionally defining herself across a variety of identity dimensions, including spirituality, and coming to a place of ownership and choice in her life.

The cases of Sasha and Clarissa highlight important aspects of the differentiation process. They both grew up in families that fostered poor boundaries and high levels of reactivity and did not readily support their connection with their Real Self. They both lacked personal authority and struggled to cultivate an inner compass. Instead, they adopted roles, reacted to external needs of others, and struggled into their adult lives. Both made reactive rather than intentional choices of an intimate partner. Thankfully, both utilized therapy as a way to increase their awareness and intentionality, and eventually, ownership for their life.

Increasing Therapist Spiritual-Differentiation

I recently provided consultation to an experienced therapist who was struggling with a client that he described as a "fundamentalist Christian." Among other labels, he said that she was "hiding behind her beliefs" and "psychologically immature." He believed that the therapy was "stuck" because she clung to "childish beliefs about God," which stopped her from taking control of her own life and dealing with her fears. Instead, he saw her as passively waiting for God to make changes for her, while she complained about the circumstances of her life.

My consultation with the therapist included questions about his past experiences with spirituality. He reported that he is "a very spiritual person" and that he had spent time in seminary, before abandoning his desire to be a priest in favor of being a therapist. He recounted numerous events where he saw students and faculty at seminary that were "blind to their psychological issues" because of their fundamentalist spiritual lens. He also reported experiences at seminary where he felt judged and oppressed by teachers and other students. As we talked, he spontaneously acknowledged that his past experiences were coloring his view of his client.

I introduced the idea that spirituality can be understood as a dimension of culture and that we could consider his client from a multicultural perspective. We began to look at how his client's up-bringing and culture had influenced her spiritual identity develop-ment. The cultural lens and client conceptualization resonated with him and were helpful, but the experiences at seminary continued to be deeply intrusive. We then focused on processing specific experi-ences from seminary that contributed to his reactivity. He began to alternate between a pathologizing stance and a softer view of his client. By the end of the consultation session, the therapist indicated that he was amazed at how "someone who knew scripture so well" (him) could have so much reactivity with a Christian client. He felt as if he had regained some perspective on his client and agreed that some additional personal reflection and clinical supervision would help him continue to work through his emotional reactivity and increase his spiritual-differentiation.

Spiritual-differentiation refers to one's level of awareness, res-olution, and ownership versus emotional reactivity in regard to spiritual and religious issues. The goal of spiritual-differentiation is to allow therapists to be genuinely interested in learning about clients' spiritual experiences, beliefs, and practices without becoming emotionally reactive and imposing their own views onto clients. Spiritual-differentiation allows therapists to utilize clients' spiritual beliefs and practices for the benefit of client healing and growth. Just like with clients, differentiation starts for therapists with self-awareness. It is essential for therapists to learn how their own history may influence their ability to work ethically and effectively with clients from a variety of faiths and philosophical positions.

When I conduct trainings for therapists on spiritually oriented therapy, in addition to asking how they personally define, experience, and access spirituality, I have therapists consider their own personal experiences with spirituality and unique spiritual journeys, including nodal events in their spiritual identity process. I have workshop attendees reflect on questions such as:

- What were your experiences of spirituality when you were growing up?
- What were you taught about God or a higher power?
- What has been your spiritual journey in relation to what you were taught as a child/teenager?
- Did you rebel against what you were taught? If yes, what happened?
- What are your current spiritual beliefs and practices?
- What were the nodal events and significant experiences that have shaped your current spiritual beliefs and practices?
- Have you experienced any judgment, oppression, or violence in the context of spirituality?
- Do you think you have the *right way* of considering and practicing spirituality?
- How open are you to your clients' unique and personal ways of defining, experiencing, and accessing spirituality?

♦ How might you respond if your clients have views that are similar or different from what you were taught as a child/teenager as well as your current views?

Therapists need to spend time reflecting on their experiences with spirituality throughout their lives, especially ones that were emotionally intrusive. Emotionally intrusive spiritual experiences tend to lead to blindly adopting and/or reacting against those experiences, and often inhibit the spiritual-differentiation process. These experiences will likely have the most influence on the development of therapists' beliefs and values and, therefore, have an impact on their ability to work with spiritually oriented clients. When therapists lack self-awareness, they run the risk of projecting their biases on clients, which will be favorable of certain terminology and ideologies and critical of others, even subtly.

Thus, another aspect of training therapists to work with spiritual issues is desensitizing them to their hot-button memories and words. Each therapist has hot-button words based on his or her unique history with spirituality. In general, higher levels of spiritual violence are associated with more intense hot-button words and lower levels of spiritual-differentiation, for clients and therapists. When I conduct workshops and trainings, one of the exercises that I use is reading a lengthy list of spiritual words while participants mindfully notice their internal reactions to each word. This way, therapists can become more aware of their hot-button words and memories and then understand the etiology of their reactivity. High levels of spiritual-differentiation lead to therapists having low levels of reactivity in relation to specific words that clients may use as they discuss spirituality. Again, the goal is to increase therapist self-awareness and decrease reactivity.

In addition to reflecting on their spiritual identity journey and increasing their awareness of words and memories that generate emotional reactivity, I also suggest that therapists practice mindfulness, regardless of their spiritual beliefs. Research has shown that one of the most effective ways to reduce therapist reactivity and increase cognitive flexibility is through the use of mindfulness (Davis & Hayes, 2011). In particular, individuals who practice mindfulness meditation are able to focus better on cognitive tasks after being exposed to emotionally upsetting stimuli than those who do not meditate (Ortner, Kilner, & Zelazo, 2007). Meditation is associated with more adaptive responses to stressful or negative situations (Cahn & Polich, 2006; Davidson et al., 2003) and leads to faster recovery after being negatively provoked (Davidson, 2000; Davidson, Jackson, & Kalin, 2000). Mindfulness has also been linked to increased counseling efficacy (Greason & Cashwell, 2009) as well as decreased therapist burnout (Shapiro & Carlson, 2009), among other benefits (Davis & Hayes, 2011).

While mindfulness has been shown to decrease burnout, any life-affirming spiritual practice can increase therapist self-soothing and self-care. I recommend that therapists *walk the talk* and practice their spirituality in ways that increase their connection with their Real Self, which supports differentiation. Spiritual-differentiation occurs when therapists embrace their own beliefs while being non-reactively open to the likelihood that their clients have equally valid ways of understanding and practicing spirituality. I encourage therapists to learn from their clients about the many different ways that spirituality can manifest. When therapists are open to engaging with this very personal material without judging or imposing their beliefs, clients inevitably share about their views and experiences. Thus, spiritually differentiated therapists are able to have their own personal beliefs and practices and are nonreactive to their clients' spiritual worldviews.

References

Adyashanti. (2006). *Emptiness dancing.* Boulder, CO: Sounds True.

Ainsworth, M. D., Blehar, M. C., Waters, E., & Wall, S. (1978). *Patterns of attachment: Assessed in the strange situation and at home.* Hillsdale, NJ: Erlbaum.

Alford, K. M. (1998). Family roles, alcoholism, and family dysfunction. *Journal of Mental Health Counseling, 20,* 250–260.

Allport, G. W. (1950). *The individual and his religion: A psychological interpretation.* New York, NY: Macmillan.

American Psychological Association (2007). Guidelines for psychological practice with girls and women. *American Psychologist, 62,* 949–979.

Anderson, T., Lunnen, K. M., & Ogles, B. M. (2010). Putting models and techniques in context. In B. L. Duncan, S. D. Miller, B. E. Wampold, & M. A. Hubble (Eds.), *The heart and soul of change* (2nd ed., pp. 143–166). Washington, DC: American Psychological Association.

Association for Spiritual, Ethical, and Religious Values in Counseling (ASERVIC). (2009). Competencies for addressing spiritual and religious issues in counseling. Retrieved from http://www.aservic. org/resources/spiritual-competencies/

Bar-on, R., Maree, J. G., & Elias, M. J. (Eds.). (2007). *Educating people to be emotionally intelligent.* Westport, CT: Praeger Publishers/Greenwood Publishing Group.

Bass, R. (1996). *The book of yaak*. Boston, MA: Houghton Mifflin.

Benjamin, L. S. (1996). *Interpersonal diagnosis and treatment of personality disorders*. New York, NY: Guilford Press.

Benson, H., & Proctor, W. (2010). *Relaxation revolution*. New York, NY: Simon & Schuster.

Black, C. (2001). *It will never happen to me*. Bainbridge Island, WA: MAC Publishing.

Bohart, A. C., & Tallman, K. (1999). *How clients make therapy work*. Washington, DC: American Psychological Association.

Bohart, A. C., & Tallman, K. (2010). Clients: The neglected common factor in psychotherapy. In B. L. Duncan, S. D. Miller, B. E. Wampold, & M. A. Hubble (Eds.), *The heart and soul of change* (2nd ed., pp. 83–111). Washington, DC: American Psychological Association.

Boorstein, S. (1996). Psychodynamic therapy and the transpersonal quest. In S. Boorstein (Ed.), *Transpersonal psychotherapy* (pp. 67–75). Albany: State University of New York Press.

Bowen, M. (1976). Theory in the practice of psychotherapy. In P. J. Guerin Jr. (Ed.), *Family therapy: Theory and practice*. New York, NY: Garner.

Bowen, M. (1978). *Family therapy in clinical practice*. New York, NY: Aronson.

Bowlby, J. (1988). *A secure base*. New York, NY: Basic Books.

Brach, T. (2003). *Radical acceptance*. New York, NY: Bantam Books.

Bray, J. H., Harvey, D. M., & Williamson, D. S. (1987). Intergenerational family relationships: An evaluation of theory and measurement. *Psychotherapy, 24*, 516–528.

Bray, J. H., Williamson, D. S., & Malone, P. E. (1986). An evaluation of an intergenerational consultation process to increase personal authority in the family system. *Family Process, 25*, 423–435.

Breuer, J., & Freud, S. (1962). Studies on hysteria. In *The standard edition of the complete psychological works of Sigmund Freud*

(Vol. 2, pp. 1–309). London, UK: Hogarth Press. (Original work published 1895).

Bublotz, W. C., Johnson, P., & Woller, K. M. P. (2003). Psychological reactance in college students: Family-of-origin predictors. *Journal of Counseling and Development, 81,* 311–317.

Cahn, B. R., & Polich, J. (2006). Meditation states and traits: EEG, ERP, and neuroimaging studies. *Psychological Bulletin, 132,* 180–211.

Cameron, J. (1992). *The artist's way.* New York, NY: Tarcher/Putnam.

Caplan, M. (2009). *Eyes wide open: Cultivating discernment on the spiritual path.* Boulder, CO: Sounds True.

Carter, B., & McGoldrick, M. (1999). *The expanded family lifecycle: Individual family and social perspectives* (3rd ed.). Boston, MA: Allyn & Bacon.

Cashdan, S. (1988). *Object relations therapy.* New York, NY: W. W. Norton.

Castro, D. M., Jones, R. A., & Mirsalimi, H. (2004). Parentification and the imposter phenomenon: An empirical investigation. *American Journal of Family Therapy, 32,* 205–216.

Chase, N. D. (Ed.). (1999). *Burdened children: Theory, research and treatment of parentification.* Thousand Oaks, CA: Sage.

Chase, N. D. (2001). Parentified children grow up: Dual patterns of high and low functioning. In B. E. Robinson & N. D. Chase (Eds.), *High performing families: Causes, consequences, and clinical solutions* (pp. 157–189). Alexandria, VA: American Counseling Association.

Chen, M.-W., & Rybak, C. J. (2004). *Group Leadership Skills.* Belmont, CA: Brooks/Cole.

Chopra, D., & Mlodinow, L. (2011). *War of the worldviews.* New York, NY: Harmony Books.

Christopher, J. C., & Smith, A. J. (2006). A hermeneutic approach to culture and psychotherapy. In R. Moodley & S. Palmer (Eds.), *Race, culture and psychotherapy.* Philadelphia, PA: Routledge/Taylor & Francis Group.

Cloitre, M., Cohen, L. R., & Koenen, K. C. (2006). *Treating survivors of sexual abuse*. New York, NY: Guilford Press.

Comstock, D. L., Hammer, T. R., Strentzsch, J., Cannon, K., Parsons, J., & Salazar, G. (2008). Relational-cultural theory: A framework for bridging relational, multicultural, and social justice competencies. *Journal of Counseling and Development, 86*, 279–287.

Cortright, B. (1997). *Psychotherapy and spirit: Theory and practice in transpersonal psychotherapy*. Albany: State University of New York Press.

Courtois, C. A., & Ford, J. D. (2009). *Treating complex traumatic stress disorder*. New York, NY: Guilford Press.

Crits-Christoph, P., & Gibbons, M. C. (2002). Relational interpretation. In J. C. Norcross (Ed.), *Psychotherapy relationships that work* (pp. 285–300). New York, NY: Oxford University Press.

Dalai Lama (2005). *The universe in a single atom*. New York, NY: Morgan Road Books.

Davidson, R. J. (2000). Affective styles, psychopathology, and resilience: Brain mechanisms and plasticity. *American Psychologist, 55*, 1196–1214.

Davidson, R. J., Jackson, D. C., & Kalin, N. H. (2000). Emotion, plasticity, context, and regulation: Perspectives from affective neuroscience. *Psychological Bulletin, 126*, 890–909.

Davidson, R. J., Kabat-Zinn, J., Schumacher, J., Rosenkranz, M., Muller, D., Santorelli, S. F., & Sheridan, J. F. (2003). Alterations in brain and immune function produced by mindfulness meditation. *Psychosomatic Medicine, 66*, 149–152.

Davis, D. M., & Hayes, J. A. (2011). What are the benefits of mindfulness? A practice review of psychotherapy-related research. *Psychotherapy, 48*, 198–208.

Devine, C., & Braithwaite, V. (1993). The survival roles of children of alcoholics: Their measurement and validity. *Addiction, 88*, 69–78.

Donatelli, J. L., Bybee, J. A., & Buka, S. L. (2007). What do mothers make adolescents feel guilty about? Incidents, reactions and relation to depression. *Journal of Child and Family Studies, 16,* 859–875.

Dreher, D. (1990). *The Tao of inner peace.* New York, NY: HarperCollins.

Duncan, B. L., Miller, S. D., Wampold, B. E., & Hubble, M. A. (Eds.). (2010). *The heart and soul of change.* Washington, DC: American Psychological Association.

Eisman, J. (2001). *The Hakomi method and re-creation of the self.* Ashland: Hakomi Institute of Oregon.

Elliott, R., Bohart, A. C., Watson, J. C., & Greenberg, L. S. (2011). Empathy. *Psychotherapy, 48,* 43–49.

Ellis, A. (1980). Psychotherapy and atheistic values: A response to A. E. Bergin's "Psychotherapy and Religious Values." *Journal of Consulting and Clinical Psychology, 48,* 635–639.

Enns, C. Z., & Byars-Winston, A. (2010). Multicultural feminist therapy. In H. Landrine & N. F. Russo (Eds.), *Handbook of diversity in feminist psychology* (pp. 367–388). New York, NY: Springer.

Epstein, M. (2007). *Psychotherapy without the self: A Buddhist perspective.* New Haven, CT: Yale University Press.

Erikson, E. H. (1959). *Identity and the life cycle.* New York, NY: W. W. Norton.

Erikson, E. H. (1963). *Childhood and society.* New York, NY: W. W. Norton.

Erikson, E. H. (1968). *Identity: Youth in crisis.* New York, NY: W. W. Norton.

Fairbairn, W. R. D. (1954). *An object relations theory of the personality.* New York, NY: Basic Books.

Faiver, C., Ingersoll, R. E., O'Brien, E., & McNally, C. (2001). *Explorations in counseling and spirituality.* Belmont, CA: Thompson Learning.

Farber, B. A., & Doolin, E. M. (2011). Positive regard. *Psychotherapy,* *48,* 58–64.

Fonagy, P. (2001). *Attachment theory and psychoanalysis.* New York, NY: Other Press.

Fonagy, P., Gergely, G., Jurist, E. L., & Target, M. (2002). *Affect regulation, mentalization, and the development of the self.* New York, NY: Other Press.

Ford, G., Waller, G., & Mountford, V. (2011). Invalidating childhood environments and core beliefs in women with eating disorders. *European Eating Disorders Review, 19,* 316–321.

Forman, M. (2010). *A guide to integral psychotherapy.* New York: State University of New York Press.

Fowler, J. W. (1981). *Stages of faith.* New York, NY: HarperCollins.

Fowler, J. W. (1991). Stages of faith consciousness [Special Issue: Religious development in childhood and adolescence]. *New Directions for Child Development, 52,* 27–45.

Fowler, J. W. (1996). *Faithful change.* Nashville, TN: Abingdon Press.

Freud, S. (1920/1966). *Introductory lectures on psycho-analysis.* New York, NY: W. W. Norton.

Freud, S. (1949). *An outline of psycho-analysis.* New York, NY: W. W. Norton.

Fukuyama, M. A., Siahpoush, F., & Sevig, T. D. (2005). Religion and spirituality in a cultural context. In C. S. Cashwell & J. S. Young (Eds.), *Integrating spirituality and religion into counseling: A guide to competent practice* (pp. 123–142). Alexandria, VA: American Counseling Association.

Gallup. (2007). *Religion in America: The Gallup report.* Retrieved from http://www.gallup.com/poll/1690/Religion.aspx

Geffner, R., & Tishelman, A. C. (2011). Child and adolescent trauma across the spectrum of experience: Underserved populations and psychological abuse. *Journal of Child and Adolescent Trauma, 4,* 87–89.

Genia, V. (1995). *Counseling and psychotherapy of religious clients: A developmental approach.* Westport, CT: Praeger.

Germer, C. K., Siegel, R. D., & Fulton, P. R. (2005). *Mindfulness and psychotherapy.* New York, NY: Guilford Press.

Gold, J. M. (2010). *Counseling and spirituality: Integrating spiritual and clinical orientations.* Upper Saddle River, NJ: Merrill.

Greason, P. B., & Cashwell, C. S. (2009). Mindfulness and counseling self-efficacy: The mediating role of attention and empathy. *Counselor Education and Supervision, 49,* 2–19.

Greenberg, L., & Goldman, R. (2008). *Emotion-focused couples therapy: The dynamics of emotion, love, and power.* Washington, DC: American Psychological Association.

Hagedorn, W. B., & Gutierrez, D. (2009). Integration versus segregation: Applications of the spiritual competencies in counselor education programs. *Counseling and Values, 54,* 32–47.

Halifax, J. (1993). *The fruitful darkness.* San Francisco, CA: HarperCollins.

Hall, T. W., Brokaw, B. F., Edwards, K. J., & Pike, P. L. (1998). An empirical exploration of psychoanalysis and religion: Spiritual maturity and object relations development. *Journal for the Scientific Study of Religion, 37,* 305–315.

Hanh, T. N. (1995). *Living Buddha, living Christ.* New York, NY: Riverhead Books.

Harris Interactive Inc. (2009). What people do and do not believe in. Retrieved from http://www.harrisinteractive.com/vault/Harris_Poll_2009_12_15.pdf

Harvey, D. M., Curry, C. J., & Bray, J. H. (1991). Individuation and intimacy in intergenerational relationships and health: Patterns across two generations. *Journal of Family Psychology, 5,* 204–236.

Hayes, J. A., Gelso, C. J., & Hummel, A. M. (2011). Managing countertransference. *Psychotherapy, 48,* 88–97.

Hayes, S. C., Follette, V. M., & Linehan, M. M. (Eds.). (2004). *Mindfulness and acceptance: Expanding the cognitive-behavioral tradition.* New York, NY: Guilford Press.

Hayes, S. C., & Smith, S. (2005). *Get out of your mind and into your life: The new acceptance and commitment therapy.* Oakland, CA: New Harbinger.

Hayes, S. C., Strosahl, K., & Wilson, K. G. (1999). *Acceptance and commitment therapy: An experiential approach to behavior change.* New York, NY: Guilford Press.

Hickson, J., Housley, W., & Wages, D. (2011). Counselors' perceptions of spirituality in the therapeutic process. *Counseling and Values, 45,* 58–66.

Hill, P. C., Pargament, K. I., Hood, R. W., Jr., McCullough, M. E., Swyers, J. P., Larson, D. B., & Zinnbauer, B. J. (2000). Conceptualizing religion and spirituality: Points of commonality, points of departure. *Journal for the Theory of Social Behaviour, 30,* 51–77.

Hodges, S. (2002). Mental health, depression, and dimensions of spirituality and religion. *Journal of Adult Development, 9,* 109–115.

Hollins, S. (2005). Spirituality and religion: Exploring the relationship. *Nursing Management, 12,* 22–26.

Hollis, J. (1996). *Swamplands of the soul: New life in dismal places.* Toronto, Canada: Inner City Books.

Hollis, J. (2000). *The archetypal imagination.* College Station, TX: A&M University Press.

Hollis, J. (2005). *Finding meaning in the second half of life.* New York, NY: Gotham Books.

Hollis, J. (2009). *What matters most.* New York, NY: Gotham Books.

Hong, P. Y., Ilardi, S. S., & Lishner, D. A. (2011). The aftermath of trauma: The impact of perceived and anticipated invalidation of childhood sexual abuse on borderline symptomatology. *Psychological Trauma, 3,* 360–368.

Horney, K. (1945). *Our inner conflicts.* New York, NY: W. W. Norton.

Horney, K. (1950). *Neurosis and human growth: The struggle toward self-realization*. New York, NY: W. W. Norton.

Horvath, A. O., Del Re, A. C., Fluckiger, C., & Symonds, D. (2011). Alliance in individual psychotherapy. *Psychotherapy, 48*, 9–16.

Hubble, M. A., Duncan, B. L., Miller, S. D., & Wampold, B. E. (2010). Introduction. In B. L. Duncan, S. D. Miller, B. E. Wampold, & M. A. Hubble (Eds.), *The heart and soul of change* (2nd ed., pp. 23–46). Washington, DC: American Psychological Association.

Ingram, C. (2003). *Passionate presence*. New York, NY: Gotham Books.

Jenkins, S. M., Buboltz, W. C., Schwartz, J. P., & Johnson, P. (2005). Differentiation of self and psychosocial development. *Contemporary Family Therapy, 27*, 251–261.

Johnson, J. M., & DelCampo, R. L. (1995, November). *A comparison of Mexican Americans and Anglo Americans on age onset of personal authority in the family system*. Poster session presented at the National Council on Family Relations annual conference, Portland, OR.

Johnson, P., & Buboltz, W. C. (2000). Differentiation of self and psychological reactance. *Contemporary Family Therapy, 22*, 91–102.

Johnson, P., Buboltz, W. C., & Seemann, E. (2003). Ego identity status: A step in the differentiation process. *Journal of Counseling & Development, 81*, 191–195.

Johnson, P., & Nelson, M. D. (1998). Parental divorce, family functioning, and college student development: An intergenerational perspective. *Journal of College Student Development, 39*, 355–363.

Johnson, P., Schamuhn, T. D., Nelson, D. B., & Buboltz, W. C. (2012). *Differentiation levels of young adults: Effects on career development*. Manuscript submitted for publication.

Johnson, P., & Smith, A. J. (2011). Social interest and differentiation of self. *Professional Issues in Counseling*, http://www.shsu.edu/~piic/

Johnson, P., Smith, A. J., & Nelson, M. D. (2003). Predictors of social interest in young adults. *Journal of Individual Psychology*, *59*, 281–292.

Johnson, P., & Stone, R. (2009). Parental alcoholism and family functioning: Effects on differentiation levels of young adults. *Alcoholism Treatment Quarterly*, *27*, 3–18.

Johnson, P., Thorngren, J. M., & Smith, A. J. (2001). Parental divorce and family functioning: Effects on differentiation levels of young adults. *The Family Journal*, *9*, 265–272.

Johnson, P., & Waldo, M. (1998). Integrating Minuchin's boundary continuum and Bowen's differentiation scale: A curvilinear representation. *Contemporary Family Therapy*, *20*(3), 403–413.

Johnson, R. (1983). *We: Understanding the psychology of romantic love*. New York, NY: HarperCollins.

Johnson, R. (1993). *Owning your own shadow: Understanding the dark side of the psyche*. San Francisco, CA: HarperCollins.

Johnson, R. (2009). *Reclaiming your real self: A psychological and spiritual integration*. North Charleston, SC: BookSurge Publishing.

Johnson, R., & Ruhl, J. (2009). *Living your unlived life: Coping with unrealized dreams and fulfilling your purpose in the second half of life*. Los Angeles, CA: Tarcher.

Johnson, S. (1996). *The practice of emotionally focused couple therapy: Creating connection* (2nd ed.). New York, NY: Brunner-Routledge.

Johnson, S., & Whiffen, R. (Eds.). (2003). *Attachment processes in couple and family therapy*. New York, NY: Guilford Press.

Jones, R. A., & Wells, M. (1996). An empirical study of parentification and personality. *American Journal of Family Therapy*, *24*, 145–152.

Jung, C. G. (1957). *The undiscovered self.* New York, NY: New American Library.

Jung, C. G. (1961). *Memories, dreams, reflections.* New York, NY: Vintage.

Jung, C. G. (1971). *The portable Jung.* London, UK: Penguin Books.

Jung, C. G. (1981). *The archetypes and the collective unconscious.* Princeton, NJ: Princeton University Press.

Kahn, M. (1991). *Between therapist and client: The new relationship.* New York, NY: W. H. Freeman.

Kasl, C. (2005). *If the Buddha got stuck.* New York, NY: Penguin Books.

Kelly, E. W., Jr. (1995). *Spirituality and religion in counseling and psychotherapy: Diversity in theory and practice.* Alexandria, VA: American Counseling Association.

Kernberg, O. (1975). *Borderline conditions and pathological narcissism.* New York, NY: Jason Aronson.

Kernberg, O. (1976). *Object relations theory and clinical psychoanalysis.* New York, NY: Jason Aronson.

Kerr, M. E. (1988). Chronic anxiety and defining a self. *The Atlantic Monthly, 9,* 35–58.

Kerr, M. E., & Bowen, M. (1988). *Family evaluation: An approach based on Bowen theory.* New York, NY: W. W. Norton.

Kiesler, D. J. (1996). *Contemporary interpersonal theory and research.* New York, NY: Wiley.

Klein, M. (1975). *The psychoanalysis of children.* New York, NY: Dell.

Klerman, G. L., Weissman, M. M., Rounsaville, B. J., & Chevron, E. S. (1984). *Interpersonal psychotherapy of depression.* New York, NY: Basic Books.

Koenig, H. (2008). *Overview of research and findings in spirituality and health.* Retrieved from http://www.dukespiritualityandhealth. org.

Kohut, H. (1971). *The analysis of the self.* New York, NY: International Universities Press.

Kohut, H. (1977). *The restoration of the self.* New York, NY: International Universities Press.

Kolden, G. G., Klien, M. H., Wang, C.-C., & Austin, S. B. (2011). Congruence/Genuineness. *Psychotherapy, 48*, 65–71.

Kosmin, B. A., & Keyser, A. (2009). *American religious identification survey (ARIS).* Retrieved from www.americanreligionsurvey-aris. org

Krause, E. D., Mendelson, T., & Lynch, T. R. (2003). Childhood emotional invalidation and adult psychological distress: The mediating role of emotional inhibition. *Child Abuse and Neglect, 27*, 199–213.

Kurtz, R. (1987). *Hakomi therapy.* Boulder, CO: Hakomi Institute.

Kurtz, R. (1990). *Body-centered psychotherapy: The Hakomi method.* Mendocino, CA: LifeRhythm.

La Torre, M. (2002). Spirituality and psychotherapy: An important combination. *Perspectives in Psychiatric Care, 38*, 108–110.

Lajoie, D. H., & Shapiro, S. I. (1992). Definitions of transpersonal psychology: The first twenty-three years. *Journal of Transpersonal Psychology, 24*, 79–98.

Lambert, M. J., & Ogles, B. (2004). The efficacy and effectiveness of psychotherapy. In M. J. Lambert (Ed.), *Bergin and Garfield's handbook of psychotherapy and behavior change* (5th ed., pp. 139–193). Hoboken, NJ: Wiley.

Lederman, L. M., & Hill, C. T. (2011). *Quantum physics for poets.* Amherst, NY: Prometheus Books.

Linehan, M. M. (1993a). *Cognitive-behavioral treatment of borderline personality disorder.* New York, NY: Guilford Press.

Linehan, M. M. (1993b). *Skills training manual for treating borderline personality disorder.* New York, NY: Guilford Press.

Loy, D. (1996). *Lack and Transcendence.* Amherst, NY: Humanity Books.

Magid, B. (2002). *Ordinary Mind.* Boston, MA: Wisdom Publications.

Mahler, M. S., Pine, F., & Bergman, A. (1975). *The psychological birth of the human infant*. New York, NY: Basic Books.

Mandara, J., & Pikes, C. L. (2008). Guilt trips and love withdrawal: Does mothers' use of psychological control predict depressive symptoms among African American adolescents? *Family Relations, 57*, 602–612.

Marcia, J. E. (1966). Development and validation of ego identity status. *Journal of Personality and Social Psychology, 3*, 551–558.

Marcia, J. E. (1980). Identity in adolescence. In J. Adelson (Ed.), *Handbook of adolescent psychology* (pp. 159–187). New York, NY: Wiley.

Masterson, J. F. (1976). *Psychotherapy of the borderline adult: A developmental approach*. New York, NY: Brunner/Mazel.

Mayseless, O., & Scharf, M. (2009). Too close for comfort: Inadequate boundaries with parents and individuation in late adolescent girls. *American Journal of Orthopsychiatry, 79*, 191–202.

McGoldrick, M., Carter, B., & Garcia-Preto, N. (2010). *The expanded family life cycle*. Boston, MA: Allyn & Bacon.

Miller, G. (2005). Religious/spiritual life span development. In C. S. Cashwell & J. S. Young (Eds.), *Integrating spirituality and religion into counseling: A guide to competent practice* (pp. 105–122). Alexandria, VA: American Counseling Association.

Miller, R. B., Anderson, S., & Keala, D. K. (2004). Is Bowen theory valid? A review of basic research. *Journal of Marital and Family Therapy, 30*, 453–466.

Miller, W. R., & Thoresen, C. E. (2003). Spirituality, religion, and health: An emerging research field. *American Psychologist, 58*.

Minuchin, S. (1974). *Families and family therapy*. Cambridge, MA: Harvard University Press.

Minuchin, S., & Fishman, H. C. (1981). *Family therapy techniques*. Cambridge, MA: Harvard University Press.

Minuchin, S., Nichols, M. P., & Lee, W.-Y. (2007). *Assessing families and couples*. Boston, MA: Pearson.

Mitchell, S. A. (1988). *Relational concepts in psychoanalysis: An integration.* Cambridge, MA: Harvard University Press.

Mitchell, S. A. (2000). *Relationality: From attachment to intersubjectivity.* Hillsdale, NJ: Analytic Press.

Morrison, J., Clutter, S., Pritchett, E., & Demmitt, A. (2009). Perceptions of clients and counseling professionals regarding spirituality in counseling. *Counseling and Values, 53*(3), 183.

New American Bible. (1992). New York, NY: Catholic Book Publishing.

New International Version Bible. (1984). Grand Rapids, MI: Zondervan Bible Publishers.

Norcross, J. C. (Ed.). (2002*). Psychotherapy relationships that work.* New York, NY: Oxford University Press.

Norcross, J. C. (2010). The therapeutic relationship. In B. L. Duncan, S. D. Miller, B. E. Wampold, & M. A. Hubble (Eds.), *The heart and soul of change* (2nd ed., pp. 113–141). Washington, DC: American Psychological Association.

Norcross, J. C., & Lambert, M. J. (2011). Psychotherapy relationships that work II. *Psychotherapy, 48,* 4–8.

Norcross, J. C., & Wampold, B. E. (2011a). What works for whom: Tailoring psychotherapy to the person. *Journal of Clinical Psychology, 67,* 127–132.

Norcross, J. C., & Wampold, B. E. (2011b). Evidence-based therapy relationships: Research conclusions and clinical practices. *Psychotherapy, 48,* 98–102.

Noricks, J. (2011). *Parts psychology: A trauma-based self-state therapy for emotional healing.* Los Angeles, CA: New University Press.

Ogden, P. (1997). Hakomi integrated somatics: Hands on psychotherapy. In C. Caldwell (Ed.), *Getting in touch: The guide to new body-centered therapies* (pp. 153–178). Wheaton, IL: Theosophical.

Orlinsky, D. E. (2010). Foreword. In B. L. Duncan, S. D. Miller, B. E. Wampold, & M. A. Hubble (Eds.), *The heart and soul of change* (2nd ed., pp. xix–xxv). Washington, DC: American Psychological Association.

Ortner, C. N. M., Kilner, S. J., & Zelazo, P. D. (2007). Mindfulness meditation and reduced emotional interference on a cognitive task. *Motivation and Emotion, 31,* 271–283.

Oser, F., & W. G. Scarlett, (Eds.) (1991). *Religious development in childhood and adolescence.* San Francisco, CA: Jossey-Bass.

Pargament, K. I., & Saunders, S. M. (2007). Introduction to the special issue on spirituality and psychotherapy. *Journal of Clinical Psychology, 63,* 903–907.

Parsons, T. (2007). *Nothing being everything.* Shaftesbury, UK: Open Secret.

Peris, T. S., Goeke-Morey, M. C., Cummings, E. M., & Emery, R. E. (2008). Marital conflict and support seeking by parents in adolescence: Empirical support for the parentification construct. *Journal of Family Psychology, 22,* 633–642.

Piaget, J. (1965). *Moral judgment of the child.* New York, NY: Free Press.

Prendergast, J. J., Fenner, P., & Krystal, S. (2003). *The sacred mirror: Nondual wisdom and psychotherapy.* St. Paul, MN: Paragon House.

Proctor, W., & Benson, H. (2011). *Christian mind-body healing strategies.* Vero Beach, FL: Inkslinger's Press.

Rakow, A., Forehand, R., Haker, K., McKee, L. G., Champion, J. E., Potts, J., . . . Compas, B. E. (2011). Use of parental guilt induction among depressed parents. *Journal of Family Psychology, 25,* 147–151.

Rakow, A., Forehand, R., McKee, L. G., Coffelt, N., Champion, J. E., Fear, J., & Compas, B. E. (2009). The relation of parental guilt induction to child internalizing problems when a caregiver has a history of depression. *Journal of Child and Family Studies, 18,* 367–377.

Rizzuto, A. M. (1979). *The birth of the living god.* Chicago, IL: University of Chicago Press.

Robertson, L. A. (2010). The Spiritual Competency Scale. *Counseling and Values, 55*, 6–24.

Robertson, L. A., Smith, H. L., Ray, S. L., & Jones, K. D. (2009). Counseling clients with chronic pain; A religiously oriented cognitive behavior framework. *Counseling and Values, 87*, 373–379.

Rogers, C. (1951). *Client-centered therapy*. Boston, MA: Houghton Mifflin.

Rogers, C. (1961). *On becoming a person*. Boston, MA: Houghton Mifflin.

Rogers, C. (1980). *A way of being*. Boston, MA: Houghton Mifflin.

Rosen, K. H., Bartle-Haring, S., & Stith, S. M. (2001). Using Bowen theory to enhance understanding of the intergenerational transmission of dating violence. *Journal of Family Issues, 22*, 124–142.

Roy, D. M. (2003). Body-centered counseling and psychotherapy. In D. Capuzzi and D. R. Gross (Eds.), *Counseling and Psychotherapy* (pp. 387–414). Upper Saddle River, NJ: Merrill Prentice Hall.

Rubin, J. B. (2003). A well-lived life: Psychoanalytic Buddhist contributions. In J. D. Saffran (Ed.). *Psychoanalysis and Buddhism* (pp. 387–425). Boston, MA: Wisdom.

Safran, J. D. (2003). *Psychoanalysis and Buddhism*. Boston, MA: Wisdom.

Safran, J. D., & Muran, J. C. (2000). *Negotiating the therapeutic alliance: A relational treatment guide*. New York, NY: Guilford Press.

Safran, J. D., Muran, J. C., & Eubanks-Carter, C. (2011). Repairing alliance ruptures. *Psychotherapy, 48*, 80–87.

Schnarch, D. (2004). Keynote address. Oregon Psychological Association annual conference, Portland, OR.

Schultz, D., & Schultz, S. E. (2009). *Theories of personality* (9th ed.). Belmont, CA: Wadsworth, Cengage Learning.

Schwartz, R. C. (1995). *Internal family systems therapy*. New York, NY: Guilford Press.

Schwartz, R. C. (2001). *Introduction to the internal family systems model.* Oak Park, IL: Trail Heads.

Shapiro, S. L., & Carlson, L. E. (2009). *The art and science of mindfulness: Integrating mindfulness into psychology and the helping professions.* Washington, DC: American Psychological Association.

Siegel, D. J. (2012). *A pocket guide to interpersonal neurobiology.* New York, NY: W. W. Norton.

Siegel, D. J., & Hartzell, M. (2003). *Parenting from the inside out.* New York, NY: Tarcher/Penguin.

Siegel, R. (September/October, 2011). West meets East. *Psychotherapy Networker.*

Skowron, E. A. (2000). The role of differentiation of self in marital adjustment. *Journal of Counseling Psychology, 47*, 229–237.

Skowron, E. A., & Dendy, A. K. (2004). Differentiation of self and attachment in adulthood: Relational correlates of effortful control. *Contemporary Family Therapy, 26*(3), 337–357.

Skowron, E., A., & Friedlander, M. L. (1998). The differentiation of self inventory: Development and initial validation. *Journal of Counseling Psychology, 45*, 235–246.

Skowron, E. A., Holmes, S. E., & Sabatelli, R. M. (2003). Deconstructing differentiation: Self regulation, interdependent relating, and well-being in adulthood. *Contemporary Family Therapy, 26*, 29–38.

Skowron, E. A., & Schmitt, T. A. (2003). Assessing interpersonal fusion: Reliability and validity of a new DSI Fusion with Others subscale. *Journal of Marital and Family Therapy, 29*, 209–222.

Smith, T. B., Bartz, J., & Richards, P. S. (2007). Outcomes of religious and spiritual adaptations to psychotherapy: A meta-analytic review. *Psychotherapy Research, 17*, 643–655.

Smith, T. B., Rodríguez, M. D., & Bernal, G. (2011). Culture. *Journal of Clinical Psychology, 67*, 166–175.

Spero, M. H. (1992). *Religious objects as psychological structures.* Chicago, IL: University of Chicago Press.

Sperry, L. (2003). Integrating spiritual direction functions in the practice of psychotherapy. *Journal of Psychology and Theology, 31,* 3–13.

Steindl-Rast, D. (1995). Foreword. In T. N. Hanh, *Living Buddha, living Christ.* New York, NY: Riverhead Books.

Sullivan, H. S. (1953). *The interpersonal theory of psychiatry.* New York, NY: W. W. Norton.

Sullivan, H. S. (1954). *The psychiatric interview.* New York, NY: W. W. Norton.

Suzuki, S. (1973). *Zen mind, beginner's mind.* New York, NY: Weatherhill.

Swift, J. K., Callahan, J. L., & Vollmer, B. M. (2011). Preferences. *Journal of Clinical Psychology, 67,* 155–165.

Teasdale, W. (1999). *The mystic heart.* Novato, CA: New World Library.

Teyber, E. (2000). *Interpersonal process in psychotherapy: A relational approach.* Belmont, CA: Brooks/Cole.

Tishelman, A. C., & Geffner, R. (2011). Child and adolescent trauma across the spectrum of experience: Research and clinical interventions. *Journal of Child and Adolescent Trauma, 4,* 1–7.

Titelman, P. (1998a). Emotional cutoff in Bowen family systems theory: An overview. In P. Titelman (Ed.), *Emotional cutoff: Bowen family systems theory perspectives* (pp. 9–65). New York, NY: Haworth Clinical Practice Press.

Titelman, P. (1998b). Overview of the Bowen theoretical-therapeutic system. In P. Titelman (Ed.), *Clinical applications of Bowen family systems theory* (pp. 7–48). New York, NY: Haworth Press.

Tolle, E. (1999). *The power of now.* Novato, CA: Namaste Publishing.

Tolle, E. (2005). *A new earth.* New York, NY: Plume.

Tryon, G. S., & Winograd, G. (2011). Goal consensus and collaboration. *Psychotherapy, 48,* 50–57.

Tuason, M. T., & Friedlander, M. L. (2000). Do parents' differentiation levels predict those of their adult children? and other tests of Bowen theory in a Philippine sample. *Journal of Counseling Psychology, 47*, 27–35.

Vacc, N. A., DeVaney, S. B., & Wittmer, J. (1995). *Experiencing and counseling multicultural and diverse populations.* Bristol, PA: Accelerated Development.

van der Kolk, B., McFarlane, A., & Weisaeth, L. (1996). *Traumatic stress.* New York, NY: Guilford Press.

Vaughan, F. (2000). *The inward arc: Healing in psychotherapy and spirituality* (2nd ed.). Lincoln, NE: iUniverse.com.

Veronie, L., & Fruehstorfer, D. B. (2001). Gender, birth order and family role identification among adult children of alcoholics. *Current Psychology, 20*, 53–67.

Walsh, R. (1999). *Essential spirituality: The 7 central practices to awaken heart and mind.* New York, NY: Wiley.

Wampold, B. E. (2001). *The great psychotherapy debate: Models, methods and findings.* Mahwah, NJ: Erlbaum.

Wampold, B. E. (2005). The psychotherapist. In J. C. Norcross, L. E. Beutler, & R. F. Levont (Eds.), *Evidence-based practices in mental health: Debate and dialogue on the fundamental questions* (pp. 200–207). Washington, DC: American Psychological Association.

Wampold, B. E. (2007). Psychotherapy: The humanistic (and effective) treatment. *American Psychologist, 62*, 857–873.

Wampold, B. E. (2010). The research evidence for the common factors models: A historically situated perspective. In B. L. Duncan, S. D. Miller, B. E. Wampold, & M. A. Hubble (Eds.), *The heart and soul of change* (2nd ed., pp. 49–81). Washington, DC: American Psychological Association.

Warren, R. (2003). *The purpose driven life.* Philadelphia, PA: Running Press.

Washburn, M. (2003). *Embodied spirituality in a sacred world.* Albany, NY: State University of New York Press.

Watkins, J. G., & Watkins, H. H. (1997). *Ego states: Theory and therapy.* New York, NY: W. W. Norton.

Weiss, J. (1993). *How psychotherapy works*. New York, NY: Guilford Press.

Weiss, J., Sampson, H., & The Mount Zion Psychotherapy Research Group. (1986). *The psychoanalytic process*. New York, NY: Guilford Press.

Weissman, M. M., Markowitz, J. C., & Klerman, G. L. (2000). *Comprehensive guide to interpersonal psychotherapy*. New York, NY: Basic Books.

Wells, M., & Jones, R. (2000). Childhood parentification and shame-proneness: A preliminary study. *American Journal of Family Therapy*, *28*, 19–27.

Welwood, J. (2000). *Toward a psychology of awakening: Buddhism, psychotherapy, and the path of personal and spiritual transformation*. Boston, MA: Shambhala.

Wilber, K. (1996). *A brief history of everything*. Boston, MA: Shambhala.

Wilber, K. (2000). *Integral psychology: Consciousness, spirit, psychology, therapy*. Boston, MA: Shambhala.

Wilber, K. (2006). *Integral spirituality: A startling new role for religion in the modern and postmodern world*. Boston, MA: Integral Books.

Williamson, D. S. (1981). Personal authority via termination of the intergenerational hierarchical boundary: A "new" stage in the family life cycle. *Journal of Marital and Family Therapy*, *7*, 441–452.

Williamson, D. S., & Bray, J. H. (1988). Family development and change across the generations: An intergenerational perspective. In C. J. Falicov (Ed.), *Family transitions: Continuity and change over the life cycle* (pp. 357–384). New York, NY: Guilford Press.

Williamson, M. (1992). *A return to love*. New York, NY: HarperCollins.

Williamson, M. (2004). *The gift of change*. New York, NY: HarperCollins.

Winnicott, D. W. (1971). *Playing and reality.* London, UK: Tavistock.

Worell, J., & Remer, P. (2003). *Feminist perspectives in therapy* (2nd ed.). Hoboken, NJ: Wiley.

Worthington, E. L. (1989). Religious faith across the life span: Implications for counseling and research. *The Counseling Psychologist, 35,* 1–19.

Worthington, E. L., Jr., & Atten, J. D. (2009). Psychotherapy with religious and spiritual clients: An introduction. *Journal of Clinical Psychology, 65,* 123–130.

Worthington, E. L., Jr., Hook, J. N., Davis, D. E., & McDaniel, M.A. (2011). Religion and spirituality. *Journal of Clinical Psychology, 67,* 204–214.

Wylie, M. S. (March/April, 2010). *The long shadow of trauma.* Psychotherapy Networker.

Yalom, I. D. (2009). *Staring at the sun: Overcoming the terror of death.* San Francisco, CA: Jossey-Bass.

Yap, M. B. H., Allen, N. D., & Ladouceur, C. D. (2008). Maternal socialization of positive affect: The impact of invalidation on adolescent emotion regulation and depressive symptomatology. *Child Development, 79,* 1415–1431.

Young, J. S., Cashwell, C., Wiggins-Frame, M., & Belaire, C. (2002). Spiritual and religious competencies: A national survey of CACREP-accredited programs. *Counseling and Values, 47,* 22–33.

AUTHOR INDEX

Adyashanti, 151
Ainsworth, M. D., 49
Alford, K. M., 75
Allen, N. D., 74
Allport, G. W., 62, 160, 195
Anderson, S., 80
Anderson, T., 170
Atten, J. D., 10
Austin, S. B., 173

Bar-on, R., 73
Bartle-Haring, S., 202
Bartz, J., 10
Bass, R., 40
Belaire, C., 8
Benjamin, L. S., 51
Benson, H., 18
Bergman, A., 49
Bernal, G., 155
Black, C., 75
Bohart, A. C., 170, 173, 187
Boorstein, S., 17, 60
Bowen, M., 15, 16, 79, 195, 198, 200,
    201, 214
Bowlby, J., 49
Brach, T., 18, 61, 178, 186
Braithwaite, V., 75
Bray, J. H., 80, 81, 209, 210, 211
Breuer, J., 12
Brokaw, B. F., 50
Buboltz, W. C., 15, 16, 80, 198, 199, 202,
    203, 206, 207, 211
Buka, S. L., 82
Byars-Winston, A., 155, 156

Bybee, J. A., 82

Cahn, B. R., 221
Callahan, J. L., 10
Cameron, J., 39
Caplan, M., 61
Carlson, S. E., 221
Carter, B., 79, 196
Cashdan, S., 49
Cashwell, C., 8
Cashwell, C. S., 221
Castro, D. M., 78
Chase, N. D., 77
Chen, M.-W., 16
Chevron, E. S., 51
Chopra, D., 152
Christopher, J. C., 155, 156
Cloitre, M., 83, 84
Clutter, S., 6
Cohen, L. R., 83
Comstock, D. L., 156
Cortright, B., 17, 60
Courtois, C. A., 83
Crits-Christoph, P., 180, 182
Cummings, E. M., 78
Curry, C. J., 81

Dalai Lama, 151, 152
Davidson, R. J., 221
Davis, D. E., 10
Davis, D. M., 109, 221
DelCampo, R. L., 197, 214
Del Re, A. C., 173
Demmitt, A., 6

Dendy, A. K., 15, 199, 202, 206
DeVaney, S. B., 8
Devine, C., 75
Donatelli, J. L., 82
Doolin, E. M., 173
Dreher, D., 36, 40
Duncan, B. L., 169, 170

Edwards, K. J., 50
Eisman, J., 18
Elias, M. J., 73
Elliott, R., 173
Ellis, A., 13
Emory, R. E., 78
Enns, C. Z., 155, 156
Epstein, M., 18, 61
Erikson, E. H., 62, 160, 195
Eubanks-Carter, C., 173

Fairbairn, W. R. D., 49
Faiver, C., 28
Farber, B. A., 173
Fenner, P., 18
Fishman, H. C., 76
Fluckiger, C., 173
Follette, V. M., 17
Fonagy, P., 49
Ford, G., 73
Ford, J. D., 83
Forman, M., 17, 60
Fowler, J. W., 62, 160, 195
Freud, S., 12, 45
Friedlander, M. L., 16, 81, 202, 206, 207, 208, 209
Fruehstorfer, D. B., 75
Fukuyama, M. A., 9, 16, 62
Fulton, P. R., 18

Garcia-Preto, N., 196
Geffner, R., 83
Gelso, C. J., 173
Genia, V., 195
Gergely, G., 49
Germer, C. K., 18, 59, 61, 90
Gibbons, M. C., 180, 182
Goeke-Morey, M. C., 78
Gold, J. M., 21

Goldman, R., 135–136
Greason, P. B., 221
Greenberg, L., 135–136
Greenberg, L. S., 173
Gutierrez, D., 6

Hagedorn, W. B., 6
Halifax, J., 34, 39, 94
Hall, T. W., 50
Hanh, T. N., 30, 34
Hartzell, M., 73, 197
Harvey, D. M., 81, 209
Hayes, J. A., 109, 173, 221
Hayes, S. C., 17, 61
Hickson, J., 8, 45, 102
Hill, C. T., 152
Hill, P. C., 21
Hodges, S., 20, 22
Hollins, S., 21
Hollis, J., 46, 47
Holmes, S. E., 15, 81
Hong, P. Y., 73
Hook, J. N., 10
Horney, K., 18, 51, 86, 131
Horvath, A. O., 173
Housley, W., 8
Hubble, M. A., 169, 170, 171
Hummel, A. M., 173

Ilardi, S. S., 73
Ingersoll, R. E., 28
Ingram, C., 34, 95

Jackson, D. C., 221
Jenkins, S. M., 198, 211
Johnson, J. M., 197, 214
Johnson, Rick, v, vi, xxiii, 15, 16, 80, 119, 156, 198, 199, 200, 201, 202, 203, 206, 207, 209, 211
Johnson, Robert, 46, 125, 126
Johnson, S., 136
Jones, K. D., 8
Jones, R. A., 78
Jung, C. G., 17, 46, 47, 126, 127
Jurist, E. L., 49

Kahn, M., 51
Kalin, N. H., 221

Kasl, C., 42
Keala, D. K., 80
Kelly, E. W., Jr., 8, 21, 62, 63
Kernberg, O., 49
Kerr, M. E., 15, 79, 195, 198, 200, 201, 204
Keyser, A., 5
Kiesler, D. J., 51, 84
Kilner, S. J., 221
Klein, M., 48–49
Klein, M. H., 173
Klerman, G. L., 51
Koenen, K. C., 83
Koenig, H., 21
Kohut, H., 49
Kolden, G. G., 173
Kosmin, B. A., 5
Krause, E. D., 73–74
Krystal, S., 18
Kurtz, R., 18

Ladouceur, C. D., 74
Lajoie, D. H., 61
Lambert, M. J., 169, 171, 172
La Torre, M., 9
Lederman, L. M., 152
Lee, W.-Y., 76
Linehan, M. M., 17, 59, 74, 109
Lishner, D. A., 73
Loy, D., 153
Lunnen, K. M., 170
Lynch, T. R., 73–74

Magid, B., 8, 32, 61
Mahler, M. S., 49
Malone, P. E., 211
Mandera, J., 82
Marcia, J. E., 62, 160, 195, 198
Maree, J. G., 73
Markowitz, J. C., 51
Masterson, J. F., 49
Mayseless, O., 82
McDaniel, M. A., 10
McFarlane, A., 83, 85
McGoldrick, M., 79, 196, 197, 198, 200, 210, 214
McNally, C., 28
Mendelson, T., 73–74

Miller, G., 62, 63, 64
Miller, R. B., 80, 200, 208
Miller, S. D., 169
Miller, W. R., 6
Minuchin, S., 76
Mirsalimi, H., 78
Mitchell, S. A., 49
Mlodinow, L., 152
Morrison, J., 6
Mountford, V., 73
Muran, J. C., 51, 173

Nelson, D. B., 198
Nelson, M. D., 119, 209, 211
Nichols, M. P., 76
Norcross, J. C., 10, 170, 171, 172, 180
Noricks, J., 184

O'Brien, E., 28
Ogden, P., 18
Ogles, B., 169
Ogles, B. M., 170
Orlinsky, D. E., 169
Ortner, C. N. M., 221
Oser, F., 195

Pargament, K. I., 10
Parsons, T., 151
Peris, T. S., 78
Piaget, J., 62, 195
Pike, P. L., 50
Pikes, C. L., 82
Pine, F., 49
Polich, J., 221
Prendergast, J. J., 18, 61
Pritchett, E., 6
Proctor, W., 18

Rakow, A., 82
Ray, S. L., 8
Remer, P., 155, 156
Richards, P. S., 10
Rizzuto, A. M., 50, 160, 195, 208
Robertson, L. A., 8, 10, 26
Rodríguez, M. D., 155
Rogers, C., 52
Rosen, K. H., 202

Rounsaville, B. J., 51
Roy, D. M., 18
Rubin, J. B., 12
Ruhl, J., 46
Rybak, C. J., 16

Sabatelli, R. M., 15, 81
Safran, J. D., 18, 51, 61, 173
Sampson, H., 54, 84
Saunders, S. M., 10
Scarlett, W. G., 195
Schamuhn, T. D., 198
Scharf, M., 82
Schmitt, T. A., 209
Schnarch, D., 200, 212
Schultz, D., 125
Schultz, S. E., 125
Schwartz, J. P., 198
Schwartz, R. C., 57, 85, 184
Seemann, E., 15
Sevig, T. D., 9
Shapiro, S. L., 61, 221
Siahpoush, F., 9
Siegel, D. J., 73, 156, 197
Siegel, R., 109
Siegel, R. D., 18
Skowron, E. A., 15, 16, 81, 199, 202, 206, 207, 208, 209
Smith, A. J., 119, 155, 156, 200
Smith, H. L., 8
Smith, S., 17, 61
Smith, T. B., 10, 19, 103, 155, 174
Spero, 195
Sperry, L., 9
Steindl-Rast, D., 30
Stith, S. M., 202
Stone, R., 201
Strosahl, K., 17
Sullivan, H. S., 51
Suzuki, S., 37, 103
Swift, J. K., 10, 19, 103, 155, 172, 174
Symonds, D., 173

Tallman, K., 170, 187
Target, M., 49
Teasdale, W., 28
Teyber, E., 51, 77, 85, 177
Thoresen, C. E., 6

Thorngren, J. M., 200
Tishelman, A. C., 83
Titelman, P., 15
Tolle, E., 89, 152
Tryon, G. S., 173
Tuason, M. T., 81

Vacc, N. A., 8
van der Kolk, B., 83, 85
Vaughan, F., 17, 60
Veronie, L., 75
Vollmer, B. M., 10

Wages, D., 8
Waldo, M., 15, 80, 201, 202
Waller, G., 73
Walsh, R., 17, 60
Wampold, B. E., 10, 169, 171, 173, 174
Wang, C.-C., 173
Warren, R., 36, 154
Washburn, M., 60
Watkins, H. H., 184
Watkins, J. G., 184
Watson, J. C., 173
Weisaeth, L., 83, 85
Weiss, J., 54, 82, 83, 84, 182
Weissman, M. M., 51
Wells, M., 78
Welwood, J., 18, 61
Whiffen, R., 136
Wiggins-Frame, M., 8
Wilber, K., 17, 60, 200
Williamson, D. S., 80, 209, 210, 211
Williamson, M., 35, 88
Wilson, K. G., 17
Winnicott, D. W., 49
Winograd, G., 173
Wittmer, J., 8
Woller, K. M. P., 199
Worell, J., 155, 156
Worthington, E. L., Jr., 10, 19, 21, 26, 62, 63, 103, 174
Wylie, M. S., 83, 84, 85

Yalom, I. D., 30, 153
Yap, M. B. H., 74
Young, J. S., 8

Zelazo, P. D., 221

SUBJECT INDEX

Abuse. *See also* Substance abuse and
  addiction; Trauma
  addictive behavior as response to, 188–189
  control-mastery theory on, 55
  humanist theory addressing, 53
  internal family systems theory
    addressing, 57–58
  interpersonal theory addressing, 51
  loss of self relationship to, 69–70,
    71–72, 83–84, 93, 96
  psychological theories on and approaches
    to treating, 51, 53, 55, 57–58
  spiritually-oriented therapy addressing,
    69–70, 110–111, 191–193
  spiritual resourcing for coping with,
    110–111
  spiritual-violence including, 16, 71–72,
    105–106, 180, 220
Acceptance and commitment therapy, 17
Addiction. *See* Substance abuse and
  addiction
Adler, Alfred, 118–119
Alcohol abuse. *See* Substance abuse and
  addiction
Alia (case example), 106
Alicia (case example), 70, 88–89, 90, 91,
  95, 98, 99
Alienation, loss of self relationship to,
  99–100
Allport's religious sentiment stage model,
  62–63
American Association for Marriage and
  Family Therapy, 6

American Counseling Association, 6
American Psychological Association, 6
Anger:
  internalization vs. externalization of, 177
  loss of self relationship to, 69, 74,
    86–87, 93, 96, 174
  shadow self relationship to, 48, 58, 127,
    134, 176–177
Anxiety:
  compensatory strategies for dealing with,
    86, 153
  dialectical behavior therapy addressing,
    59
  differentiation and emotional reactivity
    to, 16, 80–81, 207–208
  fear-based living triggering, 35
  Freudian theory on, 46, 55
  interpersonal theory approach to, 51–52
  Jungian theory on, 48
  list-making creating, 91
  loss of self relationship to, 70, 73, 74,
    78–79, 80–81, 83–84, 85, 86, 90, 91,
    95, 97–98
  mindfulness techniques addressing, 70,
    109, 110–111
  psychological theories on and
    approaches to treating, 2, 46, 48,
    49–52, 55, 59, 66
  self-soothing strategies for, 49–51, 59,
    66, 73, 74, 109–111, 207–208
  shadow self triggering, 48, 133, 137–139
  spiritually-oriented therapy addressing,
    104, 109, 110–111

Anxiety (*continued*)
    spiritual resourcing for coping with,
      109, 110–111
    therapist experiencing, 2
    traumatic events leading to, 83–84
Artistic expression. *See* Creativity and
    artistic expression
Association for Spiritual, Ethical, and
    Religious Values in Counseling
    (ASERVIC), 6–7
Attachment theory, 48–51

Balance:
    loss and recovery of, in life activities,
      91–92, 98–99
    of responsibility, 98–99, 204–206
    of shadow and personal integrity,
      125–126, 129, 141–147
    of thoughts and emotions, 206
    of work and leisure, 98, 117
Body-oriented therapies, 17–18
Boundaries:
    differentiation leading to healthy,
      201–202, 203
    familial, 76–79, 201–202
    therapeutic alliance, 1, 3, 11, 14, 189,
      201–202
Buddhist tenets:
    balance achievement through, 92
    Buddha nature and inner knowing in,
      30–31
    Buddha nature and Real Self in, 52, 159
    Buddhist psychology, as holistic,
      reflective practice, 18
    client-defined spirituality perspective
      based on, 24, 28, 30–31, 32, 34, 37
    free will, naturalness and flow in, 37
    interconnectedness in, 34, 150–151,
      152–153, 159
    no-self vs. Real Self concept in, 150–
      153, 158, 159, 161
    present moment awareness in, 32,
      151–152
    suffering awareness and acceptance in,
      96
    therapist personal spirituality including,
      3

    transcendent and ordinary experience
      perspective in, 32
    transpersonal and integral psychology
      incorporation of, 61

Carlos (case example), 2–3, 16
Case examples:
    Alia (spiritually-reactive client), 106
    Alicia (loss and recovery of self), 70,
      88–89, 90, 91, 95, 98, 99
    Carlos (therapist response to spiritually-
      oriented therapy), 2–3, 16
    Casey (loss of self), 81–82
    Clarissa (differentiation), 215–217
    Dan (client-defined spirituality), 23–25
    Darla (spiritually-uninterested client),
      108–109
    Donna (reclaiming Real Self), 163–168
    James and Judy (shadow), 137–139
    Jana (therapist response to spiritually-
      oriented therapy), 3
    Joan (spiritually-oriented therapy
      effectiveness), 190–193
    John (shadow), 133–134
    John (trauma and addictive behavior),
      188–189
    Julie (loss of self), 87
    Karl (loss of self), 74, 86–87
    Katy and Don (shadow), 139–141
    Kendra (life structure evaluation),
      121–123
    Kristi (spiritually-interested client), 1–2
    Kyle (spiritual resourcing), 110–111
    Lana (spiritually-interested client),
      104–105
    Lee (loss of self), 78–79
    Ramon (shadow), 145–146
    Sarah (shadow), 134
    Sasha (differentiation), 214–215
    Shawn (loss and recovery of self),
      69–70, 88–89, 90, 93, 94, 95, 96, 97,
      98, 99, 100
Casey (case example), 81–82
Children:
    attachment theory on parent-child
      relationships, 48–51
    boundaries for, 76–79, 201–202

control-mastery theory on pathogenic
    beliefs developed by, 55–56
de-selfing of, 53–54, 84–85
differentiation levels of, 16, 79–82,
    195–201, 213
familial roles of, 74–76
guilt, externally based, in, 82–83
humanism on self-actualization of, 53
idealized self developed in, 130–132
interpersonal theory on Real Self
    development in, 51–52
life span development theories on
    development of, 62–65
life structure evaluation of relationships
    with, 116
parental invalidation of, 73–74
parental projection onto, 16, 75, 80, 82,
    198–200
parental role modeling for, 73
parent-child relationships with, 16,
    48–52, 53, 55–56, 65–66, 73–82,
    195–202, 209–211, 213
Real Self development in, 51–52, 160–
    161, 163–164
structural family difficulties impacting,
    76–79
traumatic events impacting (*see* Abuse;
    Trauma)
Christian tenets:
    client-defined spirituality perspective
        based on, 23, 28, 30–31, 34, 35–36,
        37, 42
    free will in, 36, 37
    inner knowing and Holy Spirit in,
        30–31
    interconnectedness and Holy Spirit in,
        34, 159
    love in, 35–36
    no-self vs. Real Self concept in, 154–
        155, 157, 159
    personal relationship with God in, 42
    Real Self and Holy Spirit in, 52, 157,
        159
    spiritual-differentiation from, 2–3,
        217–218
    transpersonal and integral psychology
        incorporation of, 61

Clarissa (case example), 215–217
Client-defined spirituality:
    case example of, 23–25
    concepts and definition of spirituality
        in, 26–27
    creativity and artistic expression in,
        38–39
    external presence in, 29–30
    free will in, 36–38
    inner knowing in, 30–31
    integration of themes in, 42–43
    interconnectedness in, 33–35
    love and fear in, 35–36
    nature and natural beauty in, 39–40
    openheartedness in, 40–41
    openness to, in spiritually-oriented
        therapy, 101–109
    personal integrity in, 20, 42
    personal relationship in, 41–42, 104
    physical and sensory sensations in, 27
    present moment awareness in, 32–33
    Real Self in, 19–20
    remembering spiritual knowledge in,
        28–29, 30
    research on, 26–28
    spiritually-oriented therapy impacted by,
        5, 19–20, 23–43, 101–109
    themes in, 26–43
    transcendent and ordinary experiences
        in, 31–32
Clients:
    case examples of specific (*see* Case
        examples)
    client-defined spirituality of, 5, 19–20,
        23–43, 101–109
    foundation of spirituality for, 5–8
    life structure evaluation by, 113–123
    personal integrity of (*see* Personal
        integrity)
    psychological theories and approaches
        used with (*see* Psychological theories
        and approaches)
    readiness for change in, 170
    Real Self concept of (*see* Real Self
        concept)
    relationships of (*see* Relationships)
    self-awareness of (*see* Self-awareness)

Clients (*continued*)
self-soothing strategies for, 49–51,
59, 66, 73, 74, 109–111, 186–187,
207–208
spiritually-interested, 103–105
spiritually-oriented therapy involving
(*see* Spiritually-oriented therapy)
spiritually-reactive, 103, 105–106
spiritually-uninterested, 106–109
therapeutic alliance with, 1, 3, 11, 14,
171, 172–174, 181–184, 189, 191,
201–202
Commission on Accreditation for
Marriage and Family Therapy
Education, 6
Community, life structure evaluation of,
118–119
Compassion and loving-kindness practices,
110
Compensatory self, 86–87, 153–154,
154–155, 157–159, 161–162,
164–165
Concentration practices, 109
Control, balance of, 98–99
Control-mastery theory, 54–57
Council Accrediting Counseling Related
Educational Programs, 6
Council on Social Work Education, 6
Counseling, spiritually-oriented. *See*
Spiritually-oriented therapy
Counselors. *See* Therapists
Creativity and artistic expression:
client-defined spirituality including,
38–39
spiritual practices including focus on,
124, 178
Criminal behavior, loss of self leading to,
83, 85
Cross-generational coalitions, 77–78

Dan (case example), 23–25
Darla (case example), 108–109
Dependent origination, 151
Depression and mood disorders:
dialectical behavior therapy addressing,
59, 109
differentiation difficulties leading to, 81

loss of self relationship to, 69, 73, 74, 81,
83, 85, 86–87, 177
mindfulness techniques addressing,
109
shadow self triggering, 133, 134,
145–146
spiritually-oriented therapy addressing,
109, 177, 190–191
traumatic events leading to, 59, 69, 83,
86, 109
De-selfing, 53–54, 84–85
Determinism, free will vs., 36–38
Dialectical behavior therapy, 17, 59–60,
109
Differentiation:
adult to adult relationships with parents
in, 209–211
balance of thoughts and emotions in,
206
balance ownership of responsibility in,
204–206
case examples of, 2–3, 16, 214–217
characteristics of well-differentiated
individuals, 201–213
children's identity development and, 16,
79–82, 195–201, 213
concept and definition of, 195–196
direct communication in, 208–209
healthy boundaries in, 201–202, 203
increasing, 213–221
inner-generated convictions in, 81, 207
loss of self and difficulties of, 79–82,
195–221
low levels of emotional reactivity in,
202–204
personal authority in, 211–212
personal integrity in, 81, 212–213
projection impacting, 16, 80, 82, 102,
194, 198–200
self-soothing ability in, 207–208
spiritual-differentiation, 2–3, 5, 15–17,
101, 102, 160, 194, 195–221
Donna (case example), 163–168
Dreams, shadow awareness through,
127–129, 146
Drug abuse. *See* Substance abuse and
addiction

Eastern philosophical perspectives. *See also* Buddhist tenets; Taoist tenets; Zen tenets
 on interconnectedness, 34, 150–151, 152–153, 159
 on no-self vs. Real Self concept, 52, 150–153, 158, 159, 161
 on present moment awareness, 32, 90, 151–152
Eating disorders, loss of self relationship to, 83, 85, 92
Education. *See* Schools and education
Ellis, Albert, 13
Emotional reactivity. *See* Reactivity
Employment. *See* Work and employment
Entertainment. *See* Leisure and entertainment
Epstein, Mark, 33–34
Erikson's psychosocial and identity status models as, 63–64
Existential perspectives:
 on loss of self, 97–98
 on no-self vs. Real Self concept, 153–154, 158
External presence, client-defined spirituality including, 29–30

Families:
 adult to adult relationships with parents in, 209–211
 cross-generational coalitions in, 77–78
 de-selfing in, 53–54, 84–85
 differentiation in, 16, 79–82, 195–202, 213
 guilt, externally based, in, 82–83
 insight into relationships in, 179–180
 internal family systems theory, 57–59, 184–187
 life structure evaluation of relationships in, 116
 multigenerational transmission process in, 200
 parental invalidation in, 73–74
 parental projection in, 16, 75, 80, 82, 198–200

parental role modeling in, 73
parent-child relationships in, 16, 48–52, 53, 55–56, 65–66, 73–82, 195–202, 209–211, 213
 roles of children in, 74–76
 scarcity model in, 96
 structural difficulties in, 76–79
 trauma in (*see* Abuse; Trauma)
Fear:
 client-defined spirituality including, 35–36
 compensatory strategies for dealing with, 153, 155, 162
 internal family systems theory on, 58
 life structure evaluation creating, 121
 loss of self relationship to, 71–72, 79, 94–95, 159, 182–183
 personal integrity superseding, 111–113
 spiritually-oriented therapy addressing, 111–113
 spiritual-violence and, 71, 105
Finances and money:
 fear-based perception of, 79
 life structure evaluation of, 117–118
 shadow self influencing perspective on, 137–138
Fowler's stages-of-faith model, 64–65
Free will:
 client-defined spirituality including, 36–38
 humanism focus on, 52–54
Freudian/psychoanalytic theory, 11–12, 45–46, 51, 55

Gratitude, loss of self recovery through, 95–96
Guilt:
 loss of self relationship to, 82–83
 shadow self creating, 134
 spiritual-violence and, 105

Hinduism, 61
Humanism:
 psychoanalytic, 51–52
 psychological theory of, 52–54
 value-free therapy influenced by, 14

Idealized self, 130–132, 157–158, 164
Identity. *See also* Personality; Self
  de-selfing impacting, 53–54, 84–85
  differentiation impacting development
    of, 16, 79–82, 195–201, 213
  Erikson's and Marcia's psychosocial and
    identity status models on, 63–64
  externally based guilt impacting
    development of, 82–83
  familial role impacting, 74–76
  loss of self and (*see* Loss of self)
  parental invalidation impacting
    development of, 73–74
  shadow aspect of, 48, 58, 125–147,
    164–165, 176–177
  traumatic events impacting, 83
Incongruence, loss of self and, 92–93
Inner knowing/wisdom:
  client-defined spirituality including,
    30–31
  control-mastery theory on, 56–57
  de-selfing impacting, 85
  differentiation difficulties impacting, 81
  embracing health of, 187–189
  externally based guilt impacting, 82–83
  humanism on, 53–54
  inner-generated convictions in well-
    differentiated individuals, 207
  loss of self and loss of, 71–73, 81,
    82–83, 84, 85, 92–93
  parental role modeling of reaching, 73
  personal integrity relationship to,
    111–113
  Real Self concept of (*see* Real Self
    concept)
  spiritually-oriented therapy support for,
    187–189
  traumatic events impacting, 84
Insight, spiritually-oriented therapy
  support of, 179–180, 191
Integrity. *See* Personal integrity
Interconnectedness:
  alienation vs., 99–100
  client-defined spirituality including,
    33–35
  loss of self recovery by finding, 93–94,
    100

no-self vs. Real Self concept based on,
    150–151, 152–153, 159
Internal family systems theory, 57–59,
    184–187
Interpersonal theory, 51–52
Invalidation, parental, 73–74
Islamic tenets, 106

James and Judy (case example), 137–139
Jana (case example), 3
Joan (case example), 190–193
John (case example), 133–134, 188–189
Julie (case example), 87
Jungian/psychoanalytic mysticism, 17,
    46–48, 51, 57, 58

Karl (case example), 74, 86–87
Katy and Don (case example), 139–141
Kendra (case example), 121–123
Knowledge:
  collective unconscious, Jung on, 47–48
  inner knowing/wisdom, 30–31,
    53–54, 56–57, 71–73, 81, 82–83,
    84, 85, 92–93, 111–113, 187–189,
    207 (*see also* Real Self concept)
  remembering spiritual knowledge,
    28–29, 30
Kristi (case example), 1–2
Kyle (case example), 110–111

Lana (case example), 104–105
Lee (case example), 78–79
Leisure and entertainment:
  balance of work and, 98, 117
  life structure evaluation of, 116–117
  shadow self influencing perspective on,
    137–139
Life span development theories, 62–65
  Allport's religious sentiment stage model
    as, 62–63
  Erikson's and Marcia's psychosocial and
    identity status models as, 63–64
  Fowler's stages-of-faith model as, 64–65
  Piaget's cognitive-development stage
    model as, 63
Life structure evaluation:
  of community structures, 118–119

of financial/monetary structures,
117–118
personal integrity and Real Self guiding,
114–123
of physical structures, 115
of relationship structures, 115–116,
120–123
spiritually-oriented therapy addressing,
113–123
of spiritual/philosophical structures, 119
of work and leisure structures, 116–117
List, tyranny of the, 90–91
Loss of self:
abuse relationship to, 69–70, 71–72,
83–84, 93, 96
alienation relationship to, 99–100
anger relationship to, 69, 74, 86–87, 93,
96, 174
anxiety relationship to, 70, 73, 74,
78–79, 80–81, 83–84, 85, 86, 90, 91,
95, 97–98
case examples of, 69–71, 74, 78–79,
81–82, 86–87, 88–89, 90, 91, 93, 94,
95, 96, 97, 98, 99, 100
childhood trauma leading to, 83–84
compensatory strategies for, 86–87, 153–
154, 154–155, 157–159, 161–162,
164–165
consequences of, 42, 52, 88–100
control and responsibility balance in
recovery of, 98–99
depression relationship to, 69, 73, 74, 81,
83, 85, 86–87, 177
de-selfing leading to, 53–54, 84–85
differentiation difficulties leading to,
79–82, 195–221
existential vacuum or sleepwalking due
to, 97–98
familial role entrenchment leading to,
74–76
fear relationship to, 71–72, 79, 94–95,
159, 182–183
fighting against flow of life leading to,
93–94
guilt leading to, 82–83
humanism on, 53–54
incongruence due to, 92–93

inner knowing/wisdom disconnect
relationship to, 71–73, 81, 82–83, 84,
85, 92–93
insight into, 179–180, 191
internal family systems theory on,
58–59
loss of balance in life leading to, 91–92,
98–99
love as tool in recovery of, 94, 95
parental invalidation leading to, 73–74
parental role modeling lack leading to,
73
personal integrity relationship to, 42, 81,
82–83, 93, 111–112
present moment awareness for recovery
of, 89–90, 91
reactivity relationship to, 79–83, 85, 87,
88–89, 91–92, 174–179
reasons for, 71–85
recovery/reclaiming of self after,
69–70, 88–100, 159–168, 169–194,
201–221
relationships impacted by, 70, 76–78,
162, 176, 182–183
scarcity vs. abundance thinking due to,
95–96
self-awareness of, 174–179, 191
shadow self as sign of, 48, 58, 125–147,
176–177
spiritual perspective on, 87–100
spiritual stillness for recovery of, 88–89,
178
structural family difficulties leading to,
76–79
suffering perspective related to,
96–97
thinking of past and future only leading
to, 89
trauma relationship to, 69–70, 83–84,
86, 93, 94, 95
tyranny of the list leading to, 90–91
Love:
client-defined spirituality including,
35–36
compassion and loving-kindness
practices, 110
loss of self recovery by finding, 94, 95

Marcia's psychosocial and identity status
models as, 64
Marriage. *See also* Families; Relationships
client-defined spirituality impacting,
23–25
life structure evaluation impacting,
115–116, 121–123
loss of self impacting, 70, 76–78, 162
reclaiming of self impacting, 162, 165–
167, 190–193
shadow self impacting, 133, 134–141,
145–147, 164–165
spiritually-oriented therapy addressing
issues in, 23–25, 104, 106, 115–116,
121–123
structural difficulties in family
impacting, 76–78
traumatic events and response
impacting, 188–189, 191–193
Meditation:
client-defined spirituality including, 19,
24, 43
spiritual-differentiation increased
through, 221
spiritual practices including, 124, 178
spiritual resourcing through, 109, 178
therapist's personal growth via, 3
transcendent experiences during, 61
Mental health practitioners. *See* Therapists
Mental health theories and approaches. *See*
Psychological theories and approaches
Mind-body medicine, 18
Mindfulness:
cognitive-behavior techniques using, 2
compassion and loving-kindness
practices as, 110
concentration practices as, 109
dialectical behavior therapy focus on,
59–60, 109
loss of self recovery through, 70, 90, 91
open-field awareness as, 109–110
personal relationship with spirituality
developed through, 42
spiritual-differentiation increased
through, 220–221
spiritual practices including focus on,
124, 178, 185–186, 191–192

spiritual resourcing through, 109–111,
178
therapist's personal growth via, 3
transpersonal and integral psychology
techniques using, 61
Money. *See* Finances and money
Mood disorders. *See* Depression and mood
disorders
Morality. *See* Personal integrity
Multicultural perspective:
no-self vs. Real Self concept in, 155–156
spiritually-oriented therapy as
multicultural therapy, 5, 8–10
Multigenerational transmission process, 200
Muslim tenets, 106

National Association of Social Workers, 6
Native American spiritual tenets, 61, 94
Nature and natural beauty:
client-defined spirituality including,
39–40
loss of self recovery through appreciation
of, 69, 90
spiritual practices including focus on,
124, 178
spiritual resourcing through, 109, 178

Object relations theory, 48–51
Open-field awareness, 109–110
Openheartedness:
client-defined spirituality including,
40–41
loss of self recovery through, 94

Parents. *See* Families
Pathogenic beliefs, control-mastery theory
on, 55–56
Patients. *See* Clients
Personal authority, healthy differentiation
and, 211–212
Personal integrity:
in client-defined spirituality, 20, 42
differentiation impacting, 81, 212–213
externally based guilt impacting, 82–83
life structure based on, 114–123
loss of self and, 42, 81, 82–83, 93,
111–112

restrictive moral visions and, 125–126, 132–134

shadow integration with, 125–126, 129, 141–147

spirituality informing, 111–113, 178–179

value-driven life based on, 112–113, 146, 178–179

Personality. *See also* Identity; Self

control-mastery theory on, 55

Freudian/psychoanalytic theory on, 45–46

internal family systems theory on, 57–59, 184–187

Jungian/psychoanalytic mysticism on, 46–48

shadow aspect of, 48, 58, 125–147, 164–165, 176–177

Personal relationships. *See* Relationships

Person-centered therapy, 52–54. *See also* Humanism

Physical being:

physical and sensory sensations in client-defined spirituality, 27

physical life structure evaluation, 115

self-awareness of, 175, 178, 191

Piaget's cognitive-development stage model, 63

Post-traumatic stress disorder (PTSD), 69, 95, 110

Prayer:

client-defined spirituality including, 19, 29, 30, 31, 32, 37, 42, 43

external presence awareness during, 30

free will direction of, 37

loss of self recovery through, 69, 96

personal relationship with spirituality developed through, 42, 104

present moment awareness during, 32

psychological theory consideration of, 50, 61

remembering spiritual knowledge during, 29

Serenity Prayer, 99

spiritual practices including, 5, 124, 178, 191–192

spiritual resourcing through, 109, 110–111, 178

transcendent experiences during, 31, 61

Present moment awareness:

client-defined spirituality including, 32–33

loss of self recovery through, 89–90, 91

mindfulness of, 59, 90, 91

no-self vs. Real Self concept based on, 151–152

Projection:

parental, 16, 75, 80, 82, 198–200

of shadow characteristics, 48, 126, 137, 138, 141, 142

therapist, 102, 194

Psychoanalytic humanism, 51–52

Psychoanalytic mysticism. *See* Jungian/psychoanalytic mysticism

Psychoanalytic theory. *See* Freudian/psychoanalytic theory

Psychological theories and approaches:

acceptance and commitment therapy as, 17

attachment and object relations theories as, 48–51

body-oriented therapies as, 17–18

Buddhist psychology as, 18

control-mastery theory as, 54–57

dialectical behavior therapy as, 17, 59–60, 109

Freudian/psychoanalytic theory as, 11–12, 45–46, 51, 55

humanism as, 14, 51–52, 52–54

internal family systems theory as, 57–59, 184–187

interpersonal/psychoanalytic humanist theory as, 51–52

Jungian/psychoanalytic mysticism as, 17, 46–48, 51, 57, 58

life span development theories as, 62–65

rational-emotive behavior therapy as, 13

Real Self linking spirituality and, 5, 18–19, 45–67, 184–187

scientific rationalism as, 12–13, 72

spiritually-oriented therapy impacted by, 5, 10–15, 17–18, 45–67, 72, 109, 184–187

thematic integration of, 65–67

transpersonal and integral psychology as, 17, 60–61

value-free therapy as, 13–15

Psychotherapy, spiritually-oriented. *See*
    Spiritually-oriented therapy
Purpose, loss of self recovery by finding, 98

Ramon (case example), 145–146
Rational-emotive behavior therapy, 13
Reactivity:
    clients', to spirituality discussion, 103,
        105–106
    compensatory strategies triggering, 87
    de-selfing triggering, 85
    dialectical behavior therapy on
        emotional mind and, 59
    differentiation from emotional reactivity,
        2–3, 5, 15–17, 79–82, 101, 102, 160,
        194, 195–221
    guilt triggering, 82–83
    loss of balance triggering, 91–92
    loss of self relationship to, 79–83, 85,
        87, 88–89, 91–92, 174–179
    structural family difficulties triggering,
        78
Real Self concept:
    Christian perspective on, 52, 154–155,
        157, 159
    client-defined spirituality including,
        19–20
    compensatory vs. natural self, 86–87,
        153–154, 154–155, 157–159, 161–
        162, 164–165
    differentiation leading to acceptance of,
        201, 207
    Eastern philosophical perspectives on,
        52, 150–153, 158, 159, 161
    existential perspectives on, 153–154,
        158
    Freudian ego-id-superego on, 45–46,
        51, 55
    humanism on self-actualization, 53–54
    idealized self vs., 130–132, 157–158,
        164
    integration of self and no-self, 157–159
    internal family systems theory on, 57,
        58–59, 184–187
    interpersonal theory on, 51–52
    Jungian self archetype, 47, 51, 57
    life structure based on, 114–123

loss of Real Self (*see* Loss of self)
multicultural perspective on, 155–156
new relationship with Real Self
    developed, 184–187
no-self vs., 150–159
personal integrity based on, 20, 42,
    81, 82–83, 93, 111–113, 114–123,
    125–126, 129, 132–134, 141–147,
    178–179, 212–213
recovery/reclaiming of Real Self,
    69–70, 88–100, 159–168, 169–194,
    201–221
self-soothing strategies, 49–51, 59, 66,
    73, 74, 109–111, 186–187, 207–208
shadow aspect of, 48, 58, 125–147,
    164–165, 176–177
spiritual and philosophical views of, 52,
    149–168
spirituality and psychological theory
    linked via, 5, 18–19, 45–67, 184–187
spiritually-oriented therapy and, 5, 18–20,
    42, 45–67, 69–100, 107, 109–123,
    125–147, 149–168, 169–194, 201–221
therapeutic alliance role in reclaiming,
    172–174
transpersonal and integral psychology
    on, 61
Relationships:
    abusive (*see* Abuse)
    acceptance and change in, 135–137
    attachment and object relations theories
        on, 48–51
    compensatory strategies in, 86–87
    control-mastery theory on, 55–57
    differentiation of self in
        (*see* Differentiation)
    direction communication in, 208–209
    embracing health in, 189–190
    familial (*see* Families; Marriage)
    insight into, 179–180, 191
    interpersonal theory on, 51–52
    life structure evaluation of, 115–116,
        120–123
    loss of self impacting, 70, 76–78, 162,
        176, 182–183
    openheartedness in, 40–41, 94
    parental invalidation impacting, 74

partner as shadow self in, 134–141
pathogenic beliefs impacting, 55–56
personal relationship with spirituality,
41–42, 94, 104
psychological theories on importance of,
48–52, 53, 55–57, 65–66
Real Self, developing new relationship
with, 184–187
reclaiming of self impacting, 162, 165–
167, 190–193
reexperiencing relational dynamics,
181–184, 191
shadow self impacting, 133, 134–141,
145–147, 164–165
structural family difficulties impacting,
76–79
therapeutic (*see* Therapeutic alliances)
traumatic events and response
impacting, 188–189, 191–193
Religion and spirituality, 17, 20–22, 26,
71–72, 105–106. *See also* Spirituality;
specific religions
Remembering, in client-defined
spirituality, 28–29, 30
Resourcing, spiritual, 109–111, 178
Responsibility, balance of, 98–99, 204–206

Sarah (case example), 134
Sasha (case example), 214–215
Scarcity model of thinking, 95–96
Schools and education:
community through, 118
loss of self and failure in, 83, 85
parental projection of goals for, 198–199
spiritually-oriented therapy training in,
6, 8
Scientific rationalism, 12–13, 72
Self:
awareness of, 141–143, 174–179, 191
compensatory vs. natural, 86–87, 153–
154, 154–155, 157–159, 161–162,
164–165
de-selfing, 53–54, 84–85
differentiation of, 2–3, 5, 15–17, 79–82,
101, 102, 160, 194, 195–221
Freudian ego-id-superego on, 45–46,
51, 55

humanism on self-actualization, 53–54
idealized, 130–132, 157–158, 164
integration of self and no-self, 157–159
internal family systems theory on, 57,
58–59, 184–187
interpersonal theory on, 51–52
Jungian self archetype, 47, 51, 57
loss of (*see* Loss of self)
no-self vs., 150–159
Real Self concept, 5, 18–20, 42, 45–67,
69–100, 107, 109–123, 125–147,
149–168, 169–194, 201–221
recovery/reclaiming of, 69–70, 88–100,
159–168, 169–194, 201–221
self-soothing strategies, 49–51, 59, 66,
73, 74, 109–111, 186–187, 207–208
shadow aspect of, 48, 58, 125–147,
164–165, 176–177
spiritual and philosophical views of, 52,
149–168
transpersonal and integral psychology
on, 61
Self-awareness:
of shadow, 141–143
spiritually-oriented therapy supporting,
174–179, 191
Self-injury or suicide, loss of self
relationship to, 58, 83, 85, 92
Serenity Prayer, 99
Shadow:
awareness of, 141–143
case examples of, 133–134, 137–141,
145–146
concept and definition of, 126–129
dichotomization of experiences leading
to development of, 129–130
formation of, 129–134
idealized self impacting development of,
130–132
integration with personal integrity,
125–126, 129, 141–147
Jungian shadow archetype, 48, 58
loss of self relationship to, 48, 58,
125–147, 176–177
marriage to/impacted by shadow self,
133, 134–141, 145–147, 164–165
ownership of, 143–146

Shadow (*continued*)
  restrictive moral visions leading to
    development of, 125–126, 132–134
Shamanism, 34, 61
Shawn (case example), 69–70, 88–89, 90,
  93, 94, 95, 96, 97, 98, 99, 100
Spiritual-differentiation:
  adult to adult relationships with parents
    in, 209–211
  balance of thoughts and emotions in,
    206
  balance ownership of responsibility in,
    204–206
  case examples of, 2–3, 16, 214–217
  characteristics of well-differentiated
    individuals, 201–213
  client reclaiming of Real Self
    necessitating, 160
  concept and definition of, 195–196
  direct communication in, 208–209
  healthy boundaries in, 201–202, 203
  identity development and, 16, 195–201,
    213
  increasing, 213–221
  inner-generated convictions in, 81, 207
  low levels of emotional reactivity in,
    202–204
  openness to client-defined spirituality
    while maintaining, 102
  personal authority in, 211–212
  personal integrity in, 212–213
  self-soothing ability in, 207–208
  of therapists, 2–3, 5, 15–17, 101, 102,
    160, 194, 195–196, 201–202, 204,
    205–206, 217–221
Spirituality:
  attachment and object relations theories
    on, 48–51
  client-defined, 5, 19–20, 23–43, 101–109
  clients' interest level in, 103–105,
    106–109
  clients' reactive response to, 103,
    105–106
  concept and definition of, 22, 26–27
  control-mastery theory on, 54–57
  creativity and artistic expression in,
    38–39, 124, 178

cultural role of, 9–10
dialectical behavior therapy on, 17,
  59–60, 109
external presence awareness in, 29–30
fear in, 35–36, 58, 71–72, 79, 94–95,
  105, 111–113, 121, 153, 155, 159,
  162, 182–183
foundational role of, 5–8
free will in, 36–38, 52–54
Freudian/psychoanalytic theory on,
  11–12, 45–46, 51, 55
humanism on, 14, 51–52, 52–54
inner knowing/wisdom in, 30–31, 53–
  54, 56–57, 71–73, 81, 82–83, 84, 85,
  92–93, 111–113, 187–189, 207
interconnectedness in, 33–35, 93–94,
  99–100, 150–151, 152–153, 159
internal family systems theory on,
  57–59, 184–187
interpersonal theory on, 51–52
Jungian/psychoanalytic mysticism on,
  17, 46–48, 51, 57, 58
life span development theories on, 62–65
life structure evaluation of, 119
loss of self and (*see* Loss of self)
love in, 35–36, 94–95, 110
nature and natural beauty in, 39–40, 69,
  90, 109, 124, 178
openheartedness in, 40–41, 94
pathologization of spiritual experiences,
  105
personal integrity relationship to (*see*
  Personal integrity)
personal relationship in, 41–42, 94, 104
physical being relationship to, 27, 115,
  175, 178, 191
present moment awareness in, 32–33,
  59, 89–90, 91, 151–152
psychological theories and approaches
  on, 5, 10–15, 17–18, 45–67, 72, 109,
  184–187
Real Self concept and, 5, 18–20, 42, 45–
  67, 69–100, 107, 109–123, 125–147,
  149–168, 169–194, 201–221
recovery of self influenced by, 69–70,
  88–100, 159–168, 169–194,
  201–221

religion and, 17, 20–22, 26, 71–72, 105–106 (*see also specific religions*)
remembering spiritual knowledge in, 28–29, 30
resourcing using, 109–111, 178
scientific rationalism on, 12–13, 72
spiritual-differentiation, 2–3, 5, 15–17, 101, 102, 160, 194, 195–221
spiritual practices related to, 5, 104, 123–124, 163, 178, 185–186, 191–192 (*see also* Client-defined spirituality; Meditation; Mindfulness; Prayer)
spiritual resourcing, 109–111, 178
spiritual stillness, 88–89, 178
spiritual-violence, 16, 71–72, 105–106, 180, 220
therapist's personal beliefs on, 1–3, 7, 9–10, 11, 14
therapy including (*see* Spiritually-oriented therapy)
transcendent and ordinary experiences in, 31–32, 53, 60–61
transpersonal and integral psychology on, 17, 60–61
value-free therapy on, 13–15
Spiritually-oriented therapy. *See also* Spirituality
attachment and object relations theories applied in, 48–51
case examples for (*see* Case examples)
client-defined spirituality impacting, 5, 19–20, 23–43, 101–109
clients in (*see* Clients)
collaboration in, 172–174
control-mastery theory applied in, 54–57
dialectical behavior therapy applied in, 17, 59–60, 109
effectiveness of, reasons for, 169–194
embracing inner health in, 187–189
embracing relationship health in, 189–190
Freudian/psychoanalytic theory influencing, 11–12, 45–46, 51, 55
humanism applied in, 14, 51–52, 52–54
insight supported in, 179–180, 191

internal family systems theory applied in, 57–59, 184–187
interpersonal theory applied in, 51–52
Jungian/psychoanalytic mysticism influencing, 17, 46–48, 51, 57, 58
life span development theories applied in, 62–65
life structure evaluation in, 113–123
loss of self addressed in, 42, 52, 69–71, 87–100, 125–147, 159–168, 169–194 (*see also* Loss of self *for details*)
as multicultural therapy, 5, 8–10
new relationship with Real Self through, 184–187
openness to client-defined spirituality in, 101–109
personal integrity informed by spirituality in, 111–113, 178–179
practical steps to achieving successful, 101–124
premises of, 5–20
psychological theories and approaches on, 5, 10–15, 17–18, 45–67, 72, 109, 184–187
questions to explore spirituality in, 102–103
Real Self concept and, 5, 18–20, 42, 45–67, 69–100, 107, 109–123, 125–147, 149–168, 169–194, 201–221 (*see also* Real Self concept *for details*)
recovery of self in, 69–70, 88–100, 159–168, 169–194, 201–221
reexperiencing relational dynamics in, 181–184, 191
self-awareness supported through, 174–179, 191
spiritual-differentiation in, 2–3, 5, 15–17, 101, 102, 160, 194, 195–221
spiritually-interested clients in, 103–105
spiritually-reactive clients in, 103, 105–106
spiritually-uninterested clients in, 106–109
spiritual practice commitment supported in, 123–124
spiritual resourcing in, 109–111, 178

Spiritually-oriented therapy (*continued*)
  therapeutic alliances in, 1, 3, 11, 14,
    171, 172–174, 181–184, 189, 191,
    201–202
  therapist competencies and comfort-level
    with, 1–4, 7–8, 102–103
  training in, 6, 8
  transpersonal and integral psychology
    applied in, 17, 60–61
  utilization of, 190–193
Substance abuse and addiction:
  client-defined spirituality and issues of,
    23, 33
  dialectical behavior therapy addressing,
    59
  loss of self leading to, 83, 85, 92, 97
  shadow self impacting, 134, 139, 140
  traumatic events leading to, 83, 184,
    187–189
Suffering, loss of self and views of, 96–97
Suicide. *See* Self-injury or suicide

Taoist tenets:
  balance achievement through, 92
  client-defined spirituality perspective
    based on, 34, 36, 40
  interconnectedness in, 34
  loss of self recovery via, 70
  love in, 36
  nature and natural beauty in, 40
  transpersonal and integral psychology
    incorporation of, 61
Therapeutic alliances:
  boundaries in, 1, 3, 11, 14, 189,
    201–202
  as collaborative team, 172–174
  effectiveness of therapy influenced by,
    171, 172–174, 181–184, 189, 191
  reexperiencing relational dynamics in,
    181–184, 191
Therapeutic theories and approaches. *See*
  Psychological theories and approaches
Therapists:
  clients of (*see* Clients)
  effectiveness of therapy influenced by
    specific, 171

openness of, to client-defined
    spirituality, 101–109
pathologization of spiritual experiences
    by, 105
personal spiritual beliefs of, 1–3, 7,
    9–10, 11, 14
psychological theories and approaches
    used by (*see* Psychological theories and
    approaches)
reexperiencing relational dynamics with,
    181–184, 191
spiritual competencies and comfort-level
    of, 1–4, 7–8, 102–103
spiritual-differentiation of, 2–3, 5,
    15–17, 101, 102, 160, 194, 195–196,
    201–202, 204, 205–206, 217–221
spiritually-oriented therapy by (*see*
    Spiritually-oriented therapy)
therapeutic alliance with, 1, 3, 11, 14,
    171, 172–174, 181–184, 189, 191,
    201–202
training and education of, 6, 8
Training. *See* Schools and education
Transcendent experiences:
  client-defined spirituality including,
    31–32
  self-actualization through, 53
  transpersonal and integral psychology
    on, 60–61
Transpersonal and integral psychology, 17,
    60–61
Trauma. *See also* Abuse
  addictive behavior resulting from, 83,
    184, 187–189
  compensatory strategies for dealing
    with, 86
  control-mastery theory addressing,
    55–56
  dialectical behavior therapy addressing,
    59
  insight into effects of, 179–180, 191
  internal family systems theory
    addressing, 57–58, 184–186
  interpersonal theory addressing, 51
  loss of self relationship to, 69–70,
    83–84, 86, 93, 94, 95

pathogenic beliefs due to, 55–56
personal relationship with spirituality
    healing, 42
post-traumatic stress disorder from, 69,
    95, 110
psychological theories on and
    approaches to treating, 51, 55–59,
    65–66, 184–186
spiritually-oriented therapy addressing,
    69–70, 109, 110–111, 179–180,
    191–193
spiritual resourcing for coping with,
    109, 110–111
spiritual-violence as, 16, 71–72, 105–
    106, 180, 220

Value-driven life, 112–113, 146, 178–179.
    See also Personal integrity
Value-free therapy, 13–15

Work and employment:
    community through, 118
    life structure evaluation of, 116–117
    overworking as substitute for healthy
        behavior, 58, 70, 79, 88, 92, 97–98,
        137–138
    parental projection of goals for, 198
    shadow self influencing perspective on,
        137–139, 145

Yoga:
    spiritual practices including, 124
    therapist's personal growth via, 3
    transpersonal and integral psychology
        incorporation of, 61
    work-life balance including, 98

Zen tenets, 37, 61